Procedural Storytelling in Game Design

Procedural Storytelling in Game Design

Edited by
Tanya X. Short
Tarn Adams

CRC Press
Taylor & Francis Group
Boca Raton London New York

CRC Press is an imprint of the
Taylor & Francis Group, an **informa** business

CRC Press
Taylor & Francis Group
6000 Broken Sound Parkway NW, Suite 300
Boca Raton, FL 33487-2742

© 2019 by Taylor & Francis Group, LLC

CRC Press is an imprint of Taylor & Francis Group, an Informa business

No claim to original U.S. Government works

Printed on acid-free paper

International Standard Book Number-13: 978-1-138-59531-6 (Hardback)

International Standard Book Number-13: 978-1-138-59530-9 (Paperback)

Library of Congress Cataloging-in-Publication Data

Names: Short, Tanya X., author. | Adams, Tarn, author.
Title: Procedural storytelling in game design / Tanya X. Short, Tarn Adams.
Other titles: Procedural generation in game design
Description: Second edition. | Boca Raton : Taylor & Francis, 2019. |
Includes bibliographical references and index.
Identifiers: LCCN 2018048320| ISBN 9781138595316 (hardback : alk. paper) |
ISBN 9781138595309 (paperback : alk. paper)
Subjects: LCSH: Level design (Computer science) | Computer games–Design.
Classification: LCC QA76.76.C672 S543 2019 | DDC 794.8/1536–dc23
LC record available at https://lccn.loc.gov/2018048320

Visit the Taylor & Francis Web site at
www.taylorandfrancis.com

and the CRC Press Web site at
www.crcpress.com

Contents

SECTION 5 **Resources**

About the Editors

Tanya X. Short is the Captain of Kitfox Games, the independent studio behind Boyfriend Dungeon, The Shrouded Isle, Moon Hunters, and more. She's also a co-founder and co-director of Pixelles, an intersectionally feminist game development non-profit. Her two cats have no interest in her storytelling, procedural or otherwise.

Tarn Adams is the co-founder of Bay 12 Games with his brother Zach, where they work on their fantasy simulation, Dwarf Fortress, one of the first video games acquired by the Museum of Modern Art in New York. He has been writing (and debugging) procedural interactive narrative projects for over twenty years.

Contributors

Tarn Adams
Bay 12 Games

Matthew Bozarth
Undead Labs

George Buckenham

Geoffrey Card
Undead Labs

Dr. Kate Compton

Daniel Cook
Spry Fox

Dr. Michael Cook
Queen Mary University of London

Bruno Dias

Riad Djemili
Maschinen-Mensch

Alex Epstein
Compulsion Games

Marta Fijak
11 Bit Studios

Jason Grinblat
Freehold Games

Benjamin Hill

Jurie Horneman

Jon Ingold
Inkle

Darius Kazemi

Tim Keenan

Jongwoo Kim
Kitfox Games

Daniel Kline

Mx. Lazer-Walker

Steven Lumpkin
Guerrilla Games

Jimmy Maher
The Digital Antiquarian Blog

Cat Manning

Jill Murray
Discoglobe Interactive

Richard Rouse III
Paranoid Productions

Elan Ruskin

Adam Saltsman
Finji

Emily Short

Tanya X. Short
Kitfox Games

Kevin Snow

Jakub Stokalski
11 Bit Studios

Jørgen Tjernø
Undead Labs

1

Introduction

S ome anthropologists believe that interactive stories were invented alongside the campfire, when the elders of the tribe would incorporate audience suggestions and reactions into their performance. If this is true, then the idea of a singular author dictating the narrative is a more modern invention. Certainly, video games are an even more modern invention, and within that digital realm, system-driven storytelling is a rarely explored and nearly uncharted frontier.

The video game industry is large and growing, with tens of thousands of workers across the globe, yet for all of our specialization, there are very, very few individuals who are comfortable being called experts in procedural storytelling. In order to acquire many of the brilliant articles in this book, the editors had to promise we would not over-exaggerate the authors' mastery of the subject matter. Procedural narrative design is not a new field, yet it remains one filled with hesitation, humility, and apologies.

Through the course of this book, different authors will use the terms "procedural" and "stories" differently, as suits their individual experiences.

However, the editors hope you find

- new ideas, approaches, and philosophies to contemplate,

- new examples of implementations and process put into practice, and

- tools and resources to use in your own projects.

In this Introduction, we will begin more generally, considering the holistic problem, appeal, and purpose of system-driven narratives. The book's contents are assembled linearly, but in whatever order you choose to encounter each chapter, we hope you will approach each author's insight and experience with an open mind, welcoming the infinite possibilities of professional growth in this rich and complex field.

CHAPTER 1

Getting Started with Generators

Dr. Kate Compton

Excerpted and adapted from "So you want to build a generator ... " galaxy-kate0.tumblr.com

With so many possible kinds of generators, what advice can I give? Any advice will depend on what *kind* of generator you want to build. I'll give you a list of questions to ask yourself and advice to match your possible answers.

The first question is **What are you making?**

Write down the *thing* that your generator will make. We'll refer to this as your "artifact," but it could be anything: procedural birds, generated stories, animated dance choreography, gazpacho recipes, RPG quests, chess variants.

Now the hard part. Inhale, exhale, and start writing down everything you know about what makes one of those successful. What qualities does a good one of those *artifacts* have? Funny? Harmonic? Playable? Now go deeper: the more specific the kind of thing you are making is, the more specific and detailed you can get with these requirements. What does a "fun" level mean? "Fun" will mean very different things for *Super Mario* or *Civilization* or *Bejeweled*. I can come up with more properties of a *good paranormal regency romance novel* than rules for a *good novel*. The easiest generators to make are the ones in which you can describe "good" artifacts as set concrete properties.

Now flip the question on its head: What makes a "bad" example of this artifact? List everything you can think of, including properties that are merely unfortunate and properties that are total deal breakers. Put a star next to anything that absolutely *must not happen*. These are your *constraints*. The most reliable generators are the ones in which you can concretely describe constraints.

You now have a list of desirable properties and constraints (things that you want and don't want) for your artifacts. We want a generator with a *possibility space* (all the kinds of artifacts it can generate) in which most of the artifacts have the good properties and few (or none) of the artifacts have bad properties. We'll also want a *range* of artifacts, not just the same perfect artifact over and over and over, though how *wide* a range is a choice for you, the designer (a problem identified by Gillian Smith[1] and being explored by Michael Cook[2]).

Now we have the guidance we need to start building methods that make artifacts.

An alternative approach: The previously described method is good for inflexible situations, where you know ahead of time what you want to build. For many situations, like game jams, prototypes, or side projects, you can be more flexible and improvisational! You can start with a method or some loose pieces to figure out what they "want" to generate (what properties they are best at generating) and then revise what artifacts you are generating to better suit what the generator is good at making.

BUILDING YOUR ARTIST-IN-A-BOX

When the *Spore* editors were being designed, the engineers and designers worked closely with the art team to understand *how* an artist or animator would go about sculpting and texturing a creature. If they could understand the *process* and design an algorithm that could follow that process on demand, they would have an "Artist-in-a-box" that could make procedurally generated creatures that would be nearly as good as the original animator would have made. Designer Chaim Gingold explained this process in his 2007 GDC talk, and Art Director Ocean Quigley used a similar process to experiment with the kinds of building blocks he would want for building cities.[3]

It is helpful when making a generator to sit down with people who make the sort of artifacts you are building and have them walk you through the process of making something. What questions do they ask themselves along the way? How do they make decisions? How do they describe the trade-offs between choices? How do they describe the different problems that they have to keep in mind? How do they name all the parts of what they are working on and all the relationships between them (their ontology)?

Some fields have expert practitioners who have written *frameworks*, often controversial, to describe what they do. Music theory has proposed plenty of rule systems, for example, for jazz improvisation, Bach-style harmonies, or pop songs. Story generation has narratological theories like the hero's journey, but also informal frameworks like TV tropes. Art theory has the golden ratio, color harmonies, and composition rules (I haven't found those visual aesthetic rules to be productive in my own work, though you may feel differently). No one framework is complete or makes provable good artifacts, but each can give you guidance and inspiration.

So now, ask yourself: **How would a human solve this problem?**

FROM RULES TO GENERATIVE METHODS

Unfortunately, knowing how a human would make something isn't the same as being able to teach a computer how to do it. Humans are good at estimation, making guesses, and synthesizing a lot of knowledge about past situations. Computers know only what you tell them, and many problems require way more implicit knowledge than we think, but computers *are* good at performing lots of calculations and trying out lots of possibilities. So the methods we want to use will need to provide a way for the computer to solve problems *like* a human, or at least with a way to mirror some of the skills *of* a human. Methods that are particularly good for building generators (generative methods) will give the computer some of the following skills:

- Encapsulate knowledge of options (skill A)

- Create some structure (skill B)

- Encode conditional rules for options (A2)

- Create variability in structure (B2)

- Be able to ask itself questions about its constraints (have I solved this?) (skill C)

Distribution

This is the easiest kind of generative method. You have a bag of *stuff* and an area of space or time that you can spread them out across. Distribution methods usually don't have much overall structure (B), but they are often very sophisticated with the odds of picking each option (A). Some use weighted randomness to change the distribution percentages, or "deck shuffling" (putting all the options in a stack and discarding when they are used), which prevents accidentally picking the same option twice. The conditional rules (A2) can get quite complex as well, but specifying *arbitrary* conditions is difficult to implement in practice. Most systems have carefully chosen parameters that can be set for each option, and the conditional functions can just compare the fixed parameters to make choices.

For an RPG example, wandering monsters are distributed around the environment (A). Higher monsters are found in higher level areas, water monsters in water, etc. (A2). There may be a little structure as to how they are distributed, like several "baby" versions of a monster leading up to the "boss" version. Loot is also distributed: You may be more likely to get high level loot in high level situations (A2), but there's still some randomly selected stuff chosen from a big list of possible loots (A).

Distribution in music and language doesn't work well. Randomly selected strings of words or musical notes don't have enough structure to make interesting meaning. For structure-heavy artifacts, you might want tile-based or grammar-based methods instead, or for something with very fixed structure and not much variability, you could try the parametric approach.

Parametric Methods

You have a pretty well-built artifact already, and you know that you can *tweak* it a little. You have music, and you can transpose it up or down, make it louder or softer. You have a teapot, and you can make the spout curve out farther; you can make the body tall or short, thin or fat; and you can make the base wide or narrow. If you have a set of handmade alien creatures, you can tweak their legs to be long, fat, curved, or flat-footed, and their bellies can be slender or barrel-shaped; their voices will change as well. This is how creatures in *No Man's Sky* are varied. This is a very reliable and controllable technology! 3D models can often be encoded as a Maya animation channel, allowing them to blend with other animations (a *Spore* trick used in the rig-block animations). But your variability (A) is along fixed one-dimensional numerical paths; there is no structure variability at all (B2). You can see something "new" but never something surprising.

A more sophisticated form of parametric methods uses other forms of input and can generate new artifacts based on not only numerical, but also point-based, path-based, and graph-based input. When you draw a line in Photoshop with a tablet pen, your path becomes the input to an algorithm that renders a brushstroke, taking into account pressure, speed, and tilt as parameters at each point. The *Spore* creatures, likewise, used metaballs, a geometry creation algorithm that can create smooth tubes along paths in 3D space. Other algorithms for filling spaces and paths are Voronoi patterns, Perlin/Simplex noise, triangulation algorithms, 3D extrusion or rotation, and the diamond-square algorithm for fractal terrain. These algorithms are particularly well-suited for interactive generators, because the user can provide the input parameters for the generator.

Want more? Inconvergent.net has more intriguing specimens than you could possibly ever need, with open-source implementations. However, although these algorithms are delightfully surprising, they can often be too uncontrollable to provide the constraint-satisfaction needed for gameplay or other highly constrained artifacts.

Tile-based

Chop the problem up into modular, identically sized slots. Have a number of different handmade solutions that can fill these slots. The artifacts being created are just differently selected or ordered sets of pre-authored solutions. A familiar example is the board layout for games like *Settlers of Catan* and *Betrayal at the House on the Hill* (or *Civilization* for a digital example). The island and the mansion are constructed from the same tiles each time but laid out differently, which changes the gameplay. Some of the earliest forms of generative content I've found are the Musikalisches Würfelspiel from the 1750s and earlier, with which pianists could put together "tiles" (in this case measures) of music to produce a playable waltz.

Tile-based methods are great for small scale structure (B) because the insides of the tile are pre-authored, but they have no flexibility (B2) for small scale structure for the same reason. Large scale structure is harder to control: It can be totally random. You can have more advanced constraints about which tiles can go next to other tiles, but then you may need a complex algorithm to solve for compatible layouts of highly constrained tiles ("The beach tile can go next to a jungle tile but cannot be within two tiles of a river tile. ... "). Individual tiles have a very rigid encapsulation of possible options (A) because each possible tile has to be authored by a human. These systems don't have enough knowledge to come up with good new tiles by themselves. Tile-based methods work for problems that can be broken up into small chunks where internal structure matters but that can still create interesting (but not constraint-breaking) behavior when combined in different orders.

Interested in more analog content generation? Additional forms of board game and role-playing game content generation can be found in "An Analog History of Procedural Generation" by Gillian Smith,[4] and the exploration of comics by Chris Martens[5] shown in Figure 1.1.

FIGURE 1.1

Grammars

Grammars comprise one of my favorite generative methods, because I find that they give me a great way to make very deep and complicated structures while still also having a lot of control over my options. Grammars are a computer-science-y way of saying that big complex things are made out of other things, and those other things may themselves be made out of even smaller simpler things. Orteil's *Nested* is a lovely example of this. The universe is made of galaxies made of planets made of continents full of people who are full of thoughts and dreams and memories and atoms. Each symbol (that is, each type of thing, as shown in Figure 1.1) has a distribution of subsymbols of which it might be composed. When it "unpacks," it has to pick one of those options (and any subsymbols) and then unpack recursively. Grammars make it easy to encode knowledge about a particular artifact and its structure and its options all in one piece of data. I like them so much that I made a library to help people work with them: Tracery. This has been used to make a Twitterbot hosting service and lots of great weird creative Twitterbots including some of my own (see also Chapter 27 of this text).

The downside of grammars is that they do not have a way to handle constraints, unless the constraints are implicitly encoded in the grammars themselves (if a bed can only be in a house, then only the house can have a bed as a subchild, for example). It's harder for grammars to encode high level relationships between different things generated at different points in the grammar. If you want to have foreshadowing of the villain's death at the very beginning of the grammar, that might be difficult to do, and you might want to use the "big hammer" of a constraint solver.

Constraint Solvers

Constraint solvers are very powerful, very recent tools in our generative arsenal. They are what you use when you have a lot of hard constraints and a lot of flexible and complex structures, but you don't know how to build out the structures in a way that will be *sure* to solve your constraints.

The oldest, simplest version is brute force solving: make *every* possible variant of content, toggle every switch, make an alternative universe where you have made each different decision, and test your constraints until you find one that works. This is a viable solution for some problems, but as any mathematician will tell you, too many choices will create a number of possible artifacts greater than the number of atoms in the universe, and searching them is going to be slow.

There are often shortcuts you can take, depending on how your constraints are structured (I don't have to choose an ice cream flavor in possible futures in which I do not go out for ice cream), but this takes a long time to author by hand (just ask the Storyteller developer). Fortunately, many mathematicians and logicians find it amusing to try to solve this problem, and they have come up with general purpose solvers. Plug in your constraints, structures, and options (in a language that it can understand), and these solvers will find all the cheap shortcuts to cut the eons of brute force solver time down to something slow but accomplishable within normal gameplay time.

Because these tools are big and bulky and new, they are still hard to plug into many game engines, and there aren't many tutorials. Adam Smith has been doing good educational outreach for Answer Set Solving, a particularly powerful method. Craft by Ian Horswill is a constrained random number generator with some support that has been recently ported to Javascript. Look for these rare but powerful tools to be more common in the future!

Agents and Simulations

This is where it gets weird. Remember how I said that we could look at how humans solve problems to provide inspiration for our generators? Guess what: Humans aren't the only ones who solve problems! Some algorithms solve problems based on the colonial behaviors of ants or the social communications of fireflies. Many agents and simulations take inspiration from parts of nature, like flocks of birds, evolution, bacteria, neurons and cities. Here are a few of my favorites, but there are many more.

Steering behaviors can create remarkably complex crowd motion. Braitenberg vehicles were originally a thought experiment about simple machines with two photosensitive eyes and two wheels that could "steer" themselves just by activating one wheel more than the other, applying an asymmetrical force that changes their direction. Despite their total brainlessness, they can show "fear" and "adventure" and have been ported to many languages and physical robots.

Boids took the steering approach of the Braitenberg vehicles and applied it to flocks of birds and fish (and the wildebeest in the *Lion King* animated movie). Each bird helps keep its flock in shape by calculating and applying its own forces for cohesion, alignment, and separation. Small variations in each bird's tuning values can generate new behavior for the flock.

I've also used steering forces to generate procedural dance (Figure 1.2): You just replace the flocking forces with rhythmic forces in time to the music. Steering forces can do a lot more than pathfinding, but I don't think they have yet been explored to their full potential.

Genetic algorithms do not generate content, as you still need a generator, but they *guide* that generator toward more constraint-fulfilling and desirable-property-producing content. I used this method in a flower-evolving app (Figures 1.3, 1.4). A genetic algorithm needs three things:

1. Something you can modify (a "genotype")

2. Something you can judge (a "phenotype")

3. A way to turn the first into the second

For the flowers in my app, the genotype is an array of floats. That array is fed into a parametric generator to create a pretty animated flower (turning genotype to phenotype). Users can see which flowers

FIGURE 1.2

Don't distrust the void because the void is full of nothingness. You will be made of nothingness, too, in a while.

myThing

#concreteNoun#	mySub			#transitiveEmotion#	#myThing#		#myThing#
#natureNoun#	#substance#						
void	nothingness	Don't	distrust	the	void	because the	void

#fullOf#	#mySub#			#fullOf#	#mySub#		#someday#	
is	full of	nothingness	. You will be	made of	nothingness	, too,	in a while	myThing

mySub

FIGURE 1.3

FIGURE 1.4

they like (something you can judge). They pick their favorite; its original genotype is cloned and mutated (something you can modify), and the next generation is born from its mutant babies; over time, evolution happens. Sexual reproduction is common in genetic algorithms, but so are many other interesting kinds of reproductions and metaheuristics. There's a lot of neat research in this area!

Cellular automata rely on many very simple agents all working in parallel. The canonical example of this is Conway's Game of Life, in which many tiny automata in a grid, each with a very simple behavior, can give rise to so many strange behaviors and phenomena that many

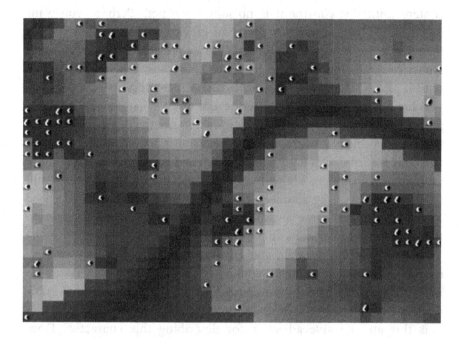

FIGURE 1.5

mathematicians make a hobby of discovering and cataloging them. This method can create outcomes like Figure 1.5. Cellular automata with more complex rules are used to create *Dwarf Fortress*, the classic *Powder* game, and with the advent of voxel-based simulation, they are taking on a new life as the engine behind Minecraft.

After you generate. ... You've browsed this list of generative methods, you've got your list of constraints and properties in hand, and you've built your generator! Now what?

WAYS THAT GENERATORS FAIL

Something has gone horribly wrong. The content looks ugly. The content all looks the same. The content looks like genitalia. The content is broken. Some of these problems are easier to solve than others. Here are a few kinds of difficult problems you will encounter.

One will be the kind in which you can *computationally identify* when something is going wrong. The solution is to generate some new content until this constraint is no longer violated. Perhaps you want a generated chair to have its center of gravity over its support points (like legs), so it won't fall over. This is possible to calculate with a physics simulation, so if the generated chair fails, generate a new one until it passes. This approach is called "generate and test."

What can go wrong with "generate and test": What if every chair you generate fails this test? Perhaps content that passes the test is very rare, or there are too many constraints (you have constraints for material thickness and cost and symmetry and comfort and more). Each chair might satisfy most constraints, but with enough constraints, most chairs will still fail one or two. Maybe you need a constraint solver. Or maybe you need to restrict your generator so that it is more conservative with its choices, though that may lose interesting possibility space.

Another difficulty is when you cannot adequately describe your constraints. This is a remarkably common situation because there are so many things that we don't want, but we can't write rules so that "I know it when I see it" can be used as a serious legal argument.

Is this an offensive adjective for describing this character? Does this color palette look too much like a corporate logo? Does this look like genitalia? Is this just ugly? This is a hard and unsolved problem, I'm afraid. If you can't define "bad" content, it becomes impossible to filter, especially when your human users are trying to get around the detection algorithm. In this case, the best path is to construct a generator that makes it *harder* or less likely to make offensive content. This also restricts your possibility space, like removing words that are harmless and useful unless combined in a particular way.

Aesthetics: The Toughest Challenge

The most common way generators fail is that they produce content that fails to be interesting. What is "interesting"? That depends on the situation. Very few generators produce only one of a thing. Most generate multiples, but a Twitterbot posting every hour will generate more content than a novel-generator outputting one novel every NaNoGenMo. So, achieving novelty with the first Twitterbot will be more difficult because there are so many artifacts being produced that any given one of them will probably start seeming less special.

Your algorithm may generate 18,446,744,073,709,551,616 planets. Each may be subtly different, but as the player is exploring them rapidly, will they be *perceived as different*? I like to call this the 10,000 **Bowls of Oatmeal** problem. I can easily generate 10,000 bowls of plain oatmeal, with each oat being in a different position and different orientation; *mathematically speaking,* they will all be completely unique. But the user will likely just see *a lot of oatmeal.* Perceptual uniqueness is the real metric, and it's darn tough.

In some situations, just perceptual differentiation is enough and an easier bar to clear. Perceptual differentiation is the feeling that this piece of content is not identical to the last. A user glancing at a line of trees can tell if they are identical or less varied than expected, suggesting unnaturalness. This fulfills an aesthetic need even if no tree is particularly memorable.

Perceptual uniqueness is much more difficult. It is the difference between an actor being a face in a crowd scene and a *character* that is memorable. Does each artifact have a distinct personality? That may be too much to ask and too much for any user to remember distinctly. Not everyone can be a main character. Instead, many artifacts can be drab background noise, highlighting the few *characterful* artifacts.

The topic of characterful artifacts is an essay for another time, but certain aesthetic principles create objects with *readable* meanings for human perception. Humans seem to like perceiving evidence of process and forces, like the pushed-up soil at the base of a tree or the grass growing in the shelter of a gravestone. These structurally generated subtleties suggest to us that there is a world alive behind this object. Kevin Lynch's influential *"Image of the City"* demonstrates that certain factors make cities memorable and describable. Perhaps there are other aesthetic rules that we can discover, too.

NOTES

1   https://games.soe.ucsc.edu/sites/default/files/smith-expressiverange-fdgpcg10.pdf
2   www.gamesbyangelina.org/2016/02/introducing-danesh-part-1/

3 http://oceanquigley.blogspot.com/2009/04/spore-early-rig-block-experi ments.html
4 http://sokath.com/main/files/1/smith-fdg15.pdf
5 http://lambdamaphone.blogspot.com/2015/12/generativity-interpreta tion-study-of.html

CHAPTER 2

Keeping Procedural Generation Simple

Darius Kazemi

As a practice, procedural generation tends to draw a technical type of person. I use "technical" in the broadest sense of the term, meaning someone who is highly interested in technique, defined as the procedures involved in completing a complicated task. This doesn't necessarily mean the task must be scientific or technological. The technique I speak of applies equally to the mathematics of graph theory and the practicalities of throwing a clay pot. An artist and an engineer are equally technical.

A common problem with the technical types of people is that it is easy for us to get lost in technique itself, seeking out ever-greater heights of technical achievement in order to impress some unseen, usually internalized spectator. Of course, this is understandable, as we find pleasure in the definition and solution of problems. It's why many of us chase procedural generation in the first place. This drive can be a positive thing in settings like academic research or the early prototyping phases of a project, but it can get in the way of finishing projects.

In other words, it is easy for us to lose sight of our ultimate goal when creating something and instead get lost in the fiddly details. We end up with projects that increase in scope until they seem like an unfinishable mess. We turn small problems into big ones. This isn't the worst thing when working in a pure research mode, but it's a very undesirable situation in the context of a project with a deadline.

One of the most life-changing pieces of advice I ever received was from the game designer and programmer Brian Reynolds. Perhaps best known for the PC strategy games *Civilization II* and *Alpha Centauri*, Reynolds was giving a lecture at the Game Developers Conference in the early 2000s about the artificial intelligence systems in his game *Rise of Nations*. Tossed off as almost an aside, he said that when you are building the AI for a strategy game, the best place to start with any computer decision-making is to pick a decision out of a hat at random; then test to see how it plays. If the AI is good enough, congratulations, you have saved yourself a bunch of time, and you can move on.

While picking a strategy out of a hat will not itself be sufficient most of the time, the important lesson in Reynolds' words is clear: when coming up with algorithms, start as simple as you can, test it to see if works, and if it doesn't, go ahead and complicate things from there.

TWO EXAMPLES FROM *SPELUNKY*

The procedural level generation in Derek Yu's roguelike platformer game *Spelunky* is often held up as a high water mark of the field, and with good reason. The level generation has been covered at length in other places, but I want to hone in on two examples from the source code of the original freeware game that illustrate two ways of approaching a procedural generation problem in the simplest possible way.

The first example is the placement of generic treasures in the level. You might think that there would be a system of treasure sub-room templates or an algorithm that intelligently creates appropriate places to store treasure in a level. *Spelunky* does nothing like this. It handles the problem simply and elegantly with the following algorithm: For any given empty ground surface on the map, the probability of a treasure existing in that space is directly proportional to the number of solid surfaces adjacent to the space.

Because *Spelunky* is based on a grid of tiles, there are four possible configurations: a tile with the ground on the bottom and nothing to the top, left, or right (an open space); a tile with ground on the bottom and one additional adjacent surface (usually a corner of a room but sometimes a crawlspace); a dead-end nook with access from only one cardinal direction; and a space completely enclosed by solid surfaces.

As the number of adjacent surfaces increases, so does the chance of treasure appearing. This makes intuitive sense: You wouldn't hide treasure in the middle of an open floor, but you might tuck it into the corner of a room or a crawlspace, and you'd definitely bury it.

This is achingly elegant, but don't worry, plenty of *Spelunky*'s code is just as simple but far more kludgy. The next example we're going to look at is the placement of the Giant Spider enemy. As you read this algorithm, compare it to the elegance of how treasure is placed: In the first cave tile set, check for a two-by-two block of empty tile spaces below every brick tile that is not the ceiling of the level itself or in a shop, in the starting room, or on the bottom half of a room. If there is a two-by-two block of empty tile spaces, and we're thus allowed to generate a Giant Spider in this level and have yet to do so, then there is a 1 in 40 chance that we generate a Giant Spider and some cobwebs right beneath this brick. If we do generate a Giant Spider, we should not generate another in this level.

The above algorithm works out to about 30 lines of code, compared to 1 line of code for the treasure placement. While one algorithm is much briefer than the other, both are simple. Neither relies on A* path finding, cellular automata, or Perlin noise, and certainly nothing more complex than those classic standbys. Both algorithms rely on simple checks against features of the game world that are already represented in the game's model. Neither algorithm introduces any additional data or systems to the game. Could we come up with better solutions than these? Probably, but these are certainly good enough and did not prevent *Spelunky* from being hailed as a modern classic.

PERCEPTION VERSUS REALITY

Another hard learned lesson from years as a videogame developer: Almost nobody who views procedural content will understand what is happening behind the scenes.

When presented with an algorithm, most people assume far more complexity than what is actually going on. For example, my Twitter bot "Two Headlines" takes the subject of one news headline and swaps it for the subject of a different news headline. I often have people ask me what kind of natural language processing code I use for it. The truth is that it's running a far less complex algorithm: It goes to Google News, clicks on a subject in the subject listing, finds a headline about that subject, and replaces the subject name with a different subject. It's a simple scraper that does a find-and-replace on some text.

People also assume machine learning where there is none. I think this is because people like to apply narratives in order to understand the world. They like to think, "This level generator seemed random at first, but now it's making more sense; it must be learning my play style." People will sometimes attribute intelligence to the algorithm rather than to themselves!

These perceptions are why Brian Reynolds' advice on prototyping artificial intelligence is so important. Simply picking a random number to make important decisions is often enough to elicit the perception of intelligence.

USING CONTEXT TO TAKE YOUR WORK FROM TRIVIAL TO IMPRESSIVE

Suppose I tell you I have written some code that gets a random noun from an English dictionary and then gives you its definition. I don't think you would be particularly impressed, and you would not consider it procedural generation except in the most trivial sense of the term.

Suppose I tell you I have written software that generates variations on a joke and that approximately three out of every five jokes it generates cause a test audience to laugh. You would probably want to see this in action.

Finally, suppose I tell you that both of these pieces of code are functionally the same, save for some window dressing.

The code I am referring to does, in fact, exist; it is a generator I made in 2011 called "You Must Be." The code is simple, and the joke is effective. The algorithm grabs a random noun and its definition, like

earthquake: a shaking of the ground caused by the movement of the earth's tectonic plates.

The window dressing, what I call the "context," is the addition of a few static words:

Girl, you must be an earthquake because you are a shaking of the ground caused by the movement of the earth's tectonic plates.

Surreal humor though it may be, it's genuinely funny stuff. Yet the core algorithm is about as simple as you can get, relying on the dictionary as its mundane data source.

The "context" part is key here. The context transforms the code from a rote algorithm to a joke generator. When you think about it, this applies to all procedurally generated content. Take Perlin noise as an example. I can describe the algorithm, a kind of randomized stepping up and down over a gradient, but the algorithm is sterile, just like our dictionary algorithm. You could have shown the algorithm for Perlin noise to any number of mathematicians who would not have made the leap that Ken Perlin did: applying the algorithm to the context of naturalistic texture generation.

In the world of procedurally generated content, the difference between a purely technical person and a craftsperson or designer is understanding that a great technical leap won't necessarily create interesting content. Rote algorithms will work just fine if you situate them within an interesting game, visual context, or music theory framework, etc.

THE PROBLEM MIGHT NOT BE YOUR PROCGEN

Imagine you have a level generator for a Mario-style platform game. It places platforms at random throughout a two-dimensional level. The player can jump from one platform to the next, but the level generator sometimes creates gaps that are too big for the player to jump. Your instinct as a programmer might tell you that this is a problem with the level generator; you need to put in a constraint that makes all gaps traversable. But maybe the solution doesn't lie in the generator.

Instead of changing the generator, you could change the way the player character controls by adding a "run" button. Maybe you include a trade-off, such as making it difficult to slow down once you've started running or causing running to use up a valuable resource. It would probably be easier to tweak the physics of the player sprite than to refactor your level generator. And when you test out these changes, you may find that what was once a "bad" level generator is now a "good" level generator.

The platform generator is responding to changes in context. When you change the physics of the player character, the meaning of the platforms themselves changes. The context also changes if you add rising lava to levels, or make the platforms crumble if they are stepped on for too long. Making technically simple changes can transform a level generator from "generator of barely noticeable terrain" to "generator of nearly insurmountable challenges." It can also do the opposite! Imagine *Spelunky*'s level generator with the main character controlled like Pac-Man. Suddenly this algorithm that was a stroke of brilliance is now just making bad Pac-Man levels.

These strategies work well outside the realm of procedural generation as well. "Write a book" is one kind of challenge. "Write a book in a month" is an entirely different challenge that completely changes the possibility space and will cause the writer to go about things in an unconventional way.

CONCLUSION

The next time you think of a question like "What is the best way to generate a system of caves?", maybe think, "What is a way that I already know to generate a system of caves, why are those caves unsatisfying to me, and what can be changed about everything but the caves themselves to make them satisfying?" If you can do this, you'll implement things faster, you'll have simpler code to maintain, and you may even gain some insights about your non-procedural systems. I'm asking you to consider the possibility that the problem with your generator is not your procedural generation. It might be everything else.

The last thing I'll say is that keeping your procedural generation implementations as simple as possible has a nearly invisible long term benefit to your career as a creator. Doing so allows you to ship more things than you would otherwise. Actually putting work out into the world means your art will have viewers, your game will have players, your music will have listeners. You will probably get feedback on your algorithms, and you will discover ways that players interact with or perceive them that you could not have predicted. This is real knowledge that you can take into your next project or your next iteration of the same project. If you spend five years building what seems like the perfect content generator, I guarantee that no matter how much testing you do you will not learn as much about its shortcomings as you will when you release it into the world. So just set it free into the world as soon as possible. The next time you make something, it will be even better.

CHAPTER 3

Generated Right in the Feels

Jill Murray

Discoglobe Interactive

W henever I speak at a conference, no matter the topic, a man approaches me when I'm done, concerned about the Future of Game Narrative.

"Let me ask you something". He adopts a wide-legged stance before lunging into a list of things he needs to tell me.

"What was your question?" I ask after a while.

"Oh uh ...", he quickly thinks of something. "What do YOU think WE, as narrative designers, are not doing enough of? What do we lack?"

My answer is always the same: "A Thorough Investigation of the Human Condition".

"So you're saying we don't innovate enough?" he replies.

As a people, we narrative designers are obsessed with the idea of innovation. That's why we give so many talks about it. What does it *mean* for a game narrative to be branching, linear, *truly* non-linear, open-world, choice-driven, player-generated, environmental, diegetic? What can procedural generation add or take away? What is the newest, freshest, cleverest delivery mechanism for story? It doesn't take long for narrative discussions to adopt a focus on structure and delivery because those are things we can measure and test.

For all our talk, how often do we innovate in ways that matter to the players? And if players are not moved to their core, is it really innovation or just a distraction from the emotional labour of story craft, an excuse to make charts?

I'm allowed to wonder. I've made my fair share of charts (Figure 3.1.)

At Ubisoft Montreal in 2011, if you finished a project and had to wait before starting the next one, you were sent to the purgatory of Inter-Project. You had a desk and regular hours but no assigned work unless someone needed help punching up a list of achievements or wanted to talk through a design issue. Depending on your work style, the unstructured time was either a blessing (paid time for research!) or a curse (why am I even here?). I landed in this state of suspended reality between my work on *Your Shape: Fitness Evolved 2012* and *Assassin's Creed: Liberation*.

I have a hard time with the ends of projects. Though some endings are better than others, each of them is a festival of mood swings—pride for what we were able to accomplish, regret for what we weren't, anticipation for how the game might be received, and relief. No matter how much we love it, we all hit a point where we just need a game to be

FIGURE 3.1

done already. But then we mourn the loss of a team, a routine, and a purpose.

To cope with these feelings, I subconsciously turn to technical things. I'm never more interested in learning a new game engine or scripting language than right after something has ended. It's comforting to imagine new possibilities arising from components and knowledge clicking tidily into place.

So it goes that roughly ten minutes into InterProject, I developed an intense curiosity for devising types of interactive fiction structures. Could the shape and execution of a story inspire its content? How might storytellers employ AI as an arbiter of fate for unsuspecting players and characters?

I wanted to create playful structures and then see what stories they suggested. I toyed with different subversions of choice, randomness, and exposure to information to make potential outcomes more and less readable to the player.

The structures that began to emerge had minds of their own, creating shapes and patterns I hadn't anticipated. The idea was actually to be able to produce each of these interactive narratives, so I mindfully controlled for scope, but as soon as I did, something strange began to happen. With the introduction of production constraints, each of my dreamy story snowflakes began to transform, one at a time, into tiny nightmares.

Another Door Opens (Figure 3.2) offered readers a simple A or B decision but then allowed them to preview all possible outcomes, of possible outcomes of their choice, ultimately presenting them with sixteen detailed scenarios to weigh. The complexity and weight of information rendered their choice paralyzing and impossible to evaluate. They might as well flip a coin.

The Quantum Circuit (Figure 3.3) created a similar problem in a different way. The players could choose to look inside container A or container B but couldn't know what might be in either container until after they chose. The act of choosing filled the container. Choice was so important as to be irrelevant, unless they played enough times to understand the possible contents of each container.

In *You Don't Know What You're Missing* (Figure 3.4), readers were required to read a chapter every day. If they missed a day, they would

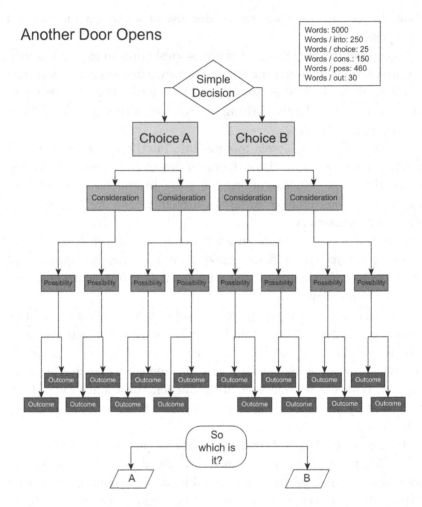

Another Door Opens

Words: 5000
Words / into: 250
Words / choice: 25
Words / cons.: 150
Words / poss: 460
Words / out: 30

FIGURE 3.2 "Another Door Opens"

not be able to go back and read the previous day's passage but instead would receive a summary of what they'd missed. The summaries would vary in reliability. The more days missed, the more the summaries would change and decay, making it impossible to trust the story after a while. Use it or lose it. Does it matter much if the voice is reliable if you're enjoying a story? What if you're not? It both emphasized and undermined the author's role.

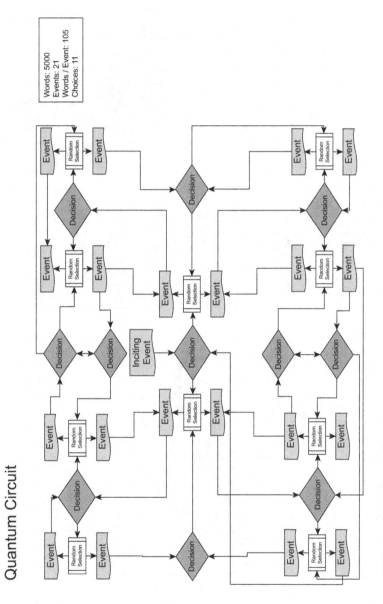

FIGURE 3.3 "The Quantum Circuit"

The Forgetting Curve?
You Don't Know What You're Missing

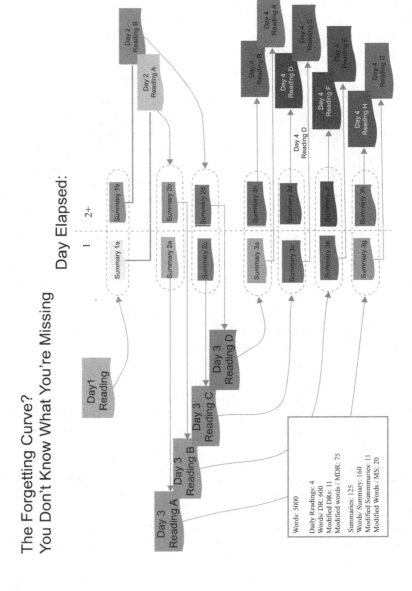

FIGURE 3.4 "You Don't Know What You're Missing"

Finally, *Down the Rabbit Hole* (Figure 3.5) was a distraction engine that allowed readers to follow tangents as they read, and then follow those tangents to deeper tangents, eventually dumping them out of the story into the internet at large if they kept accepting the offer to follow their own drive. It accelerated the author's loss of control over the readers and the readers' loss of narrative closure in the face of outside temptations for their focus and time.

Looking at my beautiful, ugly, chart-based baby, I realized that I hadn't so much innovated in game narrative as I had destroyed reading. I called the collection *Bad Dreams* and decided it was complete as it was. The structures themselves communicated volumes, but most of what they had to say was "help me". They were a series of story prisons, and I don't believe in filling a prison just because you built it.

Bad Dreams preoccupied me for a full month of InterProject, and I came out of it feeling very accomplished, but with not a word written, no characters, no drama—no actual stories. The real work of making stories—not just structuring them, but populating them with all of these important things, testing your assumptions, and letting the results change all your best plans—is messy and unpredictable. It doesn't reward us with the reassuring click of plans sliding into place; it gives questions, challenges and emptiness demanding to be contemplated or filled.

Most writers love the feeling of having *already* written. Second best is the feeling of being *about to write*—perhaps with a trip to the notebook store for fresh stationery. The discipline of narrative design allows us to consider living our whole lives in this *about to* state, replacing the drudgery and self-doubt of committing to specific details with intellectual planning for how a story *ought* to go. Innovation is next to procrastination.

Thank goodness for reality. In January 2012, I was relieved from InterProject by an invitation to write for *Assassin's Creed Liberation*. Its needs and deadlines left no time for theory. We had to get straight to work.

Although the pressures were greater, this was, in many ways, easier. I immediately fell in love with the character of Aveline de Grandpré. Born in New Orleans in the 18th century, her father was a wealthy French merchant, and her mother had been a slave. Although Aveline

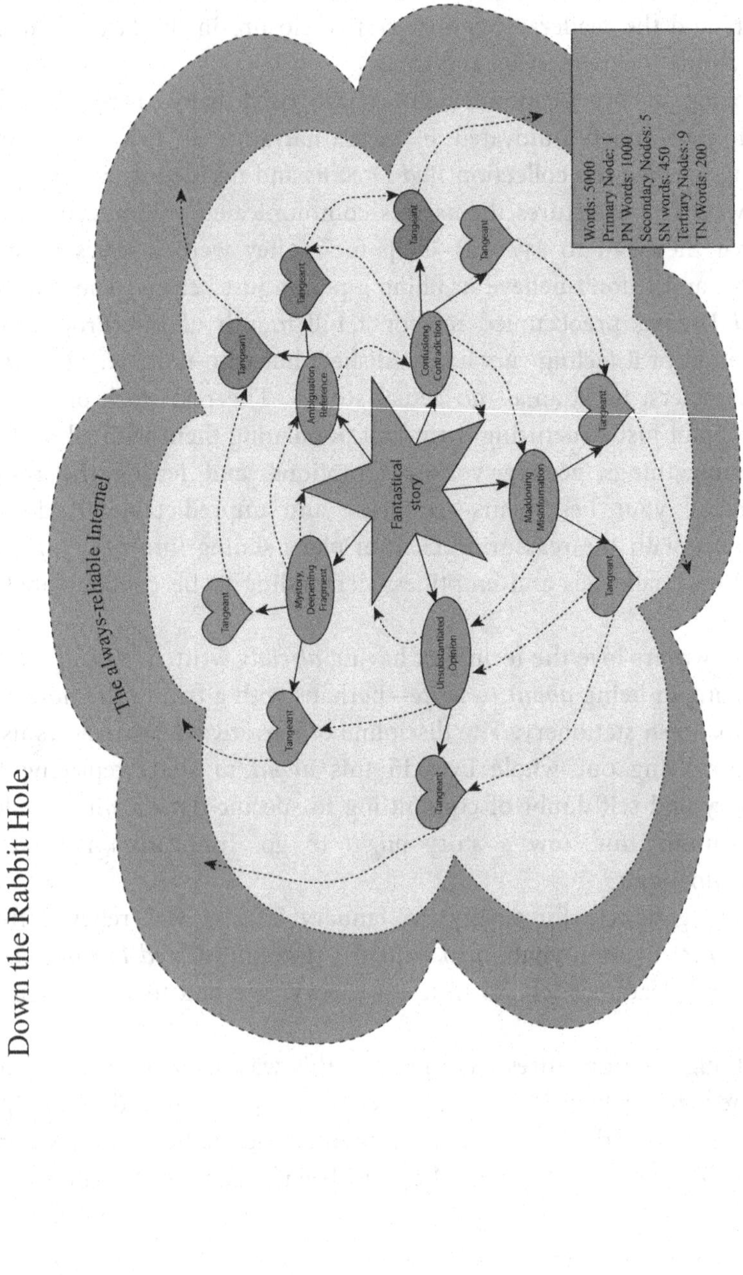

Down the Rabbit Hole

The always-reliable Internet

Fantastical story

Tangent

Ambiguation Reference

Confusing Contradiction

Mystery Deepening Fragment

Maddening Misinformation

Unsubstantiated Option

Words: 5000
Primary Node: 1
PN Words: 1000
Secondary Nodes: 5
SN words: 450
Tertiary Nodes: 9
TN Words: 200

FIGURE 3.5 "Down the Rabbit Hole"

was armed to the teeth and educated in the art of assassination, she had three father figures who watched protectively over her every breath. *That must be annoying*, I thought, and from this seed, her character grew.

Liberation, like other games in the *Assassin's Creed* franchise, ran a linear adventure story through an open world game, effectively challenging two narrative structures to co-exist. Open worlds, as we have known them so far in games, are largely about a feeling of getting lost in a world larger than oneself and then through exploration, and often combat, learning and mastering that world.

Meanwhile, adventure stories in games typically take their cues from the seventeen-step programme of the Hero's Journey. As handy as the Hero's Journey is for analysing one specific category of Western stories, players stepping into an open world on their own terms are less interested in completing a seventeen-step programme than testing the world, perhaps even breaking it, to come to their own understanding. For many people, *Skyrim* is about adopting pets or herding cheese, and questing is how they pass time until more world (and more cheese) becomes available. I'm no stranger to this player perspective. Even after working on the game, I played *Assassin's Creed Black Flag* to 53% completion by sailing around the world on the winds of my whims, consciously avoiding the linear story.

If you're going to run a linear story through an open world game (and I don't necessarily suggest that you do), you can't count on having the players' focus, and you don't have control over how they spend their time, so you lose the ability to pace their experience in any meaningful way. How, then, do you get them to advance and perhaps even one day complete the story?

On *Liberation*, it would have been easy to get lost in the bayou and never find our way out, but character guided us through production; more than that, *love* of character. Aveline led with her heart and made decisions swiftly. She could be as ruthless as she was understanding. She was a manipulator with a heart of gold who used others' assumptions and perceptions to shapeshift between the roles available to her in her time: assassin, lady, slave. In each of these guises, she challenged players to re-evaluate her world and their own. She was real and important to us, and the more we invested in her, the more we trusted that players would follow her where the story needed to go.

My own story next led me to *Assassin's Creed: Black Flag* and then to *Freedom Cry*, with Adéwalé and the Maroons of Saint-Domingue laying the foundations of revolution, and from there, to a series of dismaying events, depositing me in personal turmoil.

Caught in the emotional muck of recovery, I turned again to my old experimental, tinkering ways—but now with characters like Aveline and Adéwalé fresh in my heart. Working on a new game, for a prospective audience that would prefer to tend and befriend than stalk and assassinate, we set about asking new questions and testing our theories. In this game, every character in the world would be generated, except for the player character. Players would have the freedom to experiment with style and preference and change themselves as often as they desired. Any sense of story or progression would come down to activities players chose to engage in, the steps necessary to undertake them, and the rewards they received. With so many moving parts, no traditional stories to speak of, and the players' own identities up in the air, it was essential to find something for players to connect with emotionally, to anchor the experience.

Generating any quantity of believable characters you can feel and connect to is a challenge. Narrative generation falls prey to the same risks of repetitiveness that other types of generation do. The 10,000 Bowls of Oatmeal problem, as it applies to character generation, can yield a series of quirky quest-givers, each one with dialogue you want to skip, as easily as a series of equally ambitious enemies, indistinguishable but for their win-loss records and a birthmark here and there.

Much like Aveline's character was deeply knit into the mechanics of her persona system, designers like Emily Short (author of Chapter 28) have written about the necessity of linking generated characters to mechanics.[1] This anchors each character within the player's experience, making the characters essential, in practical terms. But how to make the player feel as attached as if they were real?

My project was small and experimental; it hadn't even been green-lit yet, so we needed to find answers on a shoestring budget. I began to wonder about the smallest, sparsest, most sketchy set of details we could generate that would make individual non-player characters seem real— to show that we cared who they were and what motivated them so we would want to get to know and befriend them, or even challenge and oppose them? What if it were less important how a character was defined and more how players attached to them? Could we elicit an emotional response to a lightly drawn character, as an artist can often make us feel the important intentions of a subject as strongly from a few loose brushstrokes as with a highly realistic rendering?

We already know that players build their own ideas of character, somewhat independently of what is authored. In the time between writing and editing this essay, I've seen *Shadow of the Tomb Raider* completed, promoted, and released. What has emerged are wildly differing portraits of Lara Croft. Some critics read her as an inconsistent narcissist. For the community, she is flawed but caring and richer for her internal struggles. There is only one Lara on screen—one set of voiced dialogue, art, and cinematics, no branching storylines creating a common gameplay vocabulary for all players. However, she lives differently in the hearts and minds of different individuals. So, we know players have a great natural capacity and enthusiasm for attachment and interpretation. Why not provoke them to use it on purpose and shift some of the processing power to players' minds, so to speak.

Back on my experimental project, I turned away from the largeness and expansiveness of open world thinking and tried instead to focus on the intimacy of getting to know a person. How many people does each of us know very well? In a crowd, do we experience each other as people or obstacles or both? I read about gossip and small talk and the many almost subconscious ways humans have of communicating and negotiating relationships. I thought about the ways we express and define ourselves, the masks we wear, and the accidents that cause us to show our hands, revealing our true character.

I devised a simple test. I wanted to know what emotional details people would connect to instantly. Using only text, I tried to strip away as much writing or dialogue style as possible. I created a simple tool in Twine (and later in Javascript) for generating simple lists of characters and their attributes. Then I let people hit the "generate" button and read and react to the skeletal details that appeared on the screen.

It soon became apparent that the list really didn't need to be long. In fact shorter was better.

The lists looked something like this*:

Name:	Nat
Age:	28
Gender:	Non-binary
Dominant trait:	Introverted
Favourite colour:	Purple
Kids:	2
Worst fear:	Spiders
Strongest childhood memory:	Bullied one friend only once and immediately regretted it
Ambition:	Go back to school and get a masters' degree
Emotional need:	Confidence
Hobby:	None

(*Re-creation. Actual lists are covered by NDA and locked away in a dusty server somewhere.)

From a grid like the one above, people not only related to the characters outlined, but also began to tell their stories to themselves and ask questions. Depending on the participant, Nat might have been an immigrant who worked hard to prove themselves. They might be introverted because they were shy or because they felt judged. Maybe they'd bullied their childhood friend under peer pressure, to fit in. Small changes to details made a big difference. If Nat's age changed from 28 to 23, then maybe they'd had their kids young and quit school. Maybe their marriage had impacted their confidence. Change their dominant personality trait from introverted to extroverted, then maybe they'd played the bully to get attention, rather than to escape it.

Too many details and Nat would turn back into a bowl of oatmeal. Users would spend more time pressing the button and trying to figure out the system and the logic behind the generated details. A sparse level of detail was more likely to tap into players' creative minds and provoke them to consider the person behind the list.

For our experiments, this was all we needed to know. If sparsely drawn characters could draw players' attention, the next set of experiments could begin to tackle how to spawn more and deeper characteristics, as players attempted to communicate and get to know characters better. It didn't matter if everyone read Nat the same way, or even if everyone cared about them equally—or at all—because even that was true to life. How often do we read each other accurately, in reality? The fact that we have to try so hard to understand each other is probably why we like stories so much in the first place.

Nat's project soon found an end, in its own unique and saddening way. We had no choice but to move on as quickly as if an unseen player had pressed the "regenerate" button. Much like Aveline, Adéwalé and Lara continue to travel with me in a small, comfortable compartment in my heart, so have the principles of Nat's game.

Innovation isn't the hard part of game narrative. Games can train players to explore by expanding and conquering or by training their focus to interpret and understand. Any structure might be the right one, and every structure can be so distracting that we forget what really matters. The difficulty in game narrative is the same thing that's hard everywhere: understanding and connecting to people, be they fictional characters, other players, developers, or even ourselves.

NOTE

1   https://emshort.blog/2016/09/21/bowls-of-oatmeal-and-text-generation/

This page intentionally left blank

CHAPTER 4

Adapting Content to Player Choices

Jurie Horneman

B ecause I wear a designer hat as well as a technical hat, it has taken me an embarrassingly long time to understand that the fact that you could generate something doesn't mean that you should. While it is certainly possible to drive your creative goals from a technical idea, it is generally better to drive your technical ideas from a creative goal: Figure out what you want to achieve, then build that.

What is the reason for using procedural storytelling or procedural content generation in general? It can be to create the unique appeal of infinite worlds (*Elite, No Man's Sky*) and extremely deep possibility spaces (*Dwarf Fortress*), replayability (*Spelunky*, roguelikes), or evocative juxtapositions and the aesthetics of randomness (Twitter bots). There are other, equally worthy, reasons. I am interested in procedural story-telling in order to adapt a game and its story to player choices (and to other dynamic elements such as game state, as in the current state of the game world). This is not one of the reasons I listed above for pursuing procedural approaches, and the methods to achieve these goals are not always seen as "procedural." Adapting to player choices allows for more player expression: It lets players have game experiences that are uniquely tailored to them, that show them the deeper consequences of a wider range of actions and is particularly important in open world games. By definition, such games give the player more choices, even if just spatial, but pacing and controlling progression are much harder when you cannot know where players will be or what they will encounter in which order. Procedural techniques can help solve this.

No matter what deep learning demos promise, it is not possible to generate every kind of content. The resulting quality may not be high enough, or the development costs may be too high. Additionally, if it does not get you closer to your creative goals, it does not make sense to generate something instead of using pre-created content. Making a game that adapts to player choices while aiming for a high level of execution quality means you have to mix pre-created content with dynamic or generated content. That creates a particular set of challenges, which this chapter will discuss.

CHOOSING WHICH PARTS TO ADAPT

In order to make a given kind of content adaptive, you first have to identify elements or aspects that tie it too much to the context in which it appears and make it hard to adapt the game to the player's choices. ("Content" is a vague word, but many of the principles in this chapter apply to many different kinds of content: levels, text, graphics, etc.) I will use missions for my examples, because missions appear in many games in some form or another, they are a powerful way of structuring the player experience, and in games that have them they are where the story happens. Spatially linear games typically don't have missions—sequences of gameplay objectives—because they don't need them as a separate concept.

Let's say you have a mission that involves finding a witch to get a magic potion, in an open world game where players can go anywhere they want whenever they want. This means that unlike in linear games, you don't know for sure where players will be when this mission makes sense in terms of story progression and pacing.

Spatial linearity is the easiest solution for solving the problem of predicting where a player will be in a given point of the story. It works very well! Naughty Dog always knows where Nathan Drake is at any point in the story of an *Uncharted* game, but in open world games it is harder. Instead of creating missions to fit locations you know ahead of time, it is useful to be able to adapt the content of missions to a dynamically determined location. You could make multiple copies of a mission, one per location, and select those at runtime. This is a brute force approach that is absolutely fine in certain cases but generally ends up being both costly and unwieldy, because you have to create and maintain all of those copies. So let's say you want to adapt your witch-finding mission so it can work in a forest as well as in a desert. How do you do that?

Let's start with a simple first step. Many games use objective texts to tell the player what to do: "Find the sword," "Kill the evil overlord," etc. In our case, we might want to tell the player "Search for the witch in the woods" or "Search for the witch in the desert." The name of the location ties the objective text to the location. You can use a text substitution system, so that you write an objective template such as "Search for the witch in the %location%." Then, when you need the actual objective, you look at the location in which the mission needs to happen and replace the magical word "%location%" with "woods" or "desert."

Text substitution is pretty well understood. In English you only need to pay attention to a few simple grammatical rules. In other languages, especially gendered ones, things get a lot harder, but that is outside the scope of this chapter. Systems like Kate Compton's Tracery, James Ryan's Expressionist, and Bruno Dias's Improv offer more sophisticated ways to do text substitution but essentially are still templates plus elements that get injected into those templates. Note that the template "Search for the witch in the %location%" is pre-created content, as are "woods" and "desert." The computer does not understand the concept of searching, or witches, or locations, or deserts. It's just replacing some letters in a sentence.

So we identified the element (the location name) that made the content (the objective text) not adaptive to the context (where the mission can occur), and then we pulled that out so it can come from elsewhere, be that generated or selected from a set of pre-created content. By doing so, we made it possible to adapt the content to a player choice (where the player went). This is the general principle to make content adaptive, and it applies broadly. Take Blizzard's multi-player game *Overwatch*, for example. At the end of each game, players see the "Play of the Game," a short clip of some particularly impressive feat a player performed. This clip is preceded by a highlight intro, showing a spiffy animation involving the hero the player selected. Players can unlock and equip both "skins" (different looks for their heroes) and highlight intro types. This means that the highlight intro players see adapts to two player choices: the hero skin and the highlight intro type.

It might surprise you to think of a fairly straightforward real-time animation as adaptive content or procedural storytelling. But it is; we just don't tend to think of it that way anymore. When I was making games in the '90s, we would have killed for the ability to show an arbitrary animation on an arbitrary character. I worked on 3D character animation technology back then in order to make that kind of thing possible. A 3D renderer is a system for procedurally generating animations and images.

Let's imagine we want to use an NPC to give our mission to the player. One approach would be to create a mission giver per setting and then activate the one you need. You create a weary explorer in the tavern near the forest who tells you about the clearing where the witch dwells. Then you create a mysterious traveler in the oasis who tells you about the cave out in the desert where another (or the same) witch lives. And so forth for any other setting that makes sense for your game. Then you use a global variable to store the setting in which this mission was activated, so it gets spawned where the player is and then never gets spawned again. We also need to make sure the witch can actually be found, so we need to define a position per setting where the witch hangs out and then activate the right one. This approach—selecting content based on player choice—is very simple and doesn't require any complicated technology. It is easy to understand, it works, and it makes the mission adaptive. It is easy to underestimate simple techniques. Procedural storytelling does not need to involve complicated technology.

This example involved creating multiple copies of a part of the content (the mission giver) and selecting and activating the right version at runtime. In this case it's OK because making multiple copies of a mission giver is usually quite cheap, but it's possible to take it further. Perhaps there can be a fixed mission giver in any tavern, like the owner—already a common thing in many games. Or perhaps any character in a tavern can be a mission giver. Or you can select or generate a mission giving character that fits the locale. The mission just needs an NPC who can give missions, it doesn't matter much who it is, because mission giving usually involves just a few lines of text. Locations can have mission givers or positions in which mission givers can be spawned. By teaching the computer what a mission giver is, we can easily make our missions even more adaptable.

However, everything we do to make our witch or mission giver more universally useful also makes it less specific. Some missions rely on having to bring a particular ring to a particular place to please a particular wizard, not just any random person in a bar. The above techniques for making mission givers adaptive are not general solutions for procedural storytelling, but rather powerful tools that are applicable in many situations. By using these tools appropriately, you can balance implementation effort and reactivity against the uniqueness of the experience. I will come back to this later in this chapter.

What more can be abstracted and factored out of missions? Since time immemorial, level designers have told stories in games by tying story progress to spatial progress. The player opens a door or walks into some invisible volume and suddenly "story happens." This is, for better or worse, one of the bedrock techniques for telling stories in games, but it's limited and laborious to set up. Whenever you want to change your story you need to adapt your space, and vice versa. If players don't move where or when you want them to, your pacing breaks down. The more spatial choices you offer the player, the more convoluted your story logic becomes.

Some types of story progression can be decoupled from spatial progression, using a technique I call a story daemon, "daemon" being a general term in computer science for an invisible entity that does things for you. In 2016 I built a little interactive fiction experiment with a story daemon called the Creepifier, which is a bit like *Left 4 Dead*'s AI Director only for slowly building dread. Its job is to introduce creepy details into scenes at an increasing pace. When it is active, it looks at its internal "creep clock" to see if it's time to show something creepy. If so, it looks at the tags of the current location and tries to find a matching entry in its library of "creep blocks" Then it injects the creep block into the description of the location. Creep blocks are typically just paragraphs of text ("You hear a scurrying noise behind the walls.") but they can also contain new player options ("A book falls open by itself. Do you read it?"). At every turn, the creep clock slowly increases until something creepy happens at every turn.

It is easy to imagine the Creepifier modifying or injecting other types of content: visual effects, music, and sound effects, but also combat scenes. The Creepifier can be turned on or off as the story requires, and it can be combined with or interact with other story daemons. A companion NPC who comments on what is happening can be implemented as a story daemon, and such an NPC system should interact with the Creepifier.

My Creepifier demo was extremely simple. Complications arise when you try to do this at higher levels of execution quality. You have to deal with repetitiveness and unintentional patterns as with any procedural technique, and it becomes tricky to make sure all creep blocks match all situations they can appear in—all problems I will discuss later in this chapter. The important thing to realize is that managing this complexity is an essential difficulty. Because we want to give the player more choice, and because at some point handling that manually no longer scales, we need to teach a computer how to help us, and that means we need to express our problem in a way a computer understands, which means we need to understand it deeply ourselves. The problem we're trying to solve is difficult, and we're making the computer help us; that costs time and effort. This is one more reason to be clear about the required investment and the expected return.

COMBINING BITS

We've made content adaptive by identifying elements that tie it to a particular context and found a way to separate those out. To create the final content when the game needs it—to adapt it to the current context or game state—you typically need to select or generate the right bit of sub-content, and combine it with a template.

For our objective text example, this is simple. We find the objective text template ("Search for the witch in the %location%") for the mission, then find the name of the target location and insert it into the template. It gets more interesting when you move away from a strict one-to-one relationship between game state and elements. In the system I built for *Mainframe*,[1] the interactive fiction game Liz England and

I made for the ProcJam game jam in 2015, it was possible to say "Give me a player option leading to a scene with a given set of properties." Those properties were expressed using tags. For example:

<injectOption tags="search, electrical"/>

would insert a player choice leading to a scene that was marked with the tags "search" and "electrical."

Tag-based content selection is simple yet powerful.[2] More sophisticated approaches exist, such as Valve's rule-based system for selecting dialogue lines or Irrational Games' gameplay pattern-matching. In 2011, I worked on an unreleased action role-playing game that used a tag-based approach to generate dungeons. Instead of generating the dungeon topology using some algorithm, we pre-defined it in a map editor. For each room of the dungeon, we added tags that specified which kind of room we wanted, for instance: "spooky," "corridor," "jungle," "exit to the east." This declarative approach did not allow us to generate an infinite amount of dungeons, but it did make editing dungeons extremely quick. The engine translated our templates into actual dungeons using a big collection of pre-defined dungeon rooms. We were able to specify that some tag requests must be satisfied, while others were nice to have. This meant that the system tried its best but had an acceptable fallback. We will see later in the chapter why that was important. Common concerns with content selection algorithms are avoiding unnecessary receptiveness and unintentional patterns, as well as implementing a weighting system so more remarkable bits occur less often. This is also quite common in NPC bark selection—and what is that if not a procedural storytelling system that involves selecting content?

CREATING THE RIGHT BITS

Selecting the right bits of content is one part of the problem. Deciding which bits of content to create is another. As a first step, you want to avoid having your system ask for a content you didn't provide. In our witch mission example, if we try to create the mission in a place where we don't have a location name, a mission giver, or a witch position, we will fail. In the action role-playing game I mentioned earlier, the game would crash hard when the dungeon template asked for a room that didn't exist. We used automated testing to make sure those cases would never occur and the "nice to have" tag type to make sure we were not over-constraining our dungeons.

The next step is to build the tools that allow you to see where you're missing content or where content is too sparse, so that you can fill your buckets of content bits appropriately.[3] Then, on the content creation side, you need to handle context. How many situations should a bit of pre-created content be able to function in? Which contexts can it appear in? Context can be implicit or explicit. With implicit context, the content creator knows which situations a piece of content can appear in and makes sure it always works, but there's no system to enforce this and sometimes no easy way to find out what the context is. This is one of the hard things about game writing: You have to know all the situations in which a line can appear and make sure it works in all of them.

With explicit context the content creator specifies in which situations a piece of context can appear, so the computer knows her intentions. This is what we did for the dungeon rooms in the action role-playing game. You get more control but it is still hard, because you need to think through the permutations and express them in a way the computer understands. The more dimensions of context a piece of adaptive content has to react to, and the more those dimensions are intertwined, the harder it gets to templatize or proceduralize that content. Our mission giver needs to tell you about the witch in the woods (*"You're looking for the witch? She lives in the forest!"*). If you were just writing this in a story, he would probably also comment on the state of the main character, the weather, etc. (*"You look like you've had some adventures on the way here. The monsters always come out in the rain."*) He might say something that is emotionally relevant to the main character's arc or that refers to the state of affairs, which the main character is in the process of changing (*"The attacks have grown more desperate lately, as if whoever is behind them is making one more attempt to wipe us out."*) You can do that all that in a few lines. You can even choose to not use dialogue, to skip the mission giver, or even to skip the entire mission, depending on what the story needs. Text has infinite nuance, and this makes adapting it extremely hard.[4]

PAPERING OVER THE SEAMS

Often, the connection between events is both crucial for high execution quality and hard to adapt dynamically. Consider a remark by an NPC between two missions. Probably you would want them to comment on what just happened, on what comes next, and on the causal relationship between those things. Branching missions, or different ways of ending missions, add even more context to adapt to (e.g., *"You convinced the witch to give you her monster-killing potion? Excellent! Now it should be easy to wipe the monsters out"* versus *"You didn't get the witch's potion? Well, you can still kill the monsters, but it will be harder."*) The same goes for transitional paragraphs in interactive fiction. These are small bits of text, but they can get complex.

The easiest way to avoid the problem is by not having any transitions. Break things up and make them modular, reducing the dependencies between them. Heavily dynamic text-based games like Dwarf Fortress use more functional text that doesn't flow nicely: *"Endok sketches pictures of stacked leather. Endok has begun a mysterious constriction."* It is effective, since the player can absorb the information in the text more quickly, if less immersive. *Fallen London* solves the same problem on a higher level by breaking the entire experience into modular bits called storylets that intentionally have no connection to each other, leaving it to the player to imagine the connections. In games that use continuous time (in other words, most games) this is not a solution that is easy to adopt. Additionally, the connections between events are the key to story. *"The king died and then the queen died of grief"* says something different from *"The king died. The queen died."* Leaving these connections to the imagination of your audience, as Fallen London does, is a valid artistic choice but not a universal solution.

CONTROL OVER SPECIFICITY

From a highly reductive perspective, and very generally speaking, the point of both stories and games is to not bore the audience, to continually surprise them with the new and unexpected. This is a challenge for procedural systems, which inevitably involve repetition and are prone to creating bland content, something Kate Compton has called the 10,000 Bowls of Oatmeal problem. The best way to deal with this risk is to make sure that you have control over the degree of "proceduralness" of your content and that you plan for content with multiple degrees of specificity. Maybe your main missions are all hand-authored with highly specific content. But even when your side missions are more generated, make sure to include some hand-authored ones to mix things up. Avoid being locked into all-procedural content or putting too much of the weight of your game onto procedural elements.

This is related to how NPC barks are typically designed. Instead of making all barks equally likely, AI voice designers and bark writers tend to weight barks differently so that the remarkable ones happen less frequently than the highly reusable ones. The key is that they have the possibility to shape things so that the repetitiveness of the most common barks is leavened by less common ones.

A COMPLETELY NEW WAY OF CREATING CONTENT

Perhaps the biggest challenge, when you are part of an existing team with previous experience shipping games, is dealing with a completely new way of creating content. Procedural or systemic content of any type often involves taking direct control away from content creators and replacing it with indirect rules and systems. This can understandably create anxiety: The tools you spent time and effort learning to master are taken away and replaced with new tools that work very differently. Because these tools are new, they often are not as sophisticated as the old ones.

An additional phenomenon with procedural content is that integration and progress work differently. Normal, static content—3D models of rocks, say—has almost no interdependencies. Each rock can be modeled in any order, the work can be divided over people arbitrarily. It behaves linearly in terms of planning. Once you've done 30% of the work, 30% of the rocks are in the game. Additionally, each rock can easily be integrated into and seen in the game. This is famously different for programming, which can have massive interdependencies and progress is not linear at all. It is fairly typical to have done 90% of the work and have nothing be visible or working. This is why project management for software is challenging.

Procedural content is a combination of the two. You can build systems that are immediately visible but produce bland content. Or all the content is there, but the systems that use them aren't there yet. A tweak to an algorithm or someone adding some data can completely change the game. Progress and visibility are often much more non-linear than with non-procedural content. This can be disconcerting for people and needs to be managed accordingly.

Procedural approaches are a fundamentally different way of developing games and slice through traditional workflows and across disciplines in unexpected ways. Developing ways of conceptualizing, measuring, and evaluating procedural work is a vital challenge. It is not enough to consider what a game does at run-time; it is equally important to design the creative process a team uses to develop games procedurally. Gray-boxing and metrics for level geometry are common techniques now. As an industry, we've figured out workflows for combining level art and gameplay geometry. But what are the equivalents for games that make heavy use of procedural techniques? What tools and workflows do content creators need to test their work in all relevant contexts? What metrics do we need to evaluate whether we've made "enough" content, or the right kind of content? As an industry, we are slowly learning how to do this, but we still have far to go. New approaches are being invented here and there and will spread in postmortems, but for now it remains a crucial challenge that should not be underestimated.

THE BIG PICTURE

On a higher level, it's important to not think of procedural storytelling as a problem we can solve the way other technical problems can be solved. 3D rendering is by now a matter of engineering: How can we get render these models in a more efficient way? Procedural storytelling is not one well-defined problem; it is a thousand differently designed solutions. This is an art not a science. You cannot "solve" storytelling in games.

The majority of storytelling techniques we have developed, over millennia, are for non-interactive media or, more precisely, for media where we have exact control over the time, space, and character of the audience's point of view. This includes techniques in stories themselves, for instance for creating tension, as well as our techniques for thinking about and developing stories. These don't work well in games, because the player can make choices that affect outcome, because time in games typically advances in a continuous manner, because players have control over their positions in space, but also because games are about systems and the potentials they enable.

Using time-honored storytelling techniques, we are able to arrange events and impressions in a precise manner that reliably evokes powerful emotions. Adapting this to games leads us to concepts such as branching and non-linearity. This a top-down approach to storytelling in games: breaking up the player-facing experience into bits. We can also create systems from which conflicts and other interesting situations arise. This is a bottom-up approach: simulating the elements from which stories are made.

However, we have not yet mastered making the top-down and bottom-up approaches work together. Bottom-up simulation does not generate the emotional experience of top-down storytelling; top-down storytelling is not as dynamic as simulations. A few years ago, I joked that the three core tools of storytelling in games are cut-scenes, invisible boxes, and environmental storytelling, but I soon realized it was not a joke.

This conflict between top-down and bottom-up is one more reason the most fruitful approach to procedural storytelling involves combining bits of pre-created, generated, and systemic content based on dynamic context.

NOTES

1 You can play the game at http://mainframe.intelligent-artifice.com.
2 While simple to understand at implementation, at larger scale tags can become unwieldy. I have written more about the pros and cons of tag-based content selection in *Game AI Pro 3*.
3 There is a lot of interesting research happening in this space in academia, as well as in interactive fiction. I recommend following the work of James Ryan, Emily Short, Jacob Garbe, and Graham Nelson.
4 Because text to speech is still very poor and speech has its own meanings and nuances, speech is the hardest form of content to generate of all.

CHAPTER 5

Ethical Procedural Generation

Dr. Michael Cook

Queen Mary University of London

There are a whole bunch of different things to worry about when you make a procedural generator. Will my generator ever make a mistake? Does it produce a lot of boring things? How much time does it need to generate something? Sometimes it can be so tricky to get your generator working that simply getting it to produce anything feels like a huge accomplishment. Worrying about what it's producing, why it's producing it or what others might think about it can get lost in the huge relief and satisfaction of finally seeing little dungeons, poems or stories coming out of your computer.

As generative software grows in popularity, we're seeing its ideas used by more people in lots of novel ways and for lots of exciting new uses. These developments are encouraging and inspiring, but they also makes it even more important that we take the time to think about the broader impact of this technology on people and society. In this chapter we're going to look at the ethical issues that can arise when making procedural generators and give you some things to keep in mind when you're making your next generator. They won't all apply to every person and every project, and you may not agree with every single thing we suggest, but with luck just reading through this chapter will give you a new perspective on procedural generation and help you think about this awesome art form in a different way. Along the way we're going to travel to some pretty extreme parts of the generative world and pose some open-ended questions about what we should let generators do, how we should talk about them and how we should let them talk about the world.

TALKING IN CODE

A procedural generator encodes a lot of different ideas and knowledge into a tiny package of rules and procedures. Each time we run it, those rules and procedures unpack bits and pieces of the knowledge we fed in and reassemble them into something new. Some of the ideas we feed into our generator are technical, and a lot of this book is given over to the broad and complicated technical challenges that surround procedural generation. We've already seen some of this in chapters about modular design and balancing chaos with predictability. Other ideas are aesthetic or artistic in nature. Procedural generators encode our ideas about how we think games should be designed: they represent what we think a good dungeon looks like, how a good story should end or what makes a beautiful colour scheme. They're little digital apprentices that we train and then trust to finish bits of our artwork in the homes of the people who view them.

Creating a procedural generator is a bit like making a work of art—some of the things we put on the canvas are intentional, but other things we paint on might be unconscious acts we don't give much thought to. Some might simply be mistakes. When we tweak the maximum size parameter of our dungeon generator, we most likely know the effects it will have on our level difficulty or how long our game takes to play—that's an example of a conscious decision. But there are lots of ways in which we can introduce accidental features to our generators, sometimes without even thinking. The tricky thing is that it can be very difficult to realise this has happened, because generators are often quite complicated and are designed to generate huge quantities of content. If there's something wrong in the system it might be hard to tell without looking at thousands and thousands of examples.

Let's explore an example of a system that ends up with an unexpected feature in it. Suppose we're making an RPG level set in a spooky graveyard, and we want the player to be able to read randomised inscriptions on each tombstone. We decide to do this using a few simple patterns, so we write a few templates for gravestone patterns, like "#NAME lies here, died #YEAR". Our templating system knows that when it sees #YEAR it replaces it with a random four-digit number, and when it sees #NAME it generates a random name by sticking a first name and a last name together. We give it a try and it works great—random names appear with random years attached. We're getting bored of the templates we've written, though, so we add one more, an inscription for couples buried together. It reads: "#NAME and #NAME, reunited in love once again, #YEAR". As a quick exercise, you can imagine a few possible outputs for this template in your head, or maybe write them down.

This template is a bit more interesting than the ones with only one name. Take a moment and imagine how we might implement the "#NAME" generator. You don't need to think about it in terms of code—imagine how you might do it with pen and paper. Depending on how we think about relationships, gender and sexuality, our first instinct might be to write two lists of names: one list of names that sound like they might be associated with "male" identity, and another of names that sound like they might be associated with "female" identity. Another approach is to simply have one big list of names and not worry too much about separating it out into a binary of any kind. You might not even think about this distinction—maybe you just used one list because it was quicker and you wanted to save time. But this decision, whatever you do, is going to have an impact on what this graveyard says about sexuality and gender in your game.

To see how, let's continue through our example. Suppose we use our two separated name generators for our new couples' template and generate a gravestone or two. The individual examples will make sense: "Jack and Jane, together again at last, 2016". They'll look fine, and you might even read a dozen or so while walking around. But "Jack and John" or "Jane and Lucy" will never appear—name pairings that might suggest non-heterosexual relationships. Because of the way we've structured the data in our generator, our graveyard is now presenting our game world in a way that implies that only heterosexual relationships exist.

Of course, this might be exactly what you want for your game! Perhaps you want to show the player that only heteronormative couples are afforded a proper burial in this town, and it becomes an important part of the plot. What matters here isn't the message sent by the generator (although for what it's worth, we highly recommend the single namelist approach). What matters is whether you as a creator realise what message your generator is broadcasting, because that means that you're in charge and able to assess whether that message is something you're happy with sending out into the world. Procedural generators can be powerful tools—they can amplify our ideas thousands of times for every single person who plays our games, but it's important to know what it's amplifying, and our little gravestone example is a case in which we might be sending a message we didn't expect to.

How can we stop these undesired features from appearing in our generators or find them when they appear? For this specific kind of problem, where the structure of our data or code is to blame, a good rule of thumb is to simply never introduce distinctions that don't mean anything in your game. If gender doesn't affect your player or your game mechanics, there's no reason to build it into the systems of your game. The more variables you introduce, the more likely there'll be something you didn't plan for, so if something doesn't need to be defined in code it's safer to simply sidestep it.

In general, though, there isn't a hard and fast rule for preventing these things from happening. Video games are big, complicated pieces of art and technology all mixed together, and part of the fun and excitement of making games is seeing things you didn't predict. The best thing you can do is always be thinking about what you make, always try to be critical of what you do and be prepared to fix mistakes when they happen. Everyone working in procedural generation is learning something new every day, and no one should feel bad for not seeing something coming. Each surprise is another learning experience.

THE BIG WIDE WORLD

A lot of the time our generators don't need to know much about the real world in order to do their job. *Spelunky*'s level generator doesn't need to know anything about how caves are formed, who Indiana Jones is or where a dog is most likely to hide if it gets stuck underground. All it needs is a big pile of level chunks and the rules for how to stick them together to make levels. For more on *Spelunky* cave generation, you can see Chapter 2.

Sometimes we want our generators to contain a little bit more information and knowledge. Maybe we want our recipe generator to name itself after random places from the real world, or maybe we want to look up the symbolic meanings of colours for our flag generator. Whether it's knowledge we don't have ourselves or it's simply faster and more flexible to do it automatically, procedural generators can easily be fed information from the Internet or other sources to make them cleverer and more powerful.

One way of doing this is to use static databases of knowledge, like Wikipedia, for information. *Argument Champion*, a 2012 game about debating, used an online resource called ConceptNet to generate content for its game. ConceptNet is a database of facts and relationships designed for use by software, especially AI programs. Some of its knowledge is input by hand, while other knowledge is automatically scraped from other sites and formatted for ease of use.

The results can seem fairly impressive, especially at first. Type in *cat* and ConceptNet can tell you that cats are capable of hunting mice, that they have four legs and whiskers, that they like playing and drinking milk. These are represented as a pair of concepts linked by a relationship, so for example "cats" and "whiskers" are connected by the "has" relationship. *Argument Champion* uses these to connect topics, allowing a debate to shift focus from schools to computers, from computers to keyboards, and from keyboards to pianos.

You might have noticed in that last connection that the sense of "keyboard" changed from something you type on, to something you play music with. ConceptNet isn't perfect and often confuses concepts (a janitor is a custodian; The Janitors are a noise rock band). If your game made these connections, the player might find them a little confusing, but might actually find them entertaining. Unfortunately, that isn't all ConceptNet thinks. If you type "woman", one of the "facts" you retrieve is "women are sluts". *Argument Champion* might not come up with that connection, but the next game to use ConceptNet could well make that mistake, and most players probably won't find that quite as entertaining, to say the least.

In fact, they might even find it as offensive as if you'd said it yourself. As humans, we tend to respond to software being intelligent by expecting it to behave in increasingly intelligent ways. When we see a game making clever connections between computers and keyboards, or cats and milk, we often assume that the software understands the meaning of what it's doing, when in practice it likely does not. That means that when it does something wrong, we don't just see it as an accident—we treat it as if it was a genuine statement, and that the software knew what it was doing. This is a great reason, as developers and designers, we need to think very carefully about the systems we build.

One approach that can solve some of these problems is using a banlist for language. Darius Kazemi (author of Chapter 2), a well-known Twitterbot creator who has done a lot of work with generative software, maintains various banlists designed to catch words that might lead to offence. These lists are often designed to be cautious, under the thought that it's better to accidentally filter out too much than to not filter out enough. One bad incident is generally all you need to ruin someone's day.

Banlists are great if you're working with language because they work by filtering the output of your generator, which means they can catch mistakes in generators that you might not ever have predicted. The original *Elite*, released in 1984, had a name generator for star systems that would stick together small collections of letters to make long words. The developers spent some time tweaking this system to make sure it never generated anything rude—a ban list can help by checking the output of even the most random words and strings of letters. But they don't solve everything, and data from the outside world can be a real source of danger when building experimental procedural generators. To give you an idea of why, we're going to look at another game which, like Argument Champion, used online data. This game was called *A Rogue Dream (Figure 5.1)*, which I made in 2013 for the 7-Day Roguelike jam.

The principle behind the game was quite simple—the player types a noun into the game at the beginning, and the game procedurally

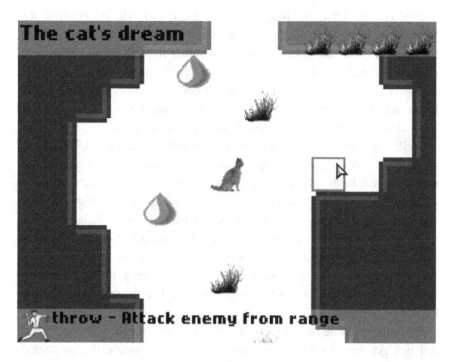

FIGURE 5.1   A screenshot of A Rogue Dream where the player is controlling
a cat.

generates a theme for itself so that the main character of the game is the
noun the player input. So for instance, if the player types in "cat" then
they control a little cat sprite, avoiding droplets of water, eating grass,
searching for cardboard boxes, using powers called "Scratch" and "Sleep".

The way the game did this was by using a technique called "Google
milking", coined by researcher Tony Veale. Google milking works by
reverse engineering the language of question-asking to get information
about the world. When someone asks Google "Why do doctors wear white
coats?" a likely reason for them asking the question is that they believe it to
be true. They're looking for a reason, but the fact that doctors wear white
coats is considered something true—we can extract the factual part out of
the question and use it as knowledge about doctors.

The more people ask a question, the more people presumably believe
the facts of the question to be true—but how do we know which

questions are popular? Google autocomplete can tell us, because it's trained to give us the most popular search queries. So if we type "why do doctors" into Google, the search queries it suggests are the most common things people ask about doctors. Why do doctors wear white coats? Why do doctors say stat? Why do doctors prescribe steroids? Our game might not know the answer to these questions, but it can use these things to understand more about what a doctor is.

So if you type "Why do cats hate ... " into Google you get "water" as an auto-completion, if you type "Why do cats eat ... " you get "grass" and so forth. Each of these specialised queries is used by the game to generate its enemies, pickups, goals and ability names. *A Rogue Dream* is entertaining to play, because unlike many knowledge databases like ConceptNet, Google is packed with popular culture, everyday observations and slang. If you choose to be a ninja you'll be fighting pirates. If you choose to be a musician, you'll be fighting music sensation Kenny G. If you choose to be a nihilist, your health packs are floating clouds of darkness.

But you might be sensing a problem here, and indeed *A Rogue Dream* did not get very far in development before unfortunate things started happening. While a lot of the most generic, innocent queries produced fun game themes, others carried more weight. If you typed in "priest" as the player character, one of your abilities would be "abuse child". If you typed in "man" your enemies were women. If you typed in "Muslim" your abilities included "kill". People don't just type into Google things that they've directly observed—they type in stereotypes, rumours, misconceptions, hate speech, conspiracy theories and worse. *A Rogue Dream*, unable to tell the difference between people who see cats eating grass and people who think French people are lazy, ends up collecting all of this information and using it as fact.

It's difficult to throw away work, and it's hard to admit an idea is bad. I almost developed *A Rogue Dream* into a museum exhibit for children to interact with and learn about procedural generation. But after weeks of trying to filter the system, improve its understanding, limit its search capabilities or change its purpose, I abandoned the project. Now it's mostly used as an example of how procedural generators with the best of intentions can end up being harmful—which, as it turns out, is quite useful. I hope it's also a great reminder of why it's important to think about the ramifications of the systems we build from an ethical standpoint.

YOU ARE WHAT YOU EAT

As an addendum to the previous section, we should talk about another way that generators can find bad things out there in the world. Previously, we focused on real-world data that we might find and want to use in our game—live data like Google results, knowledge bases like ConceptNet—and the things we might want to be wary of when doing this. Just as dangerous is opening our generator up to real people and giving them some control over the content it creates.

Outside of games, Microsoft learned this lesson the hard way in 2016 when it released Tay, a Twitterbot that interacted with users and learned words and phrases from them. Tay had a lot in common with a procedural generator in a game: it created things for other people to look at and enjoy, from a catalogue of data it could intelligently chop up and rearrange. But Microsoft wanted Tay to interact more closely with its users and to appear as intelligent as possible, so it allowed Tay to learn things from people who spoke to it. This had the unexpected (or perhaps completely expected, depending on your perspective) effect of turning Tay into a mimic for anything anyone told it, from hate speech to pure nonsense. Tay was shut down within hours of launching and led to a lot of reflection from engineers and artists about how to create systems that learn from other people.

Tay might seem like it doesn't have too much to teach us, but a number of trends in game design and development are leading in the direction of more human involvement in the games that we play. Games like *Stellaris* have built-in mod tools that allow players to edit, upload and share data lists for in-game procedural generation, which means that the game's procedural generator is partly designed by someone who may not be thinking about the game and content generation in the same way that the game's designer was. Of course, in the case of modding the player is able to choose what to install and what to ignore. But other trends—like taking game input from the chat messages on streaming services such as Twitch—opens up the game to unpredictable, hard-to-filter input from a large quantity of people. If anything, these inputs are likely to be even more problematic for a generative system than Tay's Twitter followers were.

Getting input from people can produce much more interesting and varied content: they can add a dose of human creativity into a rigid system, and they can help make a generator feel personalised and unique for a particular player. But we are always running the risk of encountering the worst side of human creativity with this, and that can be something that is hard to recover from. Just because opening up our generators is potentially dangerous doesn't mean we shouldn't try to experiment and see what new systems and games we can build, though. But we need to be aware that these problems are out there and do what we can to design our systems to limit these bad outcomes.

One way we can experiment in this area while limiting the bad outcomes is to restrict the ways we take input into our generator. If our generator can be given strings of words, then instead of letting our users have totally free input, we can limit them to the use of a set of a few hundred words to express themselves. If our generator uses artwork, we can let our users snap shapes together instead of allowing them completely freeform drawing. People will always try to circumvent whatever systems you give them, but a few restrictions here or there will make life easier and your generator safer.

Before we close out this section, let's dwell a moment longer on Tay, because in many ways the story of Tay is a good explanation of why this chapter matters and why it might have an impact on your game. One of the reasons the response to Tay was so negative and so critical was that once a piece of software is given bad patterns of behaviour, the people who see and repeat those patterns don't think about who taught them those behaviours. They only focus on what the software is doing. If our generator starts producing offensive or other kinds of bad content, people won't blame Twitch chat—they'll blame our generator. It's a totally reasonable response and something that should motivate us to do our best to be responsible in what we build, who we let it talk to, and where we let it do its work.

TALKING THE TALK

Most of this chapter was dedicated to all the things that can go wrong with our software. It can be taught bad things, it can find out bad things all on its own, it can spread ideas (both good and bad) far and wide. Of course as the designers of that software we are responsible for what it does. But sometimes we're more directly responsible for the issues surrounding our procedural generators, so before we move on from this chapter back into technical and aesthetic concerns, let's take a minute to think about how we talk about procedural generation with the wider world.

Promoting games—or anything else for that matter—is really hard. Even if money isn't involved, simply getting people to look at something you made is really difficult. Various advice is offered to developers about how to promote games in particular: advice about whom you should talk to, what you should talk about and how you should phrase it. Even if you've never read a thing about promotion, you'll probably have noticed common patterns in the way other people talk about their games or describe them in stores. It's important to summarise things, to focus on the most important points, to get across the essence of what it is that you've made and to emphasise what makes your game special. What sets it apart? What makes it unique and worth talking about?

Procedural generation is still a selling point for video games. Steam has a tag dedicated to it, and many curators recommend games solely for the presence of procedural generation, but games with generators have been popular for a very long time. "The heart of *Diablo* is the randomly created dungeon" states the very first page of the original *Diablo* design document, "providing a new gaming experience every time *Diablo* is played". Even though it can feel like so many games have procedural generation these days, people are still interested by it. So it's natural for it to come up when talking about games.

It's also very easy to get carried away when describing something amazing that you've created and are proud of. So when we talk to people about procedural generators, often we say things that express how excited we are, without thinking about what they really mean. Let's go back to that statement from the *Diablo* design document for a second: "A new gaming experience every time *Diablo* is played". What does that actually mean? Does it mean the game mechanics change? If you've played *Diablo* you'll know that's definitely not the case—you're clicking on zombies and casting spells no matter what happens. Does it mean the levels change? Well, sort of. They look different and have different layouts. You couldn't memorise a level and run it twice, certainly. But you're always going to the same places—the same caves, the same villages. They are shaped differently but painted the same.

That might sound unfairly harsh on *Diablo*, because we know what they *really* mean by "a new gaming experience". It's a euphemism, like a lot of language about procedural generation is: "limitless gameplay", "infinite replayability", "endless variety". These are all phrases we see used to describe algorithms that are usually doing the computer equivalent of shuffling a deck of cards and dealing you a new hand. Over time we've grown so used to these turns of phrase that we probably don't think much about the language any more—we instinctively know what the person speaking them means, so we don't think about how they sound to people who are less familiar with these ideas.

Relying on people to "know what we mean" when we talk about our work isn't a very good idea. People might learn over time, but all we're really doing is passing the problem on to a new community of people who will make the same mistakes. More importantly, as this book shows, new ideas are coming out of the procedural generation world every day. When we try to explain or sell these ideas to people, there will be hardly anyone who knows what you mean. You'll be deciding how people understand your work, and what expectations people have when they buy your game.

A good example of this is the idea of "uniqueness" in procedural generation. A lot of games try to count how many different dungeons or items their game has and use this to illustrate how big their procedural generator is. The 2009 shooter *Borderlands* proudly stated the game's 17.5 million guns as a key part of its marketing campaign—it even managed to find its way into the *Guinness Book of World Records* with this award. But if we made a copy of a gun in the game and added one point to its damage, most people wouldn't consider the two very different except in the most legal, technical sense. Even if we kept adding damage points until it felt different, we'd probably end up in a situation a little bit like *Diablo*'s dungeons—they're distinct from one another, but not unique. For more on perceptual uniqueness, see Chapter 1.

So what's wrong here, ethically? We're not specifically lying; we're just being a little misleading or unclear with how we're talking about the game. It probably comes from a good place, from a feeling of excitement and positivity the developers have about their game. When we put a big number in front of someone, though, we're leaving it up to them to guess at what percentage of that number will be interesting, useful, fun or relevant. If they're familiar with procedural generation in games and its limitations, they probably won't mind! But if they're less experienced, or perhaps you're offering something new, then there's more of an opportunity for misunderstanding.

That doesn't mean we can't be passionate and excited about our work, of course! It just means that we should think carefully about what we say and write about what we make. Sometimes it can be as simple as changing the kind of language you use. In *Spelunky*, the game tells you "the walls are shifting" as a new level is generated. It's a small and elegant phrase, but it tells you everything you need to know: the levels are being shuffled around, they aren't entirely new, but they're different to what you just saw. It doesn't promise too much, and it slots neatly into the game's theme.

Another approach is to think more carefully about what makes your procedural generator fun. In many ways, advertising millions of guns or billions of levels doesn't really make much sense—the average player will probably only see a few thousand. So what is it that makes our generator cool? What does it do that makes us smile or makes us want to see more of what it produces? Maybe it actually produces a lot of rubbish, and maybe that rubbish is what makes the rare discoveries of something good so wonderful and exciting. Instead of avoiding these ideas, we can play into them and build our game to be more strongly based around these ideas of rarity and surprise.

People will have their own ideas of how to talk about their procedural generation, what kind of language they feel comfortable using and what story they want to tell people about their game. Don't feel like you need to take everything we've discussed here at face value, but do bear some of these ideas in mind the next time you tell someone about a procedural generator.

THE FUTURE

One of the great things about working in procedural generation is how fresh and unexplored most of the field is. Although games have had procedural generation for many decades now, we've spent a lot of that time doing the same things over and over. We're getting really good at them now, but there are a lot of things that people have never even thought of, let alone actually attempted. This book will give you a lot of inspiring ideas to consider and experiments to try, and possibly inspire some things that we've never seen before!

With that excitement of pioneering comes the responsibility of being the first people in a strange new land. It means we should tread a little more carefully in case something unexpected happens, that we should be prepared to think in new ways and break old traditions if the situation demands it. It also means that the things that we do now, the problems we decide to solve, the issues we consider important—these become examples that are set for the people who come later. All of the ethical topics in this chapter do matter, even if they seem trivial right now, because by valuing these issues we make them valuable for the generations of procedural generation enthusiasts who will follow us.

Each reader will have a different response to this chapter, agreeing with some things, ignoring others. All that really matters is that you've thought about these things long enough to decide what they mean to you, and what you want to do in response. I hope you'll bear some of them in mind as you enjoy the inspiring chapters in the rest of this book and as you build generators of your own in the future.

2

Structure and Systems

S torytelling itself is already a complex structure, building upon the rules of vocabulary and spelling into grammar and coherent sentences, finally establishing meaning and insight through patterns of imagined behaviors, events, and consequences. How, then, does one teach all of these intersecting rules to a machine collaborator? How can this complexity be improved upon rather than diminished by the addition of programmed logic? What are our goals in doing so?

This section offers a selection of approaches to the problem from different angles. Starting with a retrospective on what may be the first significant procedural narrative in games, we will move into a series of explorations in different ways systems can define emotional outcomes of narrative.

We can know neither what kinds of procedural narrative you are trying to structure nor what your goals for your systems may be, but we can offer this encouragement: There are almost as many structures and philosophies as there are designers working in the field. There is no single method that dominates procedural narrative design. Therefore, take what processes and taxonomies you may find useful here, as a series of lenses, applicable to either creation or analysis as the need strikes.

This page intentionally left blank

CHAPTER 6

Retrospective

Murder on the Zinderneuf (1983)

Jimmy Maher

The Digital Antiquarian Blog

M ystery stories have been a staple of adventure gaming since 1978's *Mystery Mansion*. That's little surprise; no other form of traditional static literature so obviously sees itself as a form of game between reader and writer and thus is so obviously amenable to adaptation into other ludic forms. Said adaptations existed well before the computer age, in such forms as the *Baffle Books* of the 1920s, the *Dennis Wheatley Crime Dossiers* of the 1930s, and the perennial board game *Cluedo* (*Clue* in North America) of 1949.

The earliest computerized mystery games had the superficial trappings of classic mystery literature but little of the substance. Games like *Mystery Mansion* (1978) and *Mystery House* (1980) were essentially standard *Adventure*-style treasure hunts, full of mazes and static puzzles that happened to play out on the stage set of a mystery story. But Infocom's 1982 text adventure *Deadline* was a far more earnest attempt to capture the spirit and substance of classic mystery stories in addition to the window dressing. With such a proof of concept to examine (and one that proved to be a major hit at that), combined with a recent uptick in interest in the mystery genre within ludic culture in general following the republication of the old Dennis Wheatley dossiers and an elaborate new board game called *Sherlock Holmes: Consulting Detective*, other developers started diving into mysteries with similar earnestness. Some of them worked in the text-adventure form, but others branched out into other paradigms. For instance, Spinnaker's two child-oriented

Snooper Troops games and CBS Software's two adult-oriented *Mystery Master* games replaced parsers and a single complex story with a more casual form of crime solving. Each contains a series of shorter cases to be solved by traveling around a graphical city map, ferreting out clues at each location using a menu-driven interface. A top rating is achieved by solving the crime quickly, using a minimum of clues. Then there was the game that would become known mostly as that other Free Fall game after the huge success of Archon: *Murder on the Zinderneuf (Figure 6.1)*. It's that most interesting anomaly that pops up more than you might expect: an adventure game designed by someone who didn't much like adventure games.

Jon Freeman laid out his objections to traditional adventure games in an article in the December 1980 issue of *Byte*, contrasting the form and its limitations with those of the CRPG form he was then using in crafting Automated Simulations' *DunjonQuest* games. An adventure game, he says, is so static that it's hardly a game at all. It's "really a puzzle that, once solved, is without further interest." The former part of this claim became increasingly less true as more dynamic, responsive game worlds like that of *Deadline* were developed, but the latter

FIGURE 6.1

part ... well, it's hard to deny that point. The real question is to what extent this bothers you. One remedy is longer, deeper works that take as long to play once as it might take you to exhaust the interest of another type of game over many, many plays. Another, of course, is to simply say "so what," to note that no one ever criticizes other forms of art, like books, for not being infinitely re-readable (not that Shakespeare doesn't come close). But still, a re-playable adventure (or for that matter re-readable book) would, all else being held equal, be superior to a non-re-playable version of the same game. After all, people playing these games in the early 1980s were (presumably, if they were honest sorts) buying them, and for prices that can seem insane today when measured against the complexity and amount of actual content found in the average product; the average $0.99 app-store download today has far more of both than most boxed $30 or $40 AAA-level productions of the early 1980s. All of these considerations led to the dynamic, re-playable *Murder on the Zinderneuf,* which generates a brand new mystery every time you play it. Freeman, who still lists *Cluedo* amongst his favorite games of all time, recycled that game's concept on the computer but fleshed out the suspects, the setting, and the randomly generated stories behind the murders themselves to make something more in line with the expectations of adventure gamers.

The mystery may change, but the setting and the actors, the raw materials of these little computer-generated dramas, must inevitably remain the same. Luckily, they're pretty inspired. The game takes place in 1936, the heyday of the rigid airship, surely one of the most romantic and just plain cool methods of travel ever invented. On a trans-Atlantic voyage aboard the fictional German airship *Zinderneuf,* a murder has been committed. Which of the sixteen passengers was killed, and which did the killing and why ... these elements are generated anew each time. As a whole genre of pulp-action tabletop RPGs have taught us, the 1930s are a wonderful period for fans of intrigue and derring-do, and *Zinderneuf* uses that well. Freeman and Reiche work in a lot of the era's touchstones: old Hollywood, action serials, the Berlin Olympics, the Spanish Civil War, the mob, Amelia Earhart, spiritualism, adventurous archaeologists (*Raiders of the Lost Ark* was still huge while they worked on the game), and of course Communists and Nazis. It's an effervescent, pulpy version of history. (That said, our libertarian friend Freeman just can't restrain himself from taking a political shot at Franklin Delano Roosevelt that strikes a weird sourpuss note amongst all the fun: "Roosevelt was still offering his own version of "bread and circuses" as he "guided" the United States through an unprecedented four terms of depression and war.") The *Zinderneuf* itself, meanwhile, proves perfect for a *Murder on the Orient Express*-style whodunit. Playing as one of eight detectives drawn from literature or television—including homages to Mike Hammer, Miss Marple, Columbo, and the inevitable Sherlock Holmes among others (*Figure 6.2*)—you have twelve hours to solve the case before the *Zinderneuf* touches down in New York, and the suspects all scatter to the winds.

Those twelve hours translate to just 36 minutes of game time—yes, this is a real-time game. The idea here was to replace a 40-hour adventure game with a half-hour game that "can be replayed 100 times." Also replaced are the text and parser, with a top-down graphical display and an entirely joystick-driven interface (*Figure 6.3*).

Each game begins by telling you who has been murdered from among the cast of characters, each of whom receives a capsule bio in the manual. And then, as Holmes would say (and the manual happily quotes), the game is afoot. You collect evidence in two ways. First, you

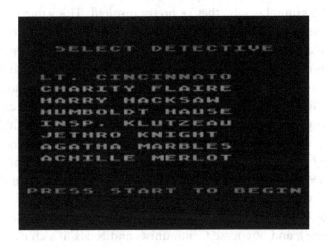

FIGURE 6.2

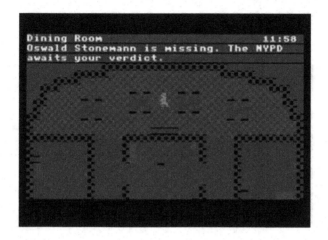

FIGURE 6.3

can search the cabins of the victim and any of the other passengers to see what connections you can discover.

In the case of Figure 6.4, I now know that the murderer of Oswald Stonemann is most likely someone with black hair; the victim is always assumed to have been killed in their cabin. This immediately narrows the suspect list down to five. A logical next step may be to search the cabins of those five suspects, to see what further connections I can turn up. Eventually, however, I will want to start questioning suspects. I can choose the approach I take to each (*Figure 6.5*). Various approaches are more or less favorable to different combinations of detective and suspect, something that must be deduced with play. If I choose wisely, perhaps I get a clue (*Figure 6.6*).

When I believe I have determined opportunity and motive (the game is oddly uninterested in the actual means of murder), I can accuse someone. A false accusation, or one based on insufficient evidence, doesn't end the game but does greatly affect your "detective rating" at the end, and prevents you from using that suspect as a source of information for the rest of the game. If you haven't accused anyone by the time twelve hours (i.e., 36 minutes) have passed, you get one last chance to make an accusation, at some cost to your detective rating, before the game reveals the murderer for you.

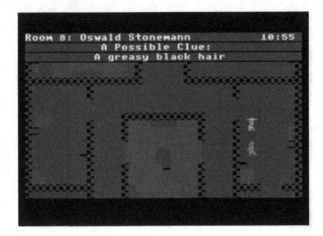

FIGURE 6.4

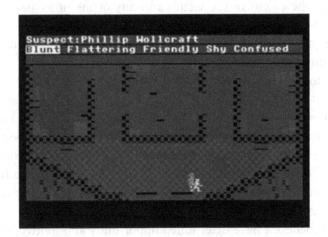

FIGURE 6.5

There's much that's very impressive here. The randomly generated cases go far beyond the likes of Colonel Mustard in the drawing room with the pistol. Most of the cases don't even involve that most reliable standby of the mystery writer, love triangles. One time, I discovered that Phillip Wollcraft, the archaeologist, had killed the

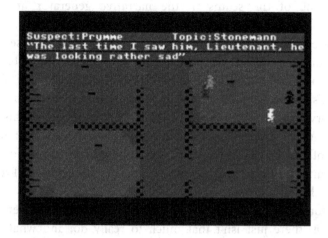

FIGURE 6.6

young Natalia Berenski because he was in thrall to certain nameless be-tentacled somethings and needed a handy virgin to sacrifice. (Yes, even the H.P. Lovecraft mythos makes an appearance in this giddy pastiche of a setting, marking what may just be its first appearance in a computer game.) Another time, I discovered that the beautiful pilot and all-around adventuress Stephie Hart-Winston had killed the Reverend Jeremiah Folmuth after learning that he had killed her beloved brother in a hit-and-run car accident years before. Other cases involve espionage (a natural given the time period), blackmail, even vampires. Most manage to tie the crime back to the period and setting and the specific persona of the characters involved with impressive grace. But for all that, and despite its superficially easy joystick-driven interface and bright and friendly on-screen graphics that actually look much nicer (at least on the Atari) than those of *Archon, Zinderneuf* doesn't quite work for me. Part of the problem derives from all of that rich background information existing only in the manual and not on the screen. The first half-dozen times you play you're frantically flipping through the pages trying to figure out just who is who as the clock steadily ticks down, an awkward experience a million miles away from Trip Hawkins's ethos for a new, more casual sort of consumer software. By the time you get over that hump, some of the seams in the narrative generator are already starting to show. You learn what combinations of clues generally lead where and start to see the same motives repeat themselves. For all the game's narrative flexibility, there are just eight master stories into which all of the other elements must be slotted. The shock of Wollcraft's doing the deed diminishes considerably after you see the same story repeat itself again, with only the name of his victim changed. All of these limitations are of course easily understandable in light of the 48 K of memory the game has at its disposal. Still, things started feeling very shopworn for me long before Freeman's ideal of a hundred plays.

I also found other elements of the design problematic. When you get down to it, there just isn't that much to really do, and what there is often ends up being more frustrating than it needs to be. Searching a cabin requires wandering about it trying to cover every square inch until the game beeps to inform you that you discovered a clue—or did not. Talking to suspects can be just as off-putting. Most will only answer a question or two before wandering off again; you then aren't allowed to speak to them again without speaking to someone else first. Thus, the game quickly devolves into a lot of sifting through denials and non-committals, struggling to figure out the right approach to use, while only being able to field one or two questions to your star witness (or suspect) at a time. The memory limitations so strangle the dialog that it's impossible to pick up clues, as you might in a real conversation, about whether or why your current interrogation approach is failing or which one might better suit. *Murder on the Zinderneuf* is fascinating and groundbreaking as a concept, but ultimately a game should be fun in addition to any other virtues it might possess, and here I'm just not sure how well it succeeds. Reading the manual with its cast of exaggerated characters was for me almost more entertaining than actually playing.

Zinderneuf's ideal of a narrative that is new every time is neat, and certainly interesting for someone like me to write about as the road almost entirely not taken in adventure games. But are there perhaps good reasons for it to be the road not taken? Maybe for someone primarily interested in games as experiential fictions, a 40-hour story, crafted by a person, is more satisfying than 100 30-minute stories generated by the computer.

At the risk of making Freeman a straw man for my argument, it's tempting to think again about the flaws that he believed he saw in existing adventures. I believe that designers who see games as rules systems to be carefully crafted and tweaked are often put off by adventure games, which are ultimately all about the fictional context, the lived experience of playing the protagonist in a story. Perhaps having the system itself generate the story could be seen, consciously or unconsciously, as a way to fix this perceived imbalance, to return the art of game design (as opposed to fiction-authoring) to the center of the equation.

Yes, *Murder on the Zinderneuf*'s narrative generator is clever, but it's not as clever as, say, Marc Blank, the author of *Deadline*—and arguably not clever enough to sustain a genre whose appeal is so deeply rooted in its fiction. *Zinderneuf* is more interesting as a system than as a playable story, in a genre whose appeal is so rooted in story. That, anyway, is how this story lover sees it. This isn't to discount *Zinderneuf*'s verve in trying something so new. We need our flawed experiments just as much as we do our masterpieces, for they push boundaries and give grist for future designers' mills.

Adapted from www.filfre.net/2013/02/free-fall-part-2-murder-on-the-zinderneuf

This page intentionally left blank

CHAPTER 7

Designing for Narrative Momentum

Jon Ingold

Inkle

> When in doubt, have a man come through the door with a gun in his hand.
>
> Raymond Chandler

This quote from Chandler seems like a pretty redundant way to start an article about game design. As an industry, we've internalised this rule all too well: nameless henchman have been springing from nowhere at our players for decades now. And yet games aren't immune to the problem that Chandler was tackling. The dreaded narrative slump: that sudden, deflating moment when the story's momentum evaporates. There is a pause in the action, and suddenly nothing much seems to be going on at all. Nathan Drake stares into space. Lara Croft adjusts her bow. The game waits, like an actor who has forgotten the next line, hoping the player will provide the cue-line that gets things rolling again.

Moments like this don't happen in modern movies: the edit suite ruthlessly enforces pace. As audiences, we have learned impatience. A great film, a great play, or a great game—whether it's football or *God of War*—is supposed to be *gripping*. Entertainment should snatch us in a giant's fist and hold us fast, not letting go until we have been carried all the way to the conclusion. We want to be swept away, whether by inescapable ratcheting tension, simmering powerful emotion, or gun-toting surprise. We wish to ride a river of narrative momentum—to be assured both that things *are* happening and that we won't *believe* what's going to happen *next*.

This momentum is precious, hard-won, and easily fumbled. And in games, the problem of conserving narrative momentum is made harder by factors Chandler did not have to consider. Games are built, not on surprise and escalation, but on loops and repetition. Players drive the experience, but players never really know what they're supposed to be doing. And while all stories talk about risk and reward, only games have to handle the outcomes of both success and failure at every turn. Philip Marlowe is never fatally wounded by a middle-act incidental gunman. He never fails to spot the laundry chit hidden under the biscuit tin in the cabin.

Worse still, Marlowe is never allowed to give up and do nothing. In games, we give our players the freedom to act, but that means also giving them freedom to do entirely unproductive things, to fail, to waste time in fruitless dead-ends, and to get horribly confused in the process.

So what hope do we have of keeping momentum alive?

ONLY FORWARDS DESIGN

In an action game, momentum is a key goal of the experience, and action games have traditionally solved the pace problem by taking their cues directly from cinema and making experiences that only go forwards. They design worlds that appear open—that may even have branches and alternative routes—but nevertheless are in fact corridors filled with exciting-yet-functional one-directional valves (mudslides, lifts, sudden drops from helicopters) to ensure that players are always in drive and never in reverse.

Some will cleverly reuse levels: flooding a room you previously ran through or making you fight your way out of somewhere you only just broke into. (If you walk through a location in a *Naughty Dog* game containing waist-high walls, you know you're in for some trouble down the line.) But whether the player's path is straight or looping, the action is all still laid out in advance, beat to beat, and the game's designers work tirelessly to ensure that at the end of each set-piece the next one is clearly signposted and preferably has already begun.

At the other end of the gameplay spectrum, the highly narrative choose-your-own-adventure books used a similarly unidirectional approach; stories structured as acyclic directed graphs, flows that branch and rejoin but are always moving forwards (Figure 7.1.) This ensured that players could not lose their way: they were always on track towards an ending, though more often than not that meant a throwaway death at the hands of a murderous yeti.

The more complex *Fighting Fantasy* books (Ian Livingstone, Steve Jackson) used their branches to create puzzles (or more accurately, to create mazes). Key information and items were hidden in obscure side paths but then required in order to proceed.

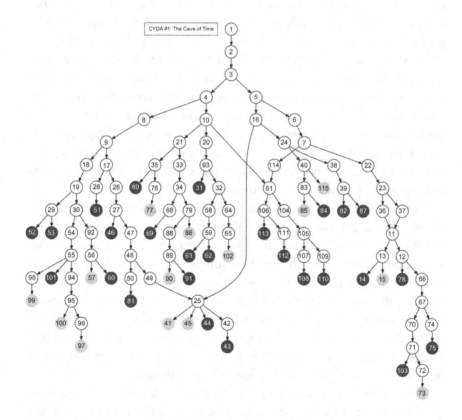

FIGURE 7.1   Courtesy of S.P. Osborne, outspaced.fightingfantasy.net.

(To minimise cheating, these hidden secrets were often coded as rules, such as "add 7 to the current paragraph number to use the gold key on a paragraph beginning with the word 'Red'". This led to a curious effect, whereby players solving *Fighting Fantasy* books often wound up reading them entirely *out* of order, so as to find the clues that would allow them to reverse-engineer what the correct order actually was.)

OPENING THE FLOW

Creating a narrative-driven digital work that doesn't rely on high-octane action-movie antics, we can replicate the CYOA structure, but the result can be unsatisfying. The "only forwards" assumption that was never questioned by readers of *Fighting Fantasy* books seems artificially restrictive in a digital context. When faced with a choice of paths, left and right, players expect to be able to explore one, backtrack, and then explore the other. When faced with a character, players expect to be able to ask every question, not one or the other. But as soon as we allow the freedom to revisit and backtrack—as text adventures, graphic adventures, and open-world games all do—or to farm through dialogue options, then our story world suffers a critical blow. It loses an entire axis, becoming frozen in time, filled with locations that remain, static and unevolving, from visit to visit. Our characters become vending machines. The game turns from a living world into a waxwork museum.

This problem scales badly. The more players explore, the more they accumulate larger and larger numbers of empty, repetitive locations: shopfronts without shops, libraries without books, smithies whose inhabitants stand patiently by their anvils day and night, bartenders who polish the same mug time and again, hoping against hope that the player will grant them the chance to deliver their line of dialogue. ("Want some rye? Course you do!") Piratical types wait endlessly in identical bars to play a board-game, either very well or very badly indeed. Villagers wring their hands about the werewolf in the woods but won't lift a finger to do anything about it themselves.

If narrative momentum can be calculated, its value is importance (mass) multiplied by rate of change (velocity); if the world is built like a mirror, unaffected by anything except the player's actions—opening doors, unlocking boxes, or inquisition of the bartender—then our mirror-world has no more momentum than the player puts in. How, then, can we sweep players off their feet?

Obviously, no game can deliver the infinite and subtle variety—and boredom!—of a living, breathing world, nor should it—the world might as well revolve around the player, springing to life like the inhabitants of Seahaven in *The Truman Show* only when the player moves into view. The player *is* the only person in the game, after all. A rich simulation, or, say, a vastly procedurally generated universe, might be fun to code but doesn't make for a very satisfying game experience unless the player is given something interesting to *do*.

So: how do we ensure our story is always moving forwards even when the player has a range of things to do at any given moment? And how do we prevent a non-linear environment from creating something tedious when experienced linearly by a temporally bound human player?

THE DESIGN OF INK

At Inkle, we've had the advantage of working largely with text content, which is cheap to produce at scale. This has allowed us to cheat: to embrace both freedom and consequence simultaneously. In *80 Days*, the player will typically see about 3% of the 750,000 words of game-script in a single playthrough; the 3% is selected entirely based on the player's choices. The design could be summarised as "only forwards, whichever way you want".

The game's central conceit—that the player is attempting to drag Phileas Fogg around the world within a tight time limit—provides a solid narrative reason to prevent backtracking, and ensures that "failing" a scenario—or simply opting out of a risky side adventure—is still an active, busy choice that pushes the player onwards to the next destination and the next opportunity to be tempted off course.

THE WEAVE STRUCTURE

The optimisation of momentum in *80 Days* was no accident. Underneath the game is the ink engine that powers the text: a mark-up based programming language, ink was specifically designed to build the assumption of "only forwards" storytelling into the fabric of the language.

The core ink structure is a "weave": a block of text and options with the assumption of "always dropping downwards" built into its flow. Here, for instance, is a somewhat abridged version of *80 Days'* opening story chunk.

```
=== london ===
-   Monsieur Phileas Fogg returned home /early/ from the
Reform  Club,  and  in  a  new-fangled  steam-carriage,
besides!
    *   I helped him down[], and the iron-lunged, steam-
driven horses clattered away.
-   "Passepartout," said he. "We are going around the
world!"
    *   (zany) "Around the world, Monsieur?"[] I asked,
utterly astonished.
    *   (dull) "Very good, Monsieur[."]," I murmured duti-
fully, not believing a word of it.
-   "We shall circumnavigate the globe within eighty days."
He was quite calm as he proposed this wild scheme. "We
leave for Paris on the 8:25. In an hour."
    *   {zany} "But I have not prepared!"[] I said wretch-
edly, quickly trying to organise a list of necessary items
in my mind.
        "Then do it now.
    *   {zany} "You are in jest!"[] I told him in dignified
affront. "You make mock of me, Monsieur."
        "I am quite serious.
    *   {dull} "But of course[."]," I answered, still extre-
mely suspicious.
        He nodded. "Good.
    * This was {dull:quite a departure|a shocking turn-
about}[!] for my master, who was, by all accounts,
a creature of inflexible habit and mechanical regularity!
Perhaps the carriage's engine-fumes had affected his
reason?
        * *   "Perhaps you should lie down, Monsieur."
        "That would be a most inefficient use of time," he
replied implacably."
        * *   "For Paris, Monsieur?"
        "To begin with, yes.
-   <> Pack my cloak and my evening jacket. There is not
a moment to waste!"
    -> DONE
```

(The real game includes additional mark-up, altering various character statistics based on the choices made here.)

Reading weave takes a little practice. The script begins at the top line, before branching across the options, marked with asterisks. Each option contains both the text of the choice (before the [] brackets), and the whole paragraph to be shown if the choice is chosen. After a set of choices, a hyphen denotes a "gather point", where divergent flows are collected again, before the next choices are shown.

The structure was designed to prevent dangling loose ends. Whatever the player chooses, the flow will fall from top to bottom. It always moves forwards and, by default, it always reaches the end.

CONTENT AS CONDITIONALS

Two choices in the example are labelled: "dull" and "zany". Labels are optional, but if a label is given, it can be queried later, to turn on or off new choices or to vary the text.

The use of paragraph labels as conditionals was originally a mere convenience—it's less typing than defining and then setting a Boolean—and so it makes branching easier to do at scale. But the design comes with two powerful restrictions. Firstly, a paragraph label condition can only be set in one place in the entire script. Secondly, once set, a paragraph conditional can *never* be unset.

This means despite *80 Days* branching interactive script running longer than *The Lord of the Rings*, if you ever want to know if the player chose the "zany" option in the first section of the game, you can be confident that "london.zany" will test exactly that and only that.

Paragraphs labels are the default way to do branching in ink, and they are intrinsically "only forwards" in design: accumulated by the player and never lost.

SEQUENCES AND LOOPS

Furthermore, options in ink are, by default, once-only. So, in a more open game, like the *Sorcery!* series, it's efficient to write a location as a hub of options that turn on as they are discovered and, once taken, cannot be repeated.

```
=== temple ===
    {The temple of Courga is decorated with the finest gold
tapestries.|You are standing in the temple of Courga once
more.} The statue of Courga himself dominates the room.
- (choices)
*   (look) [Look at the statue]
    The statue depicts Courga as his followers choose to
believe he is. Extremely large, extremely happy, and ben-
evolent{courga_has_trap:, except for the poison darts
inside his mouth}.
*   (courga_has_trap) [Look for traps]
    You scour the walls and floor for traps, but find nothing.
Then, as you stand from your stoop, you notice a curious
steel glint within the dark mouth of the statue. {look:
Darts.}
*   {look && courga_has_trap} {pick_up_rag}
    [Stuff the rag into Courga's mouth]
    You block up the statue's mouth with the filthy rag in one
quick movement. There is a quiet /thunk/ from deep inside.
The darts have fired—but you are safe.
// etc...
+   [Leave]
    {You turn and walk through the double doors back into the
sunlight.|You bid Courga farewell once more.}
        -> outside_temple
- (loop) -> choices
```

The braced content at the top indicates content printed sequentially, so the player gets a different description on entering the temple for the first time than on subsequent visits. Again, sequences are "only forwards" and cannot be reset!

The hub structure is a loop: each choice elicits a response then falls down to the "loop" point, which bounces the flow back up to offer more choices, until the "leave" option is chosen. (Leave is marked with a + bullet, which tells ink this particular option isn't once-only.) Players may or may not unlock the significant actions in the hub—they may be missing crucial items or information. Regardless of what they achieve, players will work their way through some, or all, of the available content, until they choose to leave or there is nothing else for them to do. Forwards movement is guaranteed.

NARRATIVE MOMENTUM IN A GRAPHICAL CONTEXT

This "only forwards" approach to default logic and structures in ink informs the narrative structure of both *80 Days* and *Sorcery!* Revisiting and backtracking are disallowed entirely in *80 Days* and actively discouraged in the *Sorcery!* games (as a last resort, if players enter now-empty locations, the entire text of a *Sorcery!* location will be simplified to a single sentence or omitted entirely).

Both games aim to avoid the issue of location cruft while using new locations to provide both momentum—you keep getting them—*and* player freedom—you get to choose where you go. How does this approach fare in a more graphical environment, where content production is expensive and locations can't be handed out in an arbitrary fashion like stickers in a primary school?

Heaven's Vault

In our console title *Heaven's Vault*, we built a set of detailed 3D environments, which the player can unlock and explore in more or less any order. Within each environment, the player explores, burning through actions in the world in a similar fashion to *Sorcery!*

In early prototypes of the narrative flow, narrative momentum was a problem: players would scour a room and hoover up interaction hotspots before moving to the next room to repeat the cycle. Watching testers play was like watching a Roomba execute its program.

Heaven's Vault is an archaeological adventure game and the intention was to have the player produce, test and resolve theories about what a place was and how it fitted into the world and history of the game. (Archaeologists are essentially detectives, except they arrive rather too late, and never get to bring all the suspects together at the end.) Our interactions all felt isolated; exploring one corner of a location didn't impact much on the others. We wanted to create real spaces, rather than game spaces with sliding blocks and light-beam puzzles, but as a result the spaces felt vacant and inert.

We realised that in-world interactions were not going to provide the momentum we needed. Unlike *Sorcery!*, in which every option in a room can be accessed with a tap, there's simply too much travel time from prop to prop in a 3D world. Our story needed to be about *understanding* the environment rather than manipulating it. Another game might use environmental storytelling in a passive, optional way, but we needed to foreground it and have the characters explicitly observe and work on the connections they find. We needed our momentum to come not from action but from knowledge, from a steady accumulation of insight about the world of the game.

To achieve this, we began to model not just where the players had been and what they'd done but what they *knew* and *believed* about the world. We designed a knowledge-tracking system, once again employing an "only forwards" philosophy to make the result something we could rely on and scale.

KNOWLEDGE AS AN ACYCLIC DIRECTED GRAPH

Our core principle is that knowledge starts vague and becomes increasingly specific. We model knowledge about any particular topic as a chain of states, each more detailed than the previous. We apply two rules: 1) once a fact has been learned, it can never be unlearned and 2) learning a fact automatically learns all the preceding facts.

If we had used this system in *80 Days*, we might have had the knowledge chain seen in *Figure 7.2*.

In the first moments of the game, players learn the first fact, but they are unaware of the time limit or reason for the journey. Later, Fogg might mention the 80-day target; this causes the second knowledge state to be marked as achieved. However, Fogg might instead leap ahead and tell you that the trip is a bet (apologies, Monsieur, I mean a "wager"); if he does, the game sets the third state and the second state is automatically filled in—players get the terms of the bet for free, without that fact having to be explicitly marked as learned by the writer.

The script of the game then tests against this model using "knowledge intervals" rather than knowledge states: a typical line in the script might be:

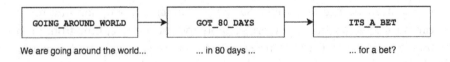

FIGURE 7.2

```
*   {between(GOING_AROUND_WORLD, ITS_A_BET)}
```
    I asked Monsieur Fogg if there was anywhere particular in
the world he wanted to see...
```
*    {between(GOT_80_DAYS, ITS_A_BET)}
```
    Why eighty days, I wondered? Was there an event Monsieur
Fogg needed to return to London for? A wedding, perhaps?

The "between" test is just prescriptive enough: it asks "do I know
enough for this to make sense, but not so much as to make it
redundant or nonsensical?" Better yet, it's future-proof: should we
later add more detail to our knowledge chain—say, inserting a state for
"We're travelling very fast" between "going around the world" and "got
80 days"—none of the existing checks need to be altered; all should still
work as intended. We only care about the ends of the interval, not the
detail inside it, so that detail can change.

A game will, of course, have a lot of parallel chains; so "between" can
happily test using states from more than one chain. Perhaps later in the
game we meet the mysterious Monsieur Fix of London, who in our take
on the novel is not a policeman at all, but is merely pretending to be
one (Figure 7.3.)

We could then combine elements of this knowledge chain with the
previous one to create subtle variations in the choices available.

```
*    {between((TRAVELLING_IN_A_HURRY, MET_MONSIEUR_FIX),
FIX_IS_A_POLICEMAN)}
```
    I wondered how on Earth Monsieur Fix had kept pace with us
[]—and why he had troubled to travel so very quickly.
```
*     {between((FIX_SAYS_FOGG_IS_A_THIEF, TRAVELLING_I-
N_A_HURRY), (ITS_A_BET, FIX_IS_A_LIAR))}
```
    My master, a thief? [] Was that why we were running so very
fast—to outstrip the grasp of the law?

MET_MONSIEUR_FIX → FIX_IS_A_POLICEMAN → FIX_IS_A_LIAR

Monsieur Fix...   ...is a Policeman...   ...No! He is a liar!

FIGURE 7.3

Here "between" is taking multiple arguments: a first set of states that must *all* be true (the minimum requirements) and a second set of states *of which none* must be true (the conditions for redundancy).

The flexibility of the "between" test also means we can split up long chains into multiple shorter chains if, as the game goes on, it turns out that one fact doesn't necessarily imply all those below it. Equally, single facts (chains of length 1) can be extended if it turns out a fact could use a little more detail after all, and such an extension again doesn't require rewriting or reviewing any existing tests against the original state.

KNOWLEDGE WEBS

Knowledge chains do not need to be entirely one-dimensional; they—like CYOA books—are really acyclic directed graphs, branching when one vague fact splits into several specific details and re-joining when a fact synthesises multiple different chains of sub-information (Figure 7.4.)

Here, knowing a later state implies knowing *all* the states leading up to that state, so discovering that Fix is in fact a saboteur will mean learning that your journey is a bet, and that Fix is not a real policeman. (And if that's more than it should imply, we restructure the web.)

In *Heaven's Vault* we have over 1,500 knowledge states split across some 700 chains, some of which are 10 states long, some of which contain only a single state and are just glorified Booleans (but that might be upgraded at any moment). Maintaining this can be tricky, but

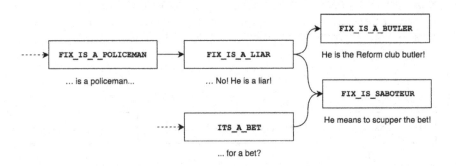

FIGURE 7.4

it's made significantly easier by the assumptions of the "only forwards" design.

Because laying out the structure of the knowledge map is separate from the business of writing actual content for the game, the writer can largely *ignore* it when they're actually writing. For any given topic, first one lays out a sensible-looking knowledge map, then one writes content that seems interesting and relevant; finally, one marks up the content with what facts the content contains and what its minimum and maximum requirements are. But that mark-up is static: there's no need to think through flow, order, or cause and effect!

USING THE KNOWLEDGE MODEL

With this knowledge system in place, the rules for authoring game content to generate narrative momentum are as follows:

Rule One: no line of dialogue, action, or scene is allowed to occur unless it is acceptable and non-redundant; that is, the player's current knowledge lies between an unlock state and a reward state. Most locations in the game have multiple unlock states and multiple reward states, so they can be triggered in a variety of contexts and for a variety of different outcomes. Since every line of dialogue is *also* gated, what the characters talk about within a scene will change automatically as well, depending on what trigger, or combination of triggers, allowed the scene to begin in the first place (and on anything else relevant as well, of course).

Rule Two: every scene, and also a decent proportion of the dialogue, should move *something* forwards. For scenes, that's the unlocking of the "reward states" as mentioned in the paragraph above—significant discoveries that move the wider game along. For individual beats of dialogue, it means that *something* in the knowledge model, whether minor or significant, should be moved forwards by whatever the characters discuss.

Rule one enforces continuity and ensures the game is always giving the player something worth doing. Rule two is the engine of our narrative momentum. If every action in the game is gated to ensure it will move some part of the knowledge model forwards, then so long as players have found *anything* to do, then *everything* they do will cause progress. The game has velocity, and hence momentum, no matter where players are or what they're doing, and no matter whether the scene they're in is tightly linear or extremely open. Because players are always stepping, and every step is only forwards, the player will, eventually, have to reach some kind of ending.

Narrative Momentum via Dialogue

The game then only needs to ensure there is *enough* content to cover all the states the knowledge model can reach so that the player will never run dry. This can be grunt work, but it's fairly low risk; a question of "just writing more" but with little requirement for one piece of content to be carefully balanced against another, as each will only show up under the correct circumstances anyway.

It also means the game can be effectively tested by an automated process, which randomly bashes through the content and moans if it runs out of things to do. (Of course, the automatic tester won't tell you if the story makes no sense; coherence is a human problem.) Of course, we still have the problem of finding things for the player to *do*. In-world actions are a limited resource—players can only look inside so many cupboards and turn on so many lamps. Indeed—let's be honest now—they can only shoot so many henchmen. But dialogue between characters is an interactive with far fewer limitations and one that suits the requirement of being powered by a knowledge model very nicely. Realising this resolved our issue with *Heaven's Vault*'s pacing. We implemented a dedicated, active-everywhere button to initiate conversation that draws content from the script based on what's currently happening within the knowledge model.

Our Roomba-style game loop becomes something more detective-like. Players enter a room and interact with an in-world prop, which stocks up the dialogue system, so as they walk to the next hotspot, they can talk with their companions about what they've just seen and done, learning and deducing new ideas and raising new questions in the process.

The moment in the game where momentum might normally dip—when the player is leaving an exhausted action point and looking about for another—now has a momentum of its own. It's a mode of momentum—discussion and reflection—that's rare in games but would be familiar to any Chandler reader. But it's all still under players' control, entirely narrative, and there's no need for any gunmen to pop out from anywhere. Well, not quite so many, anyway.

CONCLUSION

Narrative momentum is the core property of a story. It emerges from the tension between what is *happening* and what is *about* to happen; and in games it flags during those moments where nothing is happening *and* players have no idea what they are supposed to be doing next.

When progression is defined entirely by movement through space, players who are physically stuck, or stationary, are also narratively stuck. By formalising our knowledge model, *Heaven's Vault* has a second axis for creating robust, measurable narrative progression, available while players are standing still, walking around in circles, or perhaps simply looking at the view.

We can't stop players putting the controller down and walking away. We can't ensure they'll *like* the game. But we can, and should, invite players to take just *one* more step, so that, after a while, they can turn around and see how far they've come.

This page intentionally left blank

CHAPTER 8

Curated Narrative in *Duskers*

Tim Keenan and Benjamin Hill

EXPLORE, ADAPT, SURVIVE

Procedural and hand-crafted content in games seem at odds with each other. Procedural content, by its nature, is unique to each player. Algorithmically creating content allows for what we call the "player story": a unique story that players can recount to friends and forum-dwellers about their personal experiences while playing a game. Whether that's the time you forgot to close the airlock and suffocated half of your crew in *FTL* or failed to manage provisions, causing you to lose your mind and *eat* your entire crew in *Sunless Sea*, the power of personal player story is undeniable and wholly unique to games.

Thus, it can be exciting to read other players' stories, to see how similar and drastically different they are from yours. These stories, on their own, tend to not rival the great fiction of our time, but since it's *your* story, it doesn't have to. The unique nature of the story makes it special. Hand-crafted content, on its own, can be much more compelling than procedurally generated content when compared out of context. The craftsmanship of a well-curated experience can be incredibly moving. This is why we read books and watch films. Video games allow for interaction, and steering the player's interactions such that they have no options when following the intended hand-crafted content can rob games of what makes them so unique and compelling.

With our sci-fi roguelike, *Duskers*, we knew we were going to use procedurally generated content to create the player story we find so powerful in games. But with our writing team having backgrounds in creating strong hand-crafted stories, we wondered whether we could bring the strengths of hand-crafted content to *Duskers* without robbing players of their unique story.

Before answering that question, we should probably answer: What is *Duskers*? In *Duskers*, you pilot drones into derelict spaceships to find the means to survive and piece together how the universe became a giant graveyard. Each time you lose your squad of drones to the dangers of exploration, you reset to an entirely new procedurally generated universe to explore. The game creates a sense of isolation, as you creep your drones into these tombs using a command line interface reminiscent of '80s film favorites like *Alien*. With that cleared up, let's get back to the question; Could we bring the strengths of hand-crafted content to *Duskers* without robbing players of their unique stories?

WHEN ALL YOU HAVE IS A HAMMER

As traditional storytellers, our first instinct was to approach the problem as we would any other narrative-rich medium. To create the world story, we began to structure a skeleton plot for *Duskers* and attempted to give the player character a clear and grounded role within that universe. Our focus here was to tell a really rich story about the world, through exploration, whilst unveiling the characters' backstory as they progressed, eventually reconciling these fragmented worlds.

While this work was very useful in creating a type of bible for the world, it immediately became apparent that the linearity of plot created massive dissonance with the procedural nature of play. The linear structure interfered with the stories that players were creating for themselves. In our minds, the player story was king, especially in roguelikes, and we wanted to stay true to that and to our players. The game was pushing back against our well-meant efforts to place narrative boundaries around the systems that made the game of *Duskers* so much fun to play. We thought we were set-dressing the game experience, but in fact we were trying to control it.

We wanted a fiction that brought the curation of a well-authored tale but conformed itself to the player, not the other way around. How do you make static, curated narrative conform to the dynamic player story? We focused on three answers, each pushing the narrative closer and closer to the player story. The same overall curated content needed to create different meaning for different players, be responsive to players' choices, and ideally, push the gameplay in novel directions.

ORDER MATTERS

The Same Overall Curated Content Needed to Create Different Meaning for Different Players

If we start with the understanding that the curated content is static, are there ways we can have players digest that content differently, interpret it differently, such that they infer different meanings from it? At some level of granularity, the pieces we could play with were going to be statically defined, but could we be clever with how they were combined? Isn't that what procedural systems do? If letters can be combined in different ways to make different words, and words to make different sentences, could larger content like paragraphs or scenes be the same?

Her Story shows us that this is possible. The content is clearly static: short videos of a woman being interviewed about a murder. However, if you watch two people play the game, snippets of story are seen in different orders and that story is experienced in entirely different ways. It's entirely possible that this could even change the ways players interpret the story and the characters portrayed in it.

We were curious to see if that was the case, so we set up a simple test. We created two example logs that players might find on different derelict spacecraft. One log would be from a scientist that found a dead rat near a food replicator and had serious concerns that the device could be malfunctioning to disastrous effects. Another would be a conversation between two support techs, complaining that someone who found a dead animal on a spacecraft would think the replicators were going to do irreparable damage to the crew. Would reading one before the other "anchor" you to that viewpoint and then reading the second validate that viewpoint?

Example Log One

[Record Start]
@SRamirez: Stop dwelling on it man. I get complaints like this every day—filter in, filter out type of stuff. I had a complaint from someone once saying he'd a stomach ache after eating three slices of cake from a replicator. Three slices, and the guy's blaming the assemblers!! Do you know how many dead rats they find on vessels every day? You've got nothing to worry about, just a bored scientist in space.

@JMartin: Haha, yeah I get you man, and I know you're right. We made it that they can turn a brick of sludge into whatever they want for dinner. I even hear we're close on our first cured disease! Quality of life stuff you know. They don't get how much better everything is now. Seriously, do you remember how bad freeze-dried ice-cream was?

Example Log Two

[Observation Report]
We're a little unsure how the rat got down there, most probably an escapee from the labs on C-Deck. Decomposition is isolated to the lower abdomen but is inconsistent with the rest of the remains, a seemingly foreign viscous material covering what may have been an initial wound.

There have been some concerns regarding the molecular assemblers that are installed aboard the vessel, and with the rate of decomposition being so peculiar I recommend an immediate report be sent to Leyland Corp. Something isn't right, and if it is what I fear, then we need to do something about it fast.

To test this theory, we created a website that would present the two logs in a random order before asking a series of questions to answer after both were read. While not overly scientific, our initial results showed that the order that you read the logs did affect how you responded. Most of those who read the scientist's email first generally felt the scientist was onto something and the operators were being obtuse, while most of those who read the operator's conversation first were more likely to think the scientist was overreacting.

In *Figure 8.1*, the top graph shows respondents who were shown the operators' conversation first, while the bottom graph shows those who first read the scientist's email.

To be fair, as we got many more data points, the tendencies started to blur, so this was far from definitive, scientific research! However, this tendency of players to infer different meanings based upon the ordering of information is something we observed in various other experiments and when reading players feedback on other titles. The simple takeaway is that order matters. If we broke the stories into

Based on the above communications: How concerning do you think the dead rat is?
(22 responses)

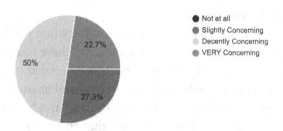

Based on the above communications: How concerning do you think the dead rat is?
(26 responses)

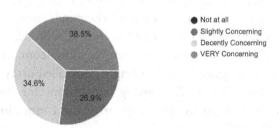

FIGURE 8.1   The top graph shows respondents who were shown the operators' conversation first, while the bottom graph shows those that first read the scientist's email.

a series of small ship logs from different points of view, we could start to have players experience the narrative differently and possibly draw different conclusions from them. This brings it one step closer to the player's story.

In order to capitalize on this more fragmented approach, we had to make sure that players had anchor points within the game's universe so it wouldn't be difficult to make connections. If we didn't, the game's narrative could become so fragmented that it'd be a struggle for the player to remember it all or so diluted that no meaning could be derived. To achieve this, we created pillars of information that would allow easy connections to be made. In *Her Story*, the words you type into the search engine help create connections directly. In *Duskers* we didn't have this feature, so instead we used a small array of consistent themes, such as corporations, people, and existential threats, across the game for people to latch on to. This also let players' imaginations run wild with conspiracy theories and, we hoped, connect themes and corporations in unexpected ways.

To add variety, we created five different storylines for how humanity may have ended. Players would stumble upon these storylines based on how they played and how the universe was generated and could attack these storylines in any order they saw fit or simultaneously. So now you could read each storyline in different orders, in addition to the logs within each storyline. We were hoping that this would not only maximize options while playing, but also further differentiate one player's experience of the narrative that of another. In addition, we created consistent corporations with specific identities (such as Muteki and Leyland) throughout the universe; we could then name drop, creating suspicion. A player could get a log from the pandemic narrative arc that mentions a shady Muteki vessel and then find a Muteki log discussing research into nano-bots, allowing them to draw connections between nano-bots and the pandemic. Creating a controlled array of repeatable subjects or characters made drawing conclusions for the player easy work. This freed us up to really support those connections with juicy context, story, and red herrings.

Finally, let's not forget the role that emotion plays in imbuing meaning into narrative. The same emotion can elicit different responses in different people. *Duskers* designs pillars centered around emotions, and we wanted the narrative to support that. One of the main pillars of the game was isolation, but after playing the game for a while players dulled to the fact of being isolated. We needed a way to remind them that they were alone.

One way to do this was to send you messages from someone that seemed to know them. This would remind them that they had no one to talk to, that they were devoid of connection, aside from the drones that they commanded (which we hoped they would anthropomorphize and realize how crazy it was to care about a machine completely devoid of autonomy). In this way, the narrative could support the emotional pillar of the game, while making players feel something in a unique way for their particular games.

We intended these messages to be delivered in order, as we had intentionally written them. But upon experimenting, we felt it more true to the game if, with the exception of the first log and the very last log received, that everything would be doled out in a random order, giving each player a unique experience with the backstory. This added yet another axis by which the game could be uniquely interpreted by each player.

LET THE PLAYER DRIVE

The Curated Content Needed to Be Responsive to the Player's Choices

One of the reasons static fiction feels so contrived in video games is that the player has agency yet can't affect the fiction. While players can make choices, they ultimately experience the fiction in the same linear manner despite those choices. This makes choices seem less meaningful and the narrative more contrived or "on rails." If we wanted the fiction to conform itself to the player, it is important to never force the player's hand. Instead, let players be the driving force. In *Duskers*, our log system allowed us to achieve this in an integrated way.

Gone Home is a game about a family that's told entirely through environmental storytelling. In it, you explore an empty house when nobody's home. Even though the stage is set, and static, the player moves through the space, deciding what to look at and when. Not only does this change what different players see, and in what order they see it, the players have agency over those choices. To make an analogy to procedural systems, it's like each player becomes the seed number that affects the content generation. Plug in different players, and what catches their eyes and how they interpret it can change the experience.

To go back to our *Her Story* example, the player doesn't get a random ordering of video snippets. Players choose the search terms as in an Internet search, which then serve them up any videos that have those terms in the transcript of the video interview. If they hear about a character and a location in a video, one player may be more interested in the character and search for that, while another may search for videos about the location. Each of these will set them on different paths and even possibly lead them to different conclusions, all with the same static content.

The lesson we learned is that not only did order matter, letting players be in control of that order was even more powerful. Given this, and the fact that we know that curated narrative can give the player mid- and long-term goals, we crafted portions of the curated narrative as a series of objectives that could be attempted in different orders. As an example, one of the storylines hypothesized that a cosmic event wiped out humanity. Scientists write back and forth about their frustration with the military and Muteki (a tech corporation largely invested in Artificial Intelligence), possibly sending them altered samples from some of the earliest ships that went dark. The scientists sent an algorithm to all research stations hoping that someone would be able to obtain a second sample to verify the accuracy of their findings from the first sample. Therefore, the player needs to commandeer an older vessel (one of those that went dark earliest) and bring it to a research station for scanning using the special algorithm.

There is a large variety of ways to accomplish this within this objective, including not attempting at all. The same player may attempt it differently depending on the run. On one run the player finds an old ship and attempt to commandeer it right away or finds a space station first then works on gathering equipment to help find an old ship. And then there's what kind of enemies are aboard that ship, what equipment players have when they board, how the ship is laid out, and what events occur while they attempt to commandeer it. These are all procedurally generated (and we'll see an example later in the chapter). The narrative and gameplay now started to complement one another and more seamlessly integrate.

Rather than be on the nose with objective pop-ups, we decided to try a more integrated approach that supported this seamless integration between story and gameplay. We fashioned an AI ship companion named JIL, who would analyze annotate logs. If JIL identified an objective, we would then store that log in a specific folder on the ship. This was an unobtrusive and cohesive way for us to integrate an objective system into a game that we wanted to be player-driven.

In addition, the narrative became the persistent element of the game; keeping all logs for reference across different runs (playthroughs). This tied into another of our design pillars: *realism*. The player remembered these logs across runs, so it felt right to incorporate that fact into the fiction rather than ignoring it. The game takes great effort to convince players that they *are* drone operators, not playing as drone operators (literally, the real-life computer screen acted as the in-game computer screen), so working the player's memory into the fiction felt in line with our design pillar of realism.

NARRATIVE AS A LURE

The Curated Content Needed to Push the Gameplay in Novel Directions

In our previous game, *A Virus Named TOM*, we found that some achievements we put in the game actually required the player to play the game entirely differently, instead of just rewarding them for playing the game normally. We always felt that these were the best form of achievements, because they brought about new gameplay. For this game, we asked: "Could we do the same with narrative, and could that strengthen the players' experience of it?"

We played a **lot** of *Duskers* while creating it. In all of this play, we started finding incredibly fun moments where our own player stories came to life. At one point we re-docked our mothership to a different airlock on the derelict ship so that our drones could escape. When the airlock opened, an alien charged out of our mothership's docking bay and destroyed the entire squad of drones in seconds. We realized the alien had somehow wandered into the docking bay of our mothership and taken a ride to the other side of the derelict ship inside of it! We remembered this experience when, in a different run, we were desperate to help our drones escape but were unable to remove an enemy from the path to an airlock. So this time, we left the docking bay open, waited for the alien to wander inside, and trapped it in the docking bay! We then re-docked on the other side of the derelict ship and let it out—thus removing it from the path to the airlock. We were now using the docking bay as an alien transport!

We loved that experience and realized that many players would never have it, so we devised a narrative that could re-create a version of it. One of the theories of how humanity died was a form of pandemic. Logs could be found from a medical scientist named Dr. J. Holmes, who created an algorithm to detect pathogen data. A subject (one of the organic alien enemies), however, needed to be scanned. To do this, the player needed to download the algorithm to the ship and lure an enemy from a quarantined derelict ship into the docking bay to initiate the scan. The player would then need to somehow find Holmes' ship to analyze the results of the scan.

By creating a narrative objective where the player needed to lure an organic enemy into the docking bay to scan it, we were able to motivate the player to experience a variation of one of the most exciting scenarios that we had stumbled upon while playtesting. We then read lots of player stories on our forums and subreddit about the variety of ways that players attempted this, with what enemy, and the narratives that the players had built up in their heads as to how and why it was all happening.

> I did it. I found Dr. J. Holmes.
>
> I was down to just 2 drones. I was doing the bare minimum for each mission, just grabbing what scrap I could from the safe first rooms. I even managed to pull off a cunning plan to capture a quarantined biological enemy in my docking bay and run the scan.
>
> Then I was just burning my resources just to keep gather and probe working, (repairing probe and replacing gather...), was running out of things to scrap; just hunting medical ships, desperately trying to

find some clue as to what 1185 meant. Dammit, I might die, I might run out of fuel, but I was gonna burn what I had if it gave me a chance to deliver that sample.

In my mind, maybe—just maybe—that would be enough to rescue whatever remained of civilisation.

And I finally found it. With barely any fuel left and no resources left to burn. The registry that, at long last, told me where Dr. J. Holmes' ship was, and what it was called. (The communication was on a med ship for me, if anyone else is also hunting.)

...

...And I'd already been there.

Reddit post from Nathin

First, that player's story shows the unique ways Nathin achieved the goal (which we talked about in the previous section) using the procedural content of the game: running out of fuel, using the *probe* and *gatherer* upgrades, coming up with a "cunning plan," etc. Second, it shows how the curated narrative led Nathin into a compelling experience they may not have otherwise had, as well as how it added color to the way they imagined and described their personal player story: "*desperately trying to find some clue as to what 1185 meant,*" "*I might die, I might run out of fuel, but I was gonna burn what I had if it gave me a chance to deliver that sample,*" etc.

COMPILING IT ALL DOWN

So during the development of *Duskers*, we found a few methods of conforming static content to the player story that we were happy with. Something as simple as breaking the story into smaller fragments and allowing them to be experienced in different orders was a start. Giving players agency in how they discovered and followed the trail of these fragments adds even more meaning and a stronger link between the player and the curated narrative. Finally, integrating that narrative into the gameplay and even forcing new ways of playing further entwines the player story and the curated narrative, so much so that the player story starts to take on elements of the curated narrative.

We found many forum posts from players, not only telling their player stories, but also incorporating the curated story into their personal fictions to give them more context and meaning! Things like "I was petrified of trying to capture one of these monsters in my docking bay, but 'for science' I tepidly boarded the ship, and you won't believe what happened. ... " This is essentially what our highest aim was, to help strengthen the player story with our own world-building and storytelling.

There's so much to explore when you add player interaction into a narrative experience and vice versa. We learned a lot on our journey developing *Duskers*, but there's so much more to discover. We hope that, by composing this story of our design journey, we inspire you to delve deeper into the abyss, and that you can tell us what insights you find lurking in the darkness.

CHAPTER 9

Uncanny Text

Blending Static and Procedural Fiction

Kevin Snow

P rocedurally generated text is a subject I have stumbled into, not intentionally sought out, over the years. So far, I have only incorporated procedural generation in ways that complement a static narrative, instead of starting projects with any fully formed ideas of how the procedural text will work or even knowing if the project will have procedural text to begin with. Still, it is in these cases a fundamental aspect of my work. At other times, it is silly and tacked on. Both of those approaches work out because procedural text has qualities that explode meaning in static narrative in complex, joyful, and uncanny ways.

SOUTHERN MONSTERS

When I demoed *Southern Monsters* at a small convention in the Midwest, one attendee playfully wanted to break the game. He read through the nightmarish introduction, had a conversation with an NPC or two, and then chose to take a shower—over and over and over. "Oh, the words changed," he said about the second shower. "Oh, this is getting sad." After showering nine or ten times, he made a *huh* sound and left the booth.

Although the shower text generation in *Southern Monsters* is simple, it was at least enough to mildly surprise that disinterested attendee. *Southern Monsters* is a combination of static and procedural text. Story events, like character conversations, have fluid structures, but their text mostly remains the same. Repetitive actions, like showering or eating food, transform in front of the player in response to the game state (*Figure 9.1*).

This came about because *Southern Monsters'* content informed the structure, a slow process in which I overhauled the core systems several times in the game's first year of development. *Southern Monsters* is a semi-autobiographical game about a teenager in south Arkansas who moderates a forum for believers in the paranormal. At night, he searches the swamp outside his house for a regional variation of Bigfoot called the Boggy Creek Monster.

All the systems in *Southern Monsters* explore how that teenager, Cripplefoot, copes with trauma from domestic violence. The character doesn't understand they're traumatized, or why they react the way they do. The game contextualizes the character's complicated routines of

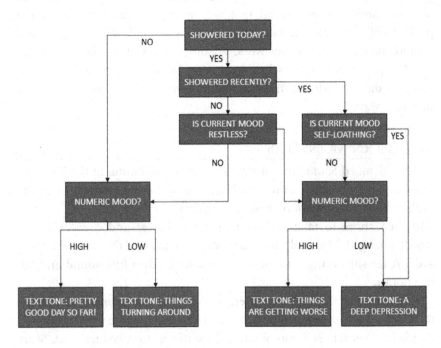

FIGURE 9.1 Shower text generation in *Southern Monsters*.

self-care and depressive impulses inside these systems. Few mechanics surface; there's no "depression meter." The player should feel as helpless as the character, like there's a logic at work too convoluted to ever comprehend. These systems are modeled after my own past behavior, after years of therapy and reflection.

Cripplefoot's mood is tracked with numbers and words. The numeric mood is a percentage that gets converted into a whole number between 1 and 3 to simplify the possibility space. With the numeric mood, there's a small amount of randomness, so although the system (and therefore Cripplefoot's behavioral trends) can be learned, it can't be reliably gamified. There's also a qualifier that adds context to the numeric mood called the "current mood" (named after the beloved LiveJournal feature). Neither mood is visible to the player, but both affect choice text and text generation. The convention attendee, through his endless showers, had achieved a current mood of "self-loathing." Effectively, the current mood adds an optional filter: *Why* does Cripplefoot feel this way?

The procedural text generation in *Southern Monsters* is guided by those systems and has to reinforce their mission. Eating a marshmallow pie can be a pleasurable activity for Cripplefoot, unless some factor turns it into a negative experience, such as eating too many in a short amount of time. So the game has to consider several factors when it decides what text is appropriate. How did Cripplefoot feel before the marshmallow pie? How did his mood affect the experience of eating and vice-versa? How about after?

When players experience story events in *Southern Monsters*, such as moderating a forum thread or speaking with an NPC, they're carrying meaning from those procedural moments. Cripplefoot's mom might comment if he hasn't showered, and his mood affects the range of choice options. The separation between static and procedural became so minor over development that the distinction's only useful to explain how it got there.

BATTLECAKES

Battlecakes is an RPG in which a batch of cupcakes goes on a quest to save the world. The game is developed by Volcano Bean; I'm the narrative designer and one of the writers. Although the structure of the script is standard for RPGs, the developers gave me creative freedom to work in small moments of procedural generation in the narrative.

Early in the game, the main character adventures to the library in the town of Butterworth Heights. If the player interacts with the shelves, the main character reads off one of the book titles and makes a generic comment about it. The names of the books are generated to have the structure of academic textbooks with the vocabulary of cookbooks (*Figure 9.2*).

Output examples:

1. Discovering Banana Cake

2. Sixty Years of Baking Mysteries

3. Ice Cream & Philosophy: The Hidden Connection

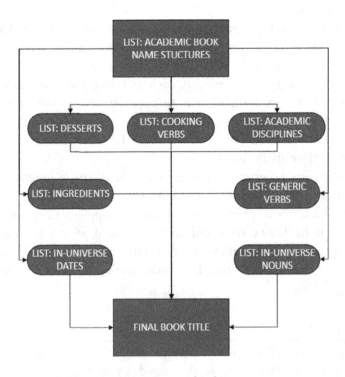

FIGURE 9.2   Book name generation in *Battlecakes*.

The capacity of procedural text to be random and unexpected makes it a perfect fit for the tone of *Battlecakes*. It's a game in which every aspect of the narrative is supposed to surprise the player, from the dialogue that takes inspiration from shows like *Steven Universe* and *Adventure Time* to the map design that encourages curiosity and exploration. Although the book generator isn't complex, it would have been easier to write a list of funny book titles and shuffle between them. The play experience would have been the same for the majority of users, but the uncanny tone of generated text is the point.

An excessively curated grammar would have removed some of the fun as much as a shuffled list. I iterated on the system just enough for the output to be diverse and for word soup to be infrequent instead of non-existent. That is accomplished by categorizing lists of words by syllable and allowing a maximum number of syllables per generated book. Ultimately, the book generator doesn't hold up to close scrutiny and doesn't need to. As with any toy, players can move on once they've become bored.

PLAYFUL TEXT

At Konsoll 2017, Jake Elliott of Cardboard Computer gave a talk titled "Playful Text," in which he presented a philosophy of procedural text design that emphasized "open, organic possibility spaces." He talked about the influence of postmodernist art on the design of procedural text in Act IV of *Kentucky Route Zero*, gently but intentionally contradicting traditional design thought that evaluates the success of procedural text in game design purely by player agency and binary dialogue choices. Elliott succinctly summarized the ability of procedural text to draw out meaning in otherwise static narrative.

The most complex text generation in *Southern Monsters* happens when the player watches cat videos. The function picks a genre, such as a cat sleeping or playing, then a paragraph structure, then individual sentence structures. Horizontal decisions are made as follows: If snow is mentioned, context is set to snow. If the function adds an additional clause to a sentence, the clause will check the context and describe an appropriate detail.

Output example:

A lean cat attacks a stuffed fish under a blanket. The cat shreds the fish, spilling cotton everywhere, while someone shrieks off camera. I rewatch the video, again and again, to absorb the scene's warmth.

Still, this text generation is simple. There's no weight given to particular words, phrases, or sentences. The context variable is flavor, not a tagging system. It's only even this complex so it creates relationships between sentences—other procedural text in *Southern Monsters* is sentence-length. The scope and specificity means it's feasible to cut down on bad output with iteration, so the procedural text doesn't need to be complicated.

Like other content in *Southern Monsters*, the cat videos both inform and respond to Cripplefoot's emotional state. That means Cripplefoot can watch a cat video and become more depressed, modeling my worst tendencies of idly scrolling through meaningless content when I really need to sleep. When the result of an action feeds back into a game state variable, it's not sophisticated: If the player is frequently making lots of small choices, the numbers can be tweaked in playtesting, with context-specific filters (the "current mood") catching exceptional situations. At heart, though, a corpus of cat videos is joyful—at least, it is if you love cats and animals like I do. *Southern Monsters* isn't miserable, or even fixated on misery. I want its procedural text to evoke the nuances of routine.

THE DOMOVOI

I released my first game, *The Domovoi*, in 2014. Made with Twine, it's a short, interactive story where the player listens to a Soviet folklorist perform a story about a domovoi, a house spirit. It has limited branching with two endings and makes heavy use of Twine's randomization features to change the text in subtle ways. "Even this performance will change—words will be different in your memories than when you first heard them," the narrator tells the player early in the story. Subtext is for cowards.

The game is not-so-secretly about my experiences with post-traumatic stress disorder, a diagnosis I received after being medically discharged from the military in 2010. If the storyteller becomes angry with the player's suggestions, she changes her story to have the domovoi beaten with a hammer. After the beating, the storyteller goes forward in time to explain how this violence affects the domovoi, a personal tangent that implies the storyteller has experienced trauma herself and is punishing her audience with the weight of its emotional burden. There are nine of these paragraphs, presented randomly to the player, each exploring a different facet of how nightmares and re-traumatization have affected my personal memories of traumatic events.

If the storyteller is satisfied with the player's suggestions, there's no beating, no trauma. The randomized elements of the text make the narrative slippery and impossible for players to retain in their memories as a static text, emphasizing the struggle I've undergone living with memories that continually recontextualize themselves.

MEMORY BLOCKS

Memory Blocks is a Twine anthology produced by Priscilla Snow that centers on the theme of memory cards and our relationship to those old relics. My own contribution to the anthology is a story about the fictional game *Animal Town*, inspired by *Animal Crossing*—more specifically, the letters sent by villager NPCs in that series. The player reads the static letters sent by the fictional owner of the *Animal Town* memory card, then reads the procedurally generated letters that the villagers send in response.

In the real series *Animal Crossing*, there are three types of response letters: positive, negative, and confused. There's very little procedural text; the content of the letter is inspired by the personality type of the NPC and a few conditional variables, such as: Did the player attach a present to the letter? *Animal Town*, in contrast, uses some light procedural generation to emphasize the uncanny nature of the NPC letters, shown in *Figure 9.3*.

Procedural text, in this instance, reinforces the story's themes about the creative imagination players bring into their relationships with

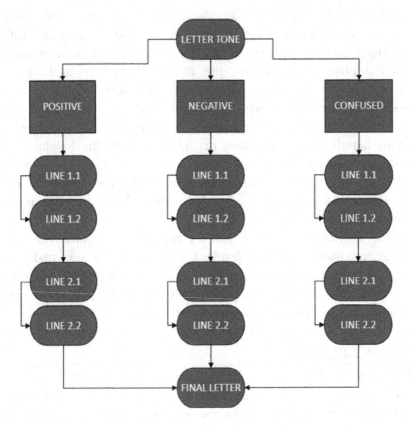

FIGURE 9.3 Letter generation in *Animal Town*.

NPCs. The owner of the *Animal Town* memory card writes sincere, personal letters to the villagers, who respond with randomized text that barely acknowledges the deeply personal nature of the original letters. The story uses that uncanniness to be funny, touching, and a little melancholy.

MATUL REMRIT

Before I made games, I wrote multimedia fanfiction: *Matul Remrit*, a Let's Play that ran from 2010 to 2013 and creatively interprets a single playthrough of *Dwarf Fortress*. The text is written in a broken, stilted style that imitates the game's uncanny procedural text. The story is a collaboration between author and machine, a record of my player imagination that *Dwarf Fortress* encourages with its highly detailed procedural systems.

All of my work with procedural text as a designer comes from fascinations I developed while creating *Matul Remrit*. Although I have yet to create or work on any games directly inspired by the complexity of *Dwarf Fortress'* systems, the experience of playing the game shaped my interest in how procedural text can explode meaning. *Matul Remrit* was a playthrough of *Dwarf Fortress* v0.31, a version in which a dwarf could throw a violent tantrum in response to a series of sometimes minor irritations. *Matul Remrit* took those factual events and ascribed narrative motivation to them, a creative process that eliminated alternative interpretations of the event and canonized a single one. Effectively, I have spent large amounts of my writing career since then doing the exact opposite, using procedural text to complicate or emphasize meaning in static narrative.

THE FUTURE

The more commercial contracts I pursue as a writer, the less I am able to incorporate procedural text. Although I didn't focus on tools because most of the procedural generation I do is simple enough to be accomplished in several, I want to stress how vital tools are to this process and how their existence allows this blending of static and procedural text. My greatest hope as a freelancer is that studios adopt dialogue tools that have options for procedural text, like Ink and the Spirit Character Engine, that make it much easier to pitch to a lead designer or editor. Voice-acting might be incompatible with procedural text, but even fully voice-acted games have tons of text lying around their environments—imagine writing a complex generator for the hundreds of books in *The Elder Scrolls* series. These tools allow these procedural moments to exist in practice.

This page intentionally left blank

CHAPTER 10

Dramatic Play in
The Sims

Daniel Kline

T here's a particular form of play that everyone does that is still rare
in video games: dramatic play. You see it in LARPing, acting,
superhero action figures, and children at the playground. Adults and
kids saying "Let's pretend we're. ..." We don't even have a clear word
for this kind of play in game design. I call it **dramatic gameplay**. Role
playing in video games has taken on a broader meaning, more about
tactics and progression then pretending. Player storytelling is sometimes
used, but these players aren't purposefully telling stories. They aren't
watching or thinking about narrative. They are

- taking on a **role,**

- making that role **personal,**

- **performing** their role, or

- expecting the game to **recognize** the role.

The Sims is both one of the most successful video game series in history
and full of dramatic gameplay. It has sold over a hundred million games
and expansion packs, spread over two decades. Players of *The Sims* talk
about how they value their characters, about how interesting they are,
and how they love playing them. *The Sims* is a great example of these
4 fundamentals of dramatic gameplay at work.

The first fundamental of dramatic gameplay is players take on a **role**. All dramatic play is *acting*, pretending to be another in the moment. It is make believe. It is empathy, in play form. Players are motivated to play their characters out, to see where they go and who they become. They often deliberately suppress knowledge, abilities, or personal desires, in seeking to play the role. Mastery is expressed, not through traditional challenge and skill tests, but through perfect impersonation. The obstacle is the role and its nature, not the game systems. These roles can be complex, even abstract. In *The Sims*, the role(s) is the active household, the Sims themselves. Sims are the center of Live mode and CAS mode. Players unconsciously identify with each Sim in the household, switching between 1st and 3rd person language. Players even adopt different roles for each Sim they control. And their play matters. If the player does nothing, the Sims won't survive. The Sim needs the player.

The second fundamental is making the role **personal**. It needs to be special to the player. It needs to be *hers*, by active choice. This is typically done by clearly contrasting elements of the role with other choices, along multiple axes. In *The Sims*, this is looks, clothes, traits, skills, careers, relationships, and more—the nouns the role is described with and represented by.

The third fundamental is the player needs to be able to **perform** the role. The player needs to be able to express the part, via its verbs. And this acting needs to feel free and deliberate, not preset by game limitations. Design-wise, this means an explosion of available choices, some of which are clearly not appropriate to the current role or situation. In *The Sims*, the pie menu provides this. Often, the mechanical differences between pie menu interactions are not significant. But each carries a different flavor that lets the player express their role.

The last fundamental is the game needs to **recognize** the role. Dramatic players are trying to inhabit the game world and feel fulfilled when the game responds as expected. This reinforcement is a reward in a classic design sense and encourages further play. In *The Sims*, this recognition can come in a host of ways: the pie menu choices available, the outcomes of each one, the target's response, the world's response, the resulting changes to the next pie menu, and the long term impact on the Sim itself.

Let's examine some key ways *The Sims* caters to dramatic play.

FIGURE 10.1 *The Sims 4: City Living* (2016). Courtesy of Electronic Arts.

DESIGN EXAMPLES IN THE SIMS

1. Go Broad

The Sims 4 is a large, sprawling, crufty game. It ships game-expanding expansions multiple times a year, and players eat it up. It runs counter to every design theory about elegance, strategic choices, and accessible controls, but it works. Why? Because each expansion delivers more dramatic gameplay (Figure 10.1).

Sims 4: Cats & Dogs adds more roles to the game—"Be a pet lover!" It adds a new axis of personality for Sims. It lets you personalize your pet's looks, traits, behaviors, skills, costumes, and more. It adds tons of choices—"Do you take care of your pets? Socialize with them? Do they sleep with you?"—and the pet is always on screen, following you around, reminding you of this. *Sims 4: Get to Work* has new careers that let you play through the work day and a business you could run to sell most anything in the game. Sell Photographs? Paintings? Your writing? All different roles to try. *Sims 4: Parenthood* adds tons of detail to parenting, fleshing out a popular role and adding new roles and behaviors for children. *Sims 4: Jungle Adventure* lets you vacation in a fictional South American jungle and play archaeologist, cultural anthropologist, or tomb raider. *Sims 4: Vampires* doesn't just give you vampires and vampire hunters, it gives you a whole new personalization axis for existing characters to layer on top. In the 4 years post-launch, *The Sims 4* has shipped 22 additional packs.

All of this can seem like clutter. When you own 10 expansion packs it can be overwhelming. But to dramatic game players, this is catnip. It hits exactly what they are looking for. And it compounds, each new axis building on the last. While not every role appeals to every player, the ones they enjoy keep them excited and engaged for years, despite not being classically "skill testing" or "content deep." Narrow, deep design is great for other game experiences, but dramatic games need a large critical mass of choices. Dramatic games want to be large and inelegant and full of orthogonal-ish stuff, to create roles that feel unique and personal and expressive, and to play these roles in new circumstances.

2. Fail Forward

Dramatic gameplay needs interesting results to reward role playing. When role playing, players choose to play sub-optimally. Unlike in most games, a character failing is not the same as the player failing. The player may actually be demonstrating role mastery! Thus, it's important that failing is fun and that characters "fail forward."

If player choices don't change the world, failure becomes a form of "save and reload" or "try, try again." This causes players to lose their sense of performance, stop role playing, and start grinding out tasks with predictable outcomes. Instead, when the character fails, change the world state. Failing forward in *The Sims* can be a cooking fire, a facepalm worthy faux pas, or an embarrassing office mistake. This actually becomes a further expression of the role's identity. "I tried cooking. I suck at cooking. I started a fire and ran out of the house screaming." Each failure builds up the character in the player's head.

Not every choice needs to lead to significant changes. Some "try again, maybe it'll work next time" is ok. But at least 20% or more should fail forward. It creates a sense that every choice can change the future. It's a key component of recognizing role play.

Another way of recognizing a role is having super successes, showing off a particular talent for a role, with outputs that improve or change future options. For example, professional Sim chefs can super-succeed at cooking, creating masterpieces. However, super successes are not usually as impactful as failing forward; "getting a bonus" is less interesting than something disruptive.

In *The Sims*, death is a common example of failing forward. Your other Sims mourn for several days, changing the nature of every future choice. They also meet Grim, a popular Sims character, and can plead for the dead Sim to be restored using different Sim skills. But even routine skill usages and socials have a chance to change your options. Cooking can burn your house down, but it can also use up your free hour or ruin dinner. Failing a social lets you apologize, get embarrassed, or get angry and start a fight. While there are times you can try again, *The Sims 4* uses different outcomes to create a mystique of "Never assume things will work the same way twice."

3. Story Surprises

The simulation in *The Sims 4* provides lots of surprises, via both interaction outcomes and simulated NPC behavior. One favorite is *"A hot guy randomly walks up to your Sim—what do you do?"* Players immediately know how they want to respond. There are a dozen possible ways, all personal to different roles. They might flirt, slap him, say they aren't interested, or apologize to a jealous wife. But players are playing their role and instinctively know what they want to do (Figure 10.2).

FIGURE 10.2 *The Sims 4: City Living* (2016). Courtesy of Electronic Arts.

These kinds of surprise scene or outcomes have powerful effects:

- They create a strong call to action, followed by strong emotions and memorable moments.

- They differentiate Sims. "But then" conflicts expose the hearts of characters, similar to a moral quandary.

- They push players out of ruts. They also make roles richer through multiple plays.

- They expose players to what's possible. One of the major challenges with dramatic play is ramping players in. The hot guy teaches you "Hey, I could be doing romantic things. I could date and get married, and maybe even have kids."

- They keep players watching. "What's going to happen next?" The mystery keeps players engaged.

4. Things to Watch

Watching, in dramatic play, is a big deal. Watching slows everything down. It disengages the twitch-action mindset and opens up creative thinking. This gives players time to reflect and find significance in their routine actions. A strong indicator of dramatic gameplay is that players are zoomed in and watch their characters. When players focus away from characters, take a lot of actions, or speed up time, they start to disengage from the role playing process.

The Sims 4 encourage players to stay and watch interactions with

- expressive and fun animations,

- speech and thought balloons over the Sim's heads when they talk, and

- surprises and variable outcomes (as previously explained)

5. Reactions

Like in any game, clear reward feedback is important. But in dramatic games, these rewards take unusual forms. Players want positive feedback from the world and other characters that they are playing their role

FIGURE 10.3 *The Sims 4: Get Together* (2015). Courtesy of Electronic Arts.

well. It's key that NPCs respond appropriately to the player's role. Over time, the world can gradually become a reflection of the player's character and the character's actions. New choices should appear that reflect the character's role, world state, and recent actions.

The Sims 4 gives special attention to NPC reactions during interactions. The game plays 1, 2, or even 3 extra back-and-forth responses for key interactions, such as a parent scolding a toddler, even though it blocks the player's next action. Sims standing nearby will also react to major interactions (Figure 10.3).

The Sims 4 does more to reflect the role. It gives players interactive objects to place in the world, so they can visibly see characters' styles, skills, and interests. Sims have different emotions, giving them new role-appropriate interactions. When players idle, Sims autonomously go off and try to represent their roles. *The Sims* exaggerates all of this for effect and makes it clear that the game is responding to the player and that the player's dramatic choices are effective.

6. Characters and Traits

Dramatic players want roles that feel unique and personal. *The Sims 4* uses systems like traits and aspirations to achieve this. But *The Sims* uses traits for 3 different purposes: NPCs, Player identities, and Dramatic gameplay. Each has different requirements:

- **NPC traits** emphasize social interactions or common NPC behaviors. If players can't see NPC traits or interact with them, then they effectively don't exist. NPC traits get bonus points if they are easy for players to push against and set up surprises or conflict. *Evil* is the classic example of a good NPC trait.

- **Player identities** are ways of defining a role that engages players at character creation. For example, the *Cheerful, Music Lover,* or *Romantic* traits in *The Sims 4* fulfill common player fantasies. They are role signposts for dramatic players, pointing them in a direction. Aspirations in Create-a-Sim also serve this function. They frame the role question as "What does this Sim want to be?" Player identity systems sometimes have no feedback during the game. That's ok. Their job is to inspire the initial role.

- **Dramatic gameplay traits** express the character during play. They want roles to feel distinct from each other, from moment to moment. In *The Sims 4,* for example, *Bro* is visible in the pie menu whenever you socialize. *Lazy* feels relevant every time your Sim naps or sleeps. *Loves Outdoors* is happy whenever outside. These are important both because they create gameplay variation and because they remind you the Sims are unique and special, each playing its own role.

Ideally, your Player Identity traits also are good NPC traits and have strong Dramatic Gameplay, but it's not required. In fact, it can become counterproductive if it restricts your content. It's far more important to enable as many roles as possible than it is to make an elegant streamlined trait system.

Notably, traits in dramatic play need not be orthogonal. Orthogonal traits are sometimes useful for dramatic gameplay needs, where opposites define strong archetypes, but they are less applicable for the NPC and Player Identity needs. In dramatic play, traits are powerful tools that should meet their purpose with as much personality as possible.

The most critical part of trait design is communicating what a trait is doing. Otherwise, players forget they exist. To show when a choice is available due to a trait, *The Sims 4* puts trait icons on pie menu buttons. If the choice is changed due to a trait, *The Sims 4* adds a tooltip to explain the change. Traits also give random buffs with tooltips. These techniques don't work for NPC traits or autonomous PC behavior, unfortunately. Whenever you're designing a trait system, think about how players will know that they are changing the game, in all the cases where traits are supposed to make characters feel distinct.

7. Realistic Fantasies

A major aid to adopting a role is using known, relatable, desirable archetypes. If players already know and dream about a role, taking it on is an instant hook. Using a realistic setting makes this connection even clearer.

Realistic settings also lend themselves to unusual or very personal roles outside the designer's original intent. (See Alice and Kev in *Sims 3*, for example.) Personal is very hard to design, but modern life is very familiar and personal by its nature. Fantasy worlds tend toward jargon

FIGURE 10.4 *The Sims 4: Cats & Dogs* (2017). Courtesy of Electronic Arts.

and made-up history that's much harder for players to relate to. *The Sims 4* is one of the few games that go all in on simulating modern life. Picking a Western suburban life familiar to its primary audience makes roles more accessible (Figure 10.4).

8. Transgressive Play

Dramatic play is more powerful when you can take on taboo and forbidden roles. It's an instant hook, particularly for young adults exploring their own identity. It's thrilling and can lead to guilty tittering and shy pleasure. It attracts players looking for something new and smoothly ramps players into a role. Breaking traditional roles gives players a taste of freedom and makes the role that much more personal. It plays directly into the core strengths and appeal of dramatic play.

The Sims has an extremely wide range of roles that are new or taboo, possibly LGBTQ relationships, transgender characters, and interracial romance or fantastical roles like vampires and witches. Even simple roles can be transgressive. Consider "pet owner" in which kids can explore owning the pet their parents have forbidden or "young mother having a baby" for teenage girls who are thinking about sex and pregnancy for the first time. Playing these roles can be extremely powerful and compelling, giving players a perspective, an outlet and a voice they often can't find in their own lives. When designing roles for your game, are there real life issues that players might want to explore?

9. Low Challenge

It's important in dramatic play that failure not be punishing. To perform a role, players need to feel empowered, creative, and free to try things. If random failures are heavily punished or success is gated by difficult skills, then players will cease role playing. This is not to say that dramatic play (or *The Sims*) has no mastery. Instead, the mastery is in performing the role expertly and knowing the game well. This can be just as rewarding as executing a difficult combo or beating a difficult boss, if designed well.

In dramatic play, one side effect of low challenge is that traditional game balance is not critical. Instead, everything should be designed to be freely rewarding, to enable you to play out the role. You *should* get rich becoming a businessman, if that's your role. Now you can explore the "rich person" role. Worst case, you can veer into another role. (New roles can be designed to be readily accessible, mid-play.) Note that *The Sims 4* has deep content that requires hours of play to unlock. But it is more a traditional progression—a reflection of investment and recognition of a role—than a reward for skill mastery or a tightly balanced pacing/unlock mechanism.

10. Player Commitments

Performing a role can be overwhelming. One trick to encourage players is giving them clear goals, like quests. Have the game make suggestions, and ask players to choose one and commit to it. Early on, these goals can be simple and instructional. Once players are experts, the goals can be more open-ended and long term. In a dramatic game, these goals should be extensions of players' current roles or opportunities to take their roles in a new direction. Completing the goal then becomes an opportunity for the game to respond to players' role playing and reward them.

The Sims has explored player commitments in multiple ways. Wishes and Promises in *The Sims 3* are a great example of this. Players had 4 wishes to "promise." Wishes were chosen from a large pool based on a Sim's recent actions, and they got deeper and deeper over time. Sims also had a lifetime wish, an ultimate "I win" goal that players choose for their Sims to strive for. The list of possible lifetime wishes is based on the Sims' traits, again reinforcing the players' roles.

11. Dramatic Currency

Games love to give out currency rewards, right? This works in dramatic games, too. Games can give out *dramatic currency* as a reward for performing a role, almost like points. These points can be attached to the player, but there's extra reinforcing power in attaching them to the role. Often, these points can be spent on internal, abstract things for growing the role or ways to control over the world (and set up the role for success).

Completing a promise in *The Sims 3* gives a Sim lifetime satisfaction points. These points can be used to buy "cheat-y" traits or objects that make the Sim feel powerful and successful or help future Sims play faster.

12. Abstraction and Humor

Dramatic play supports abstraction very well. Players are very forgiving of a game taking unrealistic shortcuts, as long as they can express their roles. *The Sims* titles have always had a sly whimsy that takes advantage of this. Sims come back to life, spin around to change clothes, teleport to their destination, make friends in a few hours, carry unrealistic loads, do magic, mind control other Sims, fight inside cartoon smoke clouds, and "Woohoo." Sims personalities are determined via traits, and their relationships by a green bar. *The Sims* is full of unrealistic abstractions. Players have expectations of being able to perform their roles, but performance is distinct from real life. As long as players can follow through on their roles and the world reacts, games can shortcut and abstract a lot of things. These shortcuts are often funny, and leaning into that helps players go along with them.

DRAMATIC DESIGN PATTERNS IN OTHER GAMES

These are some examples of how *The Sims* supports and encourages dramatic play. *Stardew Valley, Middle Earth: Shadow of Mordor, Rim-World, Mass Effect, Sim City*, and *Dwarf Fortress* are all games in other genres to research. *Skyrim* is particularly noteworthy, as a mainstream AAA game that's met with significant success with dramatic players.

It's important to note that dramatic play is not all or nothing. Games can support multiple types of players. So don't be afraid to do a few low-hanging designs for dramatic players, even if they aren't your core audience. Dramatic play is a natural fit for RPGs, simulations, and multiplayer games. It can be a good mini-game, a nice break from an action sequence, or make a narrative game's characters seem more human. Consider the celebrated scene in *Uncharted 2,* where mid-game the player explores a quiet Tibetan village.

Some common design techniques are anti-patterns to dramatic play and require care. Recall the 4 components of dramatic play and then consider

- *narrative* and *cut scenes*: The authorial voice puts players in a passive mode and often stops the player from personalizing and performing the role.

- *difficult controls, high challenge, fast pace,* or *significant learning curves*: These engage the optimization brain, creating intense emotions and occupying all of the player's attention, blocking the player from performing.

- *fixed Characters*: Avatar verbs are often heavily prescribed, with little player flexibility. A preset character can be ok—the players are opting in when they buy the game, after all. But during play, the dramatic players want to personalize and perform their roles in some way, beyond looks. The player's choices about who they are and how they express themselves need range, or dramatic play morphs into follow-the-breadcrumbs linear play.

Pen and paper role-playing games with Game Masters are often held up as the next step for emergent storytelling in video games. But this misunderstands a core reason this kind of pen and paper role-playing is *fun*. Indie games like *Fiasco* have no Game Masters. Others, like *Blades in the Dark*, put Game Masters in the backseat. It's not about the Game Master. It's about playing to explore a role, playing to see what happens to that role. *The Sims* does this and has found a passionate fan base eager for more.

Dramatic play is part of our nature. Every child does it. It's fundamental to how we learn and grow. It's part of what makes us human. *The Sims* is on the tip of a deep iceberg. There's so much more that can be done. How can you use dramatic play in your next game?

This page intentionally left blank

CHAPTER 11

Memorable Stories from Simple Rules in *Curious Expedition*

Riad Djemili

Maschinen-Mensch

The Curious Expedition features hundreds of story fragments that are procedurally combined. In this article, I will give an overview of how a simple ruleset can create personal and memorable storylines.

In the year 2014, after leaving the AAA industry, Johannes Kristmann and I founded the indie company Maschinen-Mensch in Berlin. In our debut title *The Curious Expedition* (CE) you gather party members and supplies for your trek and travel to explore the last remaining uncharted regions of the Victorian Era. We tell stories of triumph and of failure, of hubris, exploitation, and death. To achieve the sense of exploring the ever unknown, procedural world- and story-generation felt like not just an option but also a necessity for the game.

The main gameplay of CE consists of a round-based strategy mechanic, where you plan your travel route on a map that you slowly uncover (*Figure 11.1*). Selecting the best path requires you to consider traversability, dangerousness, equipment, team morale, and other factors. Each small tile represents a full day's travel, and legs can easily involve weeks of traversing the Perlin-generated terrain. Our goal was to feature traveling as the core gameplay, instead of the map being just a beautiful level selection screen.

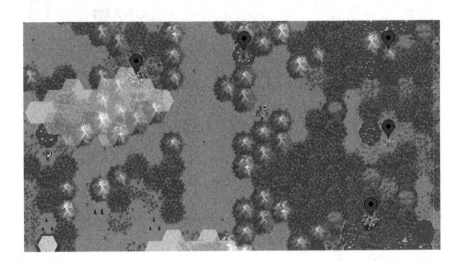

FIGURE 11.1

During your travels, we document noteworthy events using a procedural text diary screen that features a close-up of your trek and the surroundings as background art. In these diary scenes, you select from multiple-choice actions, usually aiming to find compromises among scarce resources, tense character dynamics, and questionable morals.

THREE LEVELS OF ABSTRACTION

An example of an event that might occur is that one night while setting up your camp, a trek member with the superstitious trait notices a vulture circling above the camp. They ask you to shoot down the vulture (*Figure 11.2*). As with any interesting decision, there is no obvious answer. Shooting down the vulture will consume valuable ammunition. Ignoring the plea will lower the loyalty of the person toward you.

For this event to appear, various procedural systems are layered on top of each other: world layer, event layer, and sentence layer.

World Layer

The diary screen can be deliberately triggered by either interacting with points of interest or automatically through catastrophic events. Points of interest include villages, missions, shrines, pyramids, travel merchants,

FIGURE 11.2 "This event is inspired by a real-life diary entry of Isabel Burton from 1897 while she was in Syria."

forsaken camp sites, and similar places. Catastrophic events that are checked on each turn often involve individual character ailments, like a wound becoming infected or suffering from sickness. Most importantly, an event is also forced when running out of the main resource of your trek: sanity.

Some of these catastrophic events stop the trek movement immediately; others are delayed until the trek arrives at its target destination to reduce potential player confusion caused by an interruption. Based on this general gameplay context, we know when to show the diary and which input event to use to calculate the page content.

Event Layer

CE uses a declarative text syntax to describe all events. A simple event might consist of nothing more than an ID, a text, and some basic effect.

```
{
id: evt-basic-example
sanity: +20
text: I suddenly felt better.
}
```

Events might reference other events and specify which and how many should be processed. The text and effect of each processed event is added to the same diary page. In the night camp example above, the diary was instructed to run the *evt-nightRest-sanityLow* event. That event contains an introductory text line ("I told the trek to unpack and allowed everyone to rest") and a list referencing over 50 other events. This list could be imagined as a cookbook, since each event specifies all the ingredients it needs the game to fulfill, like a recipe.

Here's an abbreviated version of that event, containing a requirement and three referenced events, from which one of the events that fulfills its requirements is randomly selected and processed:

```
{
id: evt-nightRest-sanityLow
reqSanity: 20..50
text: I laid down, but then...
select: [evt-vulture, evt-fight, evt-calmNight]
}
```

The most interesting events are those that take into account individual members of the party. The following example uses the *charEffects* keyword to specify a sub-event that is checked for each trek member individually and considered valid if at least *count* members pass the specified requirements. In this case, we're looking for two characters, who will get into an argument:

```
{
id: evt-sanity-fight
charEffects: {
    count: 2
    reqCharFlags: +humanoid -special
    text: A discussion between $name grew into a argument
    actions: {
        actionText: Arrest $name
        text: We tried to arrest $name but $he fled the
        scene.
        removeCharacter: true
        }
    }
}
```

Let's assume the system found two characters by the names of "Richard Wellington" and "Akulta." The text of this event features a special $name keyword, which is replaced by the names of all the matched trek members, resulting in: "A discussion between Richard Wellington and Akulta grew into an argument." The diary will also show two action buttons named "Arrest Richard Wellington" and "Arrest Akulta."

These systems allow us to portray events featuring various requirements and effects that are able to reference other events for increased modularization and variation.

Sentence Layer

Another layer of variation can now be applied at the sentence level. The texts declared by events also support word randomization. This text will randomly choose to show only one of the text variations in the square parentheses:

"[He|She] suggested that we should set up camp here. I [hated| agreed with] the idea. We would stay here [for now|until I felt like moving on again]."

Initially, our written text featured a large amount of synonyms, but we realized that synonyms create a big burden on localization without making events more interesting. Much more memorable are tonal and even contradictory variations that manage to fit into the general sentence meaning. In the example above, the sentence needs to communicate that the trek is setting up a camp point. Within this context, we're free to play around with the idea of the explorer being glad or angry about that decision as long as we don't negate the goal of the sentence.

SAME EVENT, DIFFERENT INTERPRETATIONS

We established three layers of abstraction that are used to build each diary page. With this simple ruleset, we're able to construct a fascinating amount of varied story telling. Let's take a look at one of my favorite diary events: One of your trek members approaches you after a nice evening of resting in one of the indigenous villages. They have fallen in love with a villager and wants to leave the expedition to stay with the village.

When players approach me at events and retell specific memorable moments, this is one that they will mention more often. Here are several real world variations that players have told me about this episode:

- a British soldier falling in love with a woman from the tribe

- a bearded sailor falling in love with a man of the tribe

- a missionary falling in love with a woman of the tribe.

Through applying the same event to different characters and applying different word variations (including different gender pronouns), we've created three scenes that hit different tones and even touch on different potential taboos. To the people that retold me these stories, they felt funny or touching or even personal.

Apples in NetHack

The reason these generated stories are able to feel relevant instead of seeming like techy text randomization exercises reminds me of how apples work in *NetHack*. First released in 1987, *NetHack* is a classic roguelike with a tremendous amount of complex systems that work together to create emergent gameplay.

In most roleplaying games you can consume food, but in *NetHack* you can choke and die from eating food. The first time I heard that apples had killed hundreds of players, my mind ran wild with the thought of how complex this and other systems would have to be, if even your dining experience was simulated to this detail. Since *NetHack* is open source, I could just look up the code in question:

```
If (food) {
You("choke over your %s.", foodword(food));
if (food->oclass == COIN_CLASS) {
killer = "a very rich meal";
} else {
```

The relevant section was only a few lines of simple code and was much less complex than I had anticipated. Little effort had been necessary to trick me into assuming a highly elaborate simulation. Similar to how I see the apples, players of CE don't know exactly how deep the rabbit hole of simulation goes. They are glad to fill up the gaps in the ruleset with their own belief in the intricacy of the system. This becomes part of the suspension of disbelief. As long as we provide enough consistency in our procedural stories so as not to break this gift, players will be happy to mentally cooperate in creating a believable world.

STORY ARCS

When we start joining together these individual events by linking cause and effect, interesting character arcs emerge organically. Here is a plausible sequence of events in CE:

We're low on sanity and start eating coca leaves to deal with the strain. Our cook Marie-Elise Alexandre has a psychotic episode and develops a strong sense of superstition (gaining the *superstitious* trait internally).

We set up the night camp, and Marie-Elise is bothered by a vulture (if she had not had the *superstition* trait, the event would not have appeared). We decline to waste scarce ammo and Marie-Elise loses loyalty, resulting in her being marked as *angry*.

At a later night camp, Marie-Elise gets into a big argument with the scout over a minor nuisance (her still being in an *angry* mood being the requirement of this event). We decide to break up the fight and chastise Marie-Elise, causing her to run off into the jungle alone. We decide not to follow her.

Many days later, we're out of resources and down on our luck, when suddenly a regretful Marie-Elise steps out of the woods. She had been following our tracks for days and asks to rejoin our trek. Thankfully she also brings food. (The previous event had removed her from the trek but stored her in a special pool of characters that we keep in the background for further purposes.)

Each of these events was allowed to be triggered due to its requirements being fulfilled. Each of these events caused an effect that potentially enabled or disabled other events. At no point was a system dedicated to crafting long-term storylines involved. Yet, by indirectly linking these individual events through a shared vocabulary of interesting hooks, a consistent and highly interactive storyline emerged.

Not all the storylines created this way will be memorable. This is partly due to the nature of characters dying or leaving the trek and partly due to our lack of forced control over the player. But when a complex storyline evolves out of this series of events, at each point highly influenceable by the player, we are rewarded with something uniquely personal and memorable. In this way, procedural story generation can feel truly magical.

CHAPTER 12

Amplifying Themes and Emotions in Systems

Daniel Cook

Spry Fox

When I prototype, I keep a watch out for the emotions that arise from playing even the simplest of the systems. Often early prototypes involve simple shapes, abstract numbers, and little evidence of what a typical player might consider plot or theming. Yet I regularly notice myself becoming excited about a variable ticking upward or crushed when I lose a resource. However, most players are not trained to watch for the emotions that arise from play. They'll experience broad moments of joy and failure; particularly when they engage with an abstract game, the subtler emotional signals can be quite weak and so they are left feeling cold about the whole experience. Beyond a very small segment of abstract thinkers, the emotional payload of the clever gameplay systems falls flat.

We want to amplify those emotional undercurrents, tie them to rich themes, and make a vibrant landscape of meaning and emotion visible to a typical game player. When I think of "narrative" in my games, I rarely think in terms of linear plotting of the sort found in static media like books or movies. Instead I follow a two-step process. First, what stimuli or feedback can we add to various interaction loops to boost the emotions of play? Second, how can we use resonant real world themes to convert raw emotions into a meaningful experience? We'll talk about applying these two steps in my game *Triple Town* as well as some of the failures that resulted.

THE EMOTIONS OF COLONIALISM IN TRIPLE TOWN

In 2010, I designed a casual puzzle game called *Triple Town*. To play, you drop objects onto a small grid, and if three of the same objects are next to one another, they merge together to form a new higher level object. Eventually the board turns into a cluttered space filled with previously combined objects, and it takes clever planning to craft the highest level of objects.

Triple Town is a very simple abstract game that produces deep emergent gameplay that has engaged players for thousands of hours. I regularly get messages from people who have been playing for years, and the basic mechanic has reappeared in popular titles like *Threes* or *2048*.

Observing Emotions in the Prototype

Mechanics generate emotions. Stephane Bura outlined the basic process in his seminal essay "Emotion Engineering in Videogames."[1] By putting the player in states in which critical variables are either constrained or move freely, we can trigger instinctual feelings of loss or plenty.

- **Variables**: The variables worth watching could be anything with in-game value: time, territory, currency, items, you name it.

- **Velocity of change**: There's a spectrum of emotional impact that stems from the velocity at which these variables are changed. A slow drain has a different emotional result than a sudden loss.

- **Direction of change**: The direction the variable changes also has an impact. A strong gain feels very different from a strong loss.

- **Predictability of change**: Emotions are also impacted by pacing and variability of change. A predictable steady decrease feels very different from a rapid unpredictable fluctuation. Much of what players do is sample the world and try to predict what is going to happen next. Their emotional state is heavily derived from those predictions.

As I played the early *Triple Town* prototypes, I was on the lookout for various emotional signals. I'm not doing anything overly theoretical here, just carefully observing my own emotional state as I play. Here's what I observed:

- **Decisiveness**: I'd make a plan for where I was going to combine pieces. I have lots of clear information so I know I can make a smart plan on how to advance in the game.

- **Anticipation**: I would wait for the right piece to appear in the random draw so that I could complete my plan. The right piece is a highly variable resource that I can't completely predict.

- **Tension**: Uncombined pieces take up space, and when the space runs out, you lose. The longer my plan went without getting the right pieces, the more cluttered the board got and the more likely it was that I would lose. In Bura's terms, I was witnessing the steady erosion of the critical territory variable and predicting my imminent failure.

- **Relief**: When the piece arrived, dropping combined multiple objects into one higher level object. This freed up space, and I could start the whole process of planning all over again.

Now, the game as I've described it so far was a bit boring in practice. Making plans and then waiting for random drops wasn't interesting enough. So we added a random moving element that would arbitrarily block you from making certain moves. Originally these were simple black squares that would randomly appear in a square each turn. With their addition, a whole new set of emotions arose.

- **Frustration**: When you got the perfect piece AND a blocker appeared in exactly the space you needed to place it ... players would be irritated. This was a sudden reduction of a hitherto reliable resource (a tactically meaningful empty space).

- **Hostility**: The blockers were moving entirely by random chance, but even using this simple simulation players felt they were intentionally being thwarted.

- **Defensiveness**: Players started ascribing motivations to the black squares and planning both desperate and diabolical counter plans for triumphing over their opponent.

From a pacing perspective, the addition of the blockers added a property of play that I love to see. Players would make plans, they would encounter new information or context, and they would be forced to revise their plans. However, smart players quickly learned that they did much better if they thought about how to balance:

- **Options planning**: Making their long terms plans robust in the face of variance.

- **Opportunism**: Staying alert to short-term opportunities.

Every move is a conscious tradeoff between the present and the future. To use Sid Meier's nomenclature, the density of interesting decisions increased dramatically. This is not merely some cold logician's complexity. Encouraging the player to operate across multiple time spans also provides *emotional richness*. Previously, a single emotional note arose from each move. Now each move resulted in a complex layer of emotions. I might feel bad about some random outcome but good that my long-term plan still remained in play. I would play this incredibly simple prototype for hours and feel deeply emotionally engaged.

IDENTIFYING A THEME

At this point in the prototyping, I was taken aback by the intensity of player hatred for abstract black squares. I design games as much as a means of personal expression and rumination as I do to create a functional commercial product. Even when building abstract games, I find it immensely useful to identify a human-centric theme to riff off and explore. A theme suggests and inspires new variations on a mechanic while giving players a familiar entrance into your game.

Many of my themes are derived from personal experiences, and this was the case for *Triple Town* as well. I grew up in a rural area of Maine. There was a river, a paper mill, and a reservation. My classmates were the descendants of both English settlers who had arrived about 400 years ago and Native Americans who had lived in the area for far longer. In school we read about the atrocities committed against the local people. Yet, we lived together, played basketball together, dated, and were close friends. There's an obvious dissonance there, and awareness of it grew perhaps too slowly over the years.

My first reaction was the dismay of walking through the summer woods and realizing this was the site of a genocide. There's a weight, a sense of this immense rolling calamity stretching back hundreds of years, the impact of which is clearly visible in the lives of the people around me. But alongside the horror, I kept coming back to an admittedly naive question: How? How could humans do such horrible things to other humans?

In that abstract game prototype with upgrading objects and hated black squares, I saw a hint of an explanation. In *Triple Town*, players learn to hate a neutral entity entirely due to the natural pressures of territory acquisition. I started to treat the prototype as a little petri dish where I could experiment with the nuts and bolts deep in human behavior. I wanted to understand, even if only a little. I didn't know it at the time, but this type of experimentation with systems has a long history in social psychology and game theory.

- You break a system down into simple rule-based interactions of agents.

- Each agent interaction has a cost and potential payoff.

- Each agent follows a strategy that tries to optimize the results. People sometimes adapt their strategies to beat the strategies of other agents. For example, in a game of Rock, Paper, Scissors, you notice your opponent always plays paper. In turn, you adapt your strategy and always play scissors.

- Given a certain set of rewards and economic tradeoffs, stable patterns of agent strategies emerge that match up well to real-world behavior.

Behaviors we might entirely ascribe to habit or history are shown to have strong structural re-enforcers; they are more economic in nature than they are arbitrary. To use game design terminology, people behave the way they do because the rules are set up to encourage certain dominant or degenerate strategies. In the world of games, Nicky Case in particular[2] is doing wonderful (and far more informed) work using these models to explore discrimination, competition, segregation, mob rule, and other aspects of human behavior.

As I played with the numbers in my prototype, I explored an idea that was new to the younger me: Colonization was a system of exploitation and conquest based in such a zero-sum value structure in which even the most innocent inevitably became marked as enemies that must be destroyed or treated as resources.

This became the core real-world theme that I wanted my abstract game to express to the player.

USING THEME TO AMPLIFY GAMEPLAY EMOTIONS

To understand how to tie a high level theme like this into the emotional output of a mechanical system, we needed to dig into how emotions work. Emotions occur on at least three levels.

1. **Body**: There is an initial physiological response when your body processes an experience: fight or flight or tend and befriend are examples of raw, instinctual body responses where adrenaline or oxytocin spikes. These are usually instinctual animal level priming that ready the body for potential action.

2. **Mind**: There's a *labeling* activity in which you consider the context of the situation and retrieve memories of similar situations.

3. **Feedback Loop**: Finally, these two earlier steps are combined to moderate or intensify the initial response. A person tackling a friend might yield a spike in heartrate preparing for action. But if you realize this is a friend being playful, that action might instead turn into delighted laughter. For more information see the two-factor theory of emotion for examples of how contextual labels can transform a base physiological response into a myriad of subtle emotions.

Much of the emotion I was observing in my initial abstract prototype can be attributed to body-level reactions, but players are also primed to look for mental labels. As a player becomes acclimated to the systems of loss and gain within a game, they engage in a brief moment of subconscious introspection: Was there something else they've experienced that this new experience resembles? It is your job as a designer to provide stimuli that suggest the labels you want experienced (*Figure 12.1.*)

In *Triple Town*, we applied the following *labels* to the abstract gameplay:

- **Territory**: The playing grid became a small island with limited space. This introduced the ideas of filling up a territory.

- **Buildings**: Upgradeable objects became forests, buildings, and mansions. This emphasized the idea of building, expansion, and growth so common to colonization.

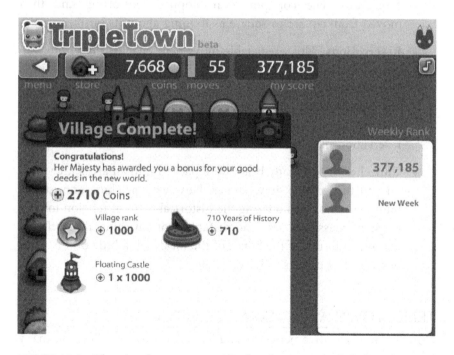

FIGURE 12.1 Theming the score screen with references to colonialism.

- **The Empire**: Score became progress toward the expansion of a fictional empire.

- **Bears**: Black squares became peaceful giant bears. I could have gone with an explicit victim of colonization, but that would have immediately triggered whatever pre-existing schema players had on the topic. It would bypass any introspection about systems and jump to a rigid narrative. I instead wanted something slightly more neutral, or the thought experiment would be less valid. Some folks do hesitate to kill the bears, but there's a long history of using explicit dehumanization (i.e., they aren't humans; they are animals) to reduce moral inhibitions; it seemed like an appropriate obfuscation.

- **Military**: Removing a black square became using a military weapon to eliminate a bear.

The theme also inspired mechanical changes.

- **Migration**: The common bear stopped teleporting and then moved from square to square as if going about its business.

- **Reservations**: This predictable movement enabled players to trap bears in an area by surrounding them by trees or other buildings. They could herd bears away from where they were building. This emergent strategy mimicked the tactics of colonizers in moving natives out of developed territories into smaller and smaller reservation-like structures.

- **Churches**: If too many bears were packed into an areas, they died off and turned into grave stones. However, matching gravestones built churches, thus offering the historical balm of religion for any angst of mass murder. The metaphor of investing in a religion literally built out of the bones of the locals felt a little on the nose, but very few players noticed.

TRIPLE TOWN AS A NARRATIVE FAILURE

Now, from a narrative perspective, *Triple Town* was a failure on many levels. Here's how I'd rate my efforts.

- **Success at personal growth**: As the designer, I feel I benefited from my exploration into the systems of colonization. I learned some deep lessons about how systems balance shapes what we think of as player morality. As mere selfish art, narrowly focused on personal growth and understanding, the game did well.

- **Failures of communication**: Very few players ended up grappling with the problems of colonization in the process of playing the game. If *Triple Town* is viewed as an interactive media trying to convey a message or express a rhetorical stance, it mostly failed to connect.

- **Failures of taste**: Of the players that did notice the theme of colonialism, many were merely offended. The raising of such a serious topic in a casual, cartoony game was considered distasteful.

FAILURES OF COMMUNICATION

My first failure can be viewed as poorly executing the *craft* of communication. In pragmatic (a.k.a. not art) communication theory, there is the author, the message and the audience. The miserable default state of a typical communication attempt is that a naive author's poorly crafted message fails to reach the audience. Communication should be seen as inherently hard, plagued by a huge range of issues ranging from noise in the communication channel to the listener's inattention, limited comprehension, and personal history. It therefore becomes the author's essential responsibility to 1. comprehend the communication constraints and 2. craft the clearest, most effective message possible.

From this perspective, many of the signals I sent were confusing to the player.

- **Cute**: The cuteness of the bears made many players think that the game couldn't possibly be dealing with serious issues. Cute is coded by Western society as either infantile or a safe and pure aspect of culture. There's a reasonable dash of sexism in this coding as well. My hope had been that the dissonance between cute and horrific would cause players to interrogate their actions. Instead, they reacted as is common when people face cognitive dissonance. They doubled down on their current biases and filtered out the dissonance.

- **Casual:** *Triple Town* is commonly grouped into the casual match-3 genre. When *Triple Town* came out, the vast majority of such games were either highly abstract or shallowly themed. Bejeweled, the most popular of match-3 titles at that time, involved matching gems for no apparent reason. With no cultural practice of serious discussion in a particular activity, players felt little reason to look for one. Or more pithily, your audience looks for wolves in a forest, not in a mall.

- **Subtle references:** Most players missed the colonization references that were there. On first read the game was about matching buildings to make bigger buildings. Oh, and there were some bears. You can think of theming in terms of First Read: what signals people immediately notice. And Second Read: what they see when looking a bit more deeply. All the little labels that I carefully played throughout the game were subtle Second Read elements.

A brief note on sexism in games: Both Cute and Casual games are often coded as activities for women. These same categories of game are labeled with a vast array of negative terms by consumers and reviewers of male-coded games. Often they are called "mindless" or "time wasters" and their players are treated as low agency "addicted" robots who are "manipulated" (by male developers) into playing. Journalists and critics write far less about such games, and when they do they almost never treat them as serious intellectual works. I cannot help but see this in the broader context of female-coded activities being historically treated as "less" than male-coded activities.

As of 2018, a popular game about men shooting other men in the head still is more likely to be treated as a thoughtful work of art than almost any game played predominantly by women. This is an interesting challenge worth trying to overcome.

FAILURES OF TASTE

It is one thing to ask if a message is well crafted, but an equally important question is if a message was even worth sending. Messages have power; they can sway opinion, inform, or misinform. They can be used as propaganda for the powerful or weapons that harm the vulnerable. These games with their systemic and narrative payloads are not neutral nothings. Whether we like it or not, they impact players. In addition to our duty to communicate well, we have an additional duty to communicate ideas that do good work in society.

There were two perceived failures of taste in *Triple Town*:

- **Enforced limits on a low art**: Considering systems of colonization in a cute commercial game treats a serious subject with a casualness that is unbefitting. This raises broader questions of whether highly commercial games with broad appeal are culturally allowed to tackle more complex social issues without being seen as merely crass.

- **Accidental reinforcement of negative norms**: A critique with more bite [https://veganithaca.wordpress.com/2013/07/25/oppres sion-in-games-what-are-we-learning/] is that the game may have caused harm by being yet another game about the unspoken yet dominant value structure of the colonizers. Specifically, there is an opportunity for harm when unthinking players engage with an "innocent game," have a pleasurable experience, and so end up being more supportive of the practices, values, and philosophies of colonization.

It is worth noting that *Triple Town* is not an "innocent game."[3] The systems and their theming were quite intentional, and to discuss it in the same bucket as other games that accidently support colonization is a poor reading of the game.

However, even intentionally crafted games can end up having an impact that is the opposite of their intention. It is entirely possible, especially with the previously discussed ambiguous theming, that *Triple Town* reinforces standard expectations about a difficult topic. I talk to players regularly and ask them about their experience. What did they get out of the game? Some understand; some do not; some bring entirely new perspectives to the work. I take notes and think about how I might do better.

CLOSING THOUGHTS

It has been many years since I designed *Triple Town,* and like all my games, it was a learning process.

The Importance of Practice

My first lesson is that the two-step process of looking for emotions and applying resonant themes benefits from practice. Often we'll read an essay like this, admire the clearly labeled bullet points and think "Oh, if I just execute this rote pattern, I'll get the clear results described here!"

Sadly, no. The path to mastery involves laboriously applying the process across multiple games and getting a little better at it each time.

- In the puzzle roguelike *Road Not Taken*, I tackled the life of someone in a traditional society who is forced to give up on having children.

- In *Leap Day*, we played with how differentiated means of production yield tight micro-communities of cooperation.

- In the multiplayer village sim *Beartopia*, I explored persistent communities where immigrant strangers slowly become close friends.

Each of these projects was a year or two of labor, and they are all deeply flawed. I repeated some of the same mistakes that I made in *Triple Town*, especially by stubbornly banging my head against regrettable player expectations around cuteness. And I made new mistakes like the high cognitive load core mechanic of *Leap Day* or the unfortunate distribution plans for *Beartopia*.

At the same time, I see clear personal progress. When I talk to players of my newer games, they tell me of rich emotional experiences similar to the ones I, the author, was attempting to amplify. They also tell me how the games made them reflect upon their own lives and consider how they might change for the better. These incremental steps are enough to encourage me to keep trying.

An Uneducated Audience

My second lesson is that the majority of game players do not have the habit of deeply reading into the subtext of the systems they engage with. So I often need to be far blunter with game players than I might desire. They need complex themes explicitly spelled out in order to overcome a limited level of systems literacy.

I'm at peace with this. Educating a large audience on new, complex forms of culture is a generational task. It is performed by a thousand authors across hundreds of meaningful works. My job is to help players understand, even just a little, that games can hold meaning. Have faith that there will be other designers who will be there to help with this grand effort.

Ongoing Conversations

My third lesson is that communication is an iterative effort. A game is not a static missive sent into the void. Instead, it is part of an ongoing, evolving communication. You start by sending a message, and then you listen. How did the audience respond? What did it hear? How did it react? Then you clarify or adjust your message in order to increase everyone's understanding. I've built *Triple Town* at least four times at this point, not including the initial prototyping. There was an e-Ink Kindle release, one for Facebook, one for Steam, and one for mobile. Each time I adjust what it says based on what I've heard. Each time the message becomes a little clearer.

At some point there will be another riff on the systemic narrative of *Triple Town*. Maybe I'll do a better job.

NOTES

1 www.stephanebura.com/emotion/
2 http://ncase.me/
3 www.lostgarden.com/2011/10/triple-town-beta-now-with-bears.html

This page intentionally left blank

CHAPTER 13

Emergent Narrative in *Dwarf Fortress*

Tarn Adams

Bay 12 Games

L ike many games, *Dwarf Fortress* doesn't have an authored story or even handwritten characters or locations. Yet *Dwarf Fortress* players themselves have produced an impressive body of fiction across different media, and the events described tie tightly into the mechanics of the game. When we talk about emergent narrative, we're referring to these kinds of stories, imagined and possibly retold by players recounting their experiences in a game, often adding details not present in the game itself, coherent and interesting beyond a simple recounting of the playthrough, but also not entering the more purely creative realm of fan fiction.

Dwarf Fortress has a reputation as a complex game that relies on procedural generation, but neither of these properties guarantees emergent narrative on its own. Complexity can harm the ability of the player to understand what's going on in their game, and procedurality can make the game world an unintelligible or boring mess. Yet, with some attention, even as a game becomes more complex and relies less on authored content, it's possible to design toward the players' ability to create their own stories.

DESIGNING FOR EMERGENT NARRATIVE

We approach this problem like other procedural generation challenges. A straightforward and usually effective method is to produce an example output and ask "what's the least I can do to generate more of these?" In this case, the example output is a story snippet as told by a theoretical player. Consider the following:

"A kobold crept into the workshop and stole Urist's masterpiece scepter. Urist was distraught for days afterward."

This is a common enough event in *Dwarf Fortress*, something one player might say to another when recounting a game, but as a guide for creating a game from scratch, even this simple example is loaded with implications:

- *A kobold*? How is this defined? Where does it come from and how often? Is it always there to steal things?

- *Crept*? Are there stealth mechanics? Do the maps support that? Can the player tell what's going on? Can the player prevent stealthy intrusions or otherwise engage with them?

- *Workshop*? How does the player make and interact with this? What control does the player have, and does that interfere with narrative formation? Are items kept inside of a workshop?

- *Stole*? Is the scepter owned by an individual or by a community? Are there laws? Do they apply to kobolds? Is theft formally punished in some way? Or is this more like a bear stealing from a picnic basket?

- *Urist*? A name! That's interesting. Where did it come from? Should the player be able to choose names or not? Does the kobold have an identity like Urist does?

- *Urist's*? Were we correct that items are owned, or is this an indicator of the artisan alone, as the workshop might imply? How do we understand Urist's connection to the scepter specifically?

- *Masterpiece*? So the item's quality seems important for this snippet. ... How does that work? Are some artisans better than others? Do we need a skill system?

- *Scepter*? An evocative-enough sort of item. How do item types work? Do they matter? Are scepters important? Does the player or the artisan decide which kinds are made?

- *Distraught?* Are we simulating emotions? Or is this a numeric event with an icon attached? Can we keep these reactions simple and maintain fresh narratives, or do we need some variety? If so, can the player understand what's going on? Do they need to understand to tell their story? How did Urist figure out the scepter was stolen? Did the quality of the scepter impact the amplitude of the emotion?

- *Days?* How does time work in this game? How is time shown to the player? If time is compressed, as is often the case, does that interfere with the flow of stories or other mechanics you might want to add?

This snippet alone has raised a lot of questions, but if we answer them in our design, we'll have a game capable of producing this story. Which questions look the most pertinent? Days is an afterthought, masterpiece an unnecessary detail; if I wanted to get a prototype up as soon as possible, I'd get a dwarf crafting objects in a workshop. For brevity's sake, the dwarf would have a name from a simple table, the crafted item type would be selected from another simple table, and the workshop would be a patch on the ground in some empty map. This is in fact what we had within a day or two of starting on *Dwarf Fortress*, along with mining into a cliff face. The kobolds came later. The emotional distress came well after that, as it's a nice part of the story, but not a driver of events until it has its own consequences ("And then Urist threw a tantrum.") Other priorities are possible, and they lead to different games as development continues, since you can't do everything. Not all of these games will produce varied and surprising player stories, but they'll have other merits.

Focusing on player stories from the start of the project has helped us home in on potent mechanics we otherwise wouldn't have noticed and steer away from mechanical details that don't occur as part of player stories (with varying success!). If you don't think about player stories in advance, you might find yourself getting invested in trivial matters, especially if your game has simulation elements. It is very easy to over-design a simulation that's intended for narrative purposes. In the example, the exact nature of the scepter is not described. An enthusiastic player might elaborate on the construction of the scepter in detail, sure, but it's not likely to occur as part of a plot beat, unless the construction itself has narrative ramifications. Detailed simulation is not always related to emergent narrative, and exposition of that detail might work against storytelling by overloading the player with insignificant facts.

At the same time, narrative potential is tied to simulation potential. Our story analysis implies a set of related elements and systems, all necessary to produce that particular snippet. An emergent story oftentimes passes through rapid plot beats that connect to each other, and if there aren't sufficient connections, that story thread will fizzle; we work to identify those mechanics and game objects that are at a nexus of story flow and try to center them. It is not sufficient to add a tangle of mechanics, throwing everything in a jar and shaking it and hoping a story comes out. You must pay attention to the kind and density of connections, and it's important to both design and expose these connections in terms that both you and the player can understand.

Once you get a feel for how stories move along the mechanical connections you create, your general design sense can kick in: how does an alteration to the game's mechanics alter the flow of possible stories? Does the story now pass more easily into richly connected subsystems, or have you created a dead end? This is yet another reason it's important to make your game playable as soon as possible in development. The emergent narrative design instincts you haven't yet obtained through practice can be compensated for by ongoing playtesting.

You can see this story flow in action, both the good and the bad, in many of *Dwarf Fortress*'s features. Research and scholarship are dead end mechanics since they don't tie into enough of the time-tested narratively potent game elements. A player can design a library, assign researchers, create and copy scientific manuscripts, produce bookshelves, place tables, and so forth, but generally, what happens in the library stays in the library. As of this writing, we haven't linked the invention of new technologies into the game mechanics; for instance, if research breakthroughs changed the division of labor and industry in the fortress, that would create some story moments. Even the interesting spats between apprentices and teachers from the game's history generation aren't yet translated into player-side mechanics. You might occasionally get a semi-interesting tale about a visiting scholar, but it's hardly ever the narrative core of a player's retelling of a fortress.

On the other side, we have, perhaps surprisingly, engraving as one of the strongest central narrative mechanisms in the game. It relates to everything. Engraving is a dwarven profession and in-game skill. Engravers can make images of historical events, other dwarves, their food preferences, and animals they are scared of, among others. The player can choose where the engraving is placed, often a location of significance, and can partially or fully determine its content or leave it up to the whim of the dwarven artist. Engravings interact with the physical descriptive systems through the wall or item selected.

These connections have consequences. Many of the most striking community stories center around fortresses that have fallen, and the decision of which engraving a dwarf makes at the end can slant the entire narrative. Does the last survivor carve a defiant picture of the demon lord being slain during the final struggle? An industrious scene recalling the foundation of the fortress when there was still hope? Or themselves, surrounded by their favorite cheese, as they descend into grief? The story flows freely into and out of engraving, as this game system is properly interconnected, both physically (through the acting dwarf) and more conceptually (through historical events and personality traits), and the choice to engrave is player-driven.

However, relative dead ends are inevitable and can be salvaged. For any given feature you've decided to add, it's important to have a "good enough" stopping point. In *Dwarf Fortress*, we've found this to be true with our book titles, for instance. They are generated using a fairly simple list and substitution method, but people enjoy them: the titles sometimes create conceptual fodder for stories, and they bring some life to the research system on a purely flavorful basis. Due to constraints in our language system, tying book titles more dynamically to other mechanics is a difficult problem, but we don't have to do that. If a system works cleanly in the game, accomplishes something, and doesn't inhibit further additions, you can polish it up, let it do its job, and move on, even if it's not a major contributor to the emergent narratives.

Just remember that the more you polish an element, the harder it may become to extend it if you later find it necessary. Stopping points won't always be permanent, and you need to choose them carefully. Indeed, as stated above, *Dwarf Fortress*'s lengthy handwritten list of book titles cannot be squared with its language system easily, and any language extension would be more difficult because of that. But polish is desirable, as emergent narrative is much more effective when the player is playing a game they enjoy. All of your design skills matter.

In fact, your broader experience is crucial; even with a healthy set of connected mechanics and a strong game loop in which the player is constantly faced with interesting choices, the amazing ability of players to fill in details and make coherent stories from imperfect information does not necessarily happen in a way that will allow them to tell their stories to other players and the outside world. What elements of your game are familiar and relatable? Which would other people understand, even people that will never play the game? *Dwarf Fortress* relies on widely understood fantasy tropes. Because it is your player building the story, you can use what the player brings to the game beforehand. Do your game elements connect to the outside world in any way? Do they resonate with you, and are they likely to resonate with other people? Can you bring that into focus mechanically or aesthetically (preferably both)? Can you think of other ways to build attachment between the player and the game elements?

For example, names and the ability to give nicknames are great here; the former will almost certainly come up if you analyze a story, and the latter almost certainly won't. That is, example output doesn't capture the full picture. Thinking about the player's role, in this case converting a passive story element into an active player ability, is a second crucial part of building emergent narrative. Let's discuss the player.

THE PLAYER'S PERSPECTIVE AND EXPOSITION

The player's place in the game determines the perspective of narratives that arise, how the player learns about what's going on, and possible ways to act to alter the narrative. You'll probably have an idea of the player's role before you begin deciding other details of your project, but it's important to consider how these choices impact emergent narrative and how you might use the player's role and abilities to enhance the story creation process.

In *Dwarf Fortress*, we conceive of the player as "the official will of the fortress," which gives the dwarves a great deal of autonomy while still allowing the player to give orders. For instance, the player indirectly induces the AI agents to create spaces through mining designations, and those spaces can be assigned functions and names, which allow them to more easily become a part of any story that develops. The player also determines most of the items that are crafted in the fort. Spaces and objects created by the player have more meaning, since players generally understand their own intentions better than the game does, and the subsequent action in the game will take place in these spaces using these objects.

There are other possibilities, of course. The player could have been assigned to a single dwarf in a leadership position or to a more personified spirit or god of some kind ordering events, and each of these potential roles has drawbacks and advantages. For us, it was important that information could plausibly be received by players abstractly, so they can be kept apprised of what's going on all over the fortress in an instant, and it was also important for the dwarves to maintain control over their own actions, especially on their free time, in order for events to happen that both surprise the player and give the dwarves a sense of being coherent characters in their shared world.

In order for any of this to matter, the player needs to know what's going on. Even in small projects, the data stream can be immense, so we need to selectively surface and highlight features of the underlying systems that we think are important. Part of this was done when we chose our mechanics, but that's just the beginning. We can use cues, such as alerts, announcements, decision windows, and other more subtle indicators, to let players know that their stories are waiting to be continued. Players can act, in which case they've potentially linked two plot beats together (the situation and their response), along with their intention and emotional context. They can observe an event, which becomes a plot beat. If the cue makes them curious enough, players might investigate the situation, using the powers you've given them through their role. This might build up to an action, but even if players are just poking around and ultimately do nothing, the entire process might lead to an impressive chain of connections that can form a portion of the story. At the other extreme, if players are uninterested in the cue, they can ignore it. This is bad if it happens too often, and sometimes players might be compelled to act, but the ability of the player to control how their stories are put together is key, and sometimes that means not engaging with everything on offer. Not having to deal with something can save the flow of the story being built in their mind: act, investigate, observe or move on.

It's also work to do a query, and it disrupts the game flow, so it's good to try to surface things that are likely to be more meaningful or narrative-building to relieve the player of as much of the burden as possible. The most important properties and relationships can be spatial (Where is X?) and naturally surfaced through the display, but they can also be social or conceptual (Why is X talking with Y? What does X believe?). It all depends on the situation and the role. The role the player occupies also limits the sorts of cues, queries, and actions that are possible or make sense.

At its worst, from the perspective of emergent narrative, we fall back on an explicit non-interactive in-the-past account for players to read, in the hopes that they can include some of it in their larger stories. *Dwarf Fortress* does this with verbose combat reports players can open if they choose. Players will often use these reports to fill in details when they are composing their stories, if they feel the specifics of the combat are narratively interesting. The upside of using openable reports is a reduction in the data stream players absorb during active play, but it requires a careful prioritization of information. In *Dwarf Fortress*, for instance, combat deaths are displayed in the main announcement queue, in addition to the combat reports, since they are too important to risk missing. This crucial information can be passively received from the main view and becomes incorporated into players' internal narratives without any effort on their part. If the death announcement makes them curious about specifics, they can check the report.

Really, players need not be able to act upon the world at all for narratives to form (though the ability to direct change certainly helps players become invested in what's going on.) It's sufficient to give players the ability to focus and query the system in order to find threads. It's possible to conceive of a simulation that does all this on its own and just presents a finished narrative to the user, but that's often clumsy. Even so, in *Dwarf Fortress*, Legends mode prepares threads for people from the generated dataset of hundreds of thousands of events and figures, and where we failed, people made mods to allow them to better sift through the data. Some people play the game exclusively in this fashion, generating histories and finding stories, even relaying them to the broader community.

On the other hand, if players are given the ability to do anything they please, they can immediately make entertaining things happen; perhaps this is good for a short story, but it is difficult for the underlying systems to "be themselves," for them to feel independent of the story-teller. Between these two extremes, consider selecting players' available actions and their ability to query the system using the nature of their roles as guides.

The overall play flow of action, observation, and investigation can be complex. Although a player's story will often end up reading as a coherent single narrative, during the preceding process of play, threads can be set down, return, join, and break off. The player is even free to leave one role and move to another. In *Dwarf Fortress*, we do this explicitly using the Fortress, Adventurer, and Legends modes. This sort of role changing is an important part of the process, since it allows people to explore a situation from a different perspective, and the meaning wrapped up in an old fortress or adventurer that was once player-controlled amplifies the narrative potential. When players' adventurers explore their previous fortresses, each room will hold old stories they'll have in mind as they play.

In multiplayer games, or serially single-player games (such as a *Dwarf Fortress* "succession" game), the narrative building process can become even more complicated. If you can't anticipate what your players are going to do (and you won't always be able to!), watch what they end up doing and try to support these new forms of story building during playtesting, updates, and subsequent games.

In the end, even with a great deal of carefully planned systems and a carefully designed player role, players will invent non-existent mechanics and be incorrect about what's going on. This is fine! We routinely and by necessity lean on players' ability to spin stories on their own, and this can require some invention. We can even empower them to change the game's rules through modding and other customization; when players brings their own understood assets to a game, the narrative connections can only increase.

In general, if players can customize the game to get the experience they want, they are more likely to play and tell stories about it. Customization can also extend the realm of the emergent narratives surrounding the game. *Dwarf Fortress* world generation has been used as a standalone tool for fantasy cartographers and people building pen-and-paper campaign settings (for more on table-top narrative generation, see Chapter 20).

As long as people are using your game creatively or otherwise edifying or enjoying themselves, the design is working as intended.

CHAPTER 14

Heavily Authored Dynamic Storytelling in *Church in the Darkness*

Richard Rouse III

Paranoid Productions

T he goal with *The Church in the Darkness* is to tell a very specific story through a very specific game. The story I wanted to tell had multiple sides, and I thought it would benefit from a dynamic narrative system. Though we invite the player into the creation of the story more than we possibly could on a linear story on the same subject, it was still conceived as a very authored experience. Our goal was not to create a complex procedural storytelling system that could be used for any number of games but instead one that would change enough for players to notice and that would help us tell the story we wanted to tell.

For context, it may be helpful for the reader to hear the trade-show-ready pitch for the game:

The Church in the Darkness is a top-down action infiltration game set inside a religious cult in the 1970s, with a story that changes every time you play. Inspired by the many outsider and new-age religious movements that sprang up during the 1970s—a period of crisis for the American people—our game features the Collective Justice Mission, a group as strongly socialist as they are Christian, led the by their charismatic cult leaders Isaac and Rebecca Walker. The group has a deep hatred for the US government and a fear/

FIGURE 14.1 The Church in the Darkness.

paranoia that the government will come to destroy them (fears not entirely unfounded based on the US government's well documented infiltration/manipulation of progressive groups in that era). Saying they just want to live peacefully, the Collective Justice Mission relocates down to the jungles of Battuela, a South American country on the Caribbean coast where they aim to build their own socialist utopia in the north end of the Amazon. They call this new community Freedom Town. The player is Vic, an ex-cop whose nephew Alex is a member of the group. When Vic's sister Stella becomes worried, the player must infiltrate the group to find Alex and check on him. But the player isn't sure whether the group is a bunch of radicals who truly are just building their own community or if something more apocalyptic and sinister is in their future.

And as a final twist to this premise, we change the nature of the cult each time a game starts, casting the player as a bit of a detective, trying to find out what's really going on. *The Church in the Darkness* is a mystery game where not only do you not know who the murderer is, but you're not sure a murder has taken place or will ever take place. It's a detective story where the antagonists may sometimes be villains but sometimes are actually the heroes.

MOTIVATIONS

Cults have long interested me as alternative societies within our larger society. As I read up on cults, what really interested me was how a cult group can be very hard to understand from the outside. Indeed, for those in the cult, the group will often not be seen as a cult at all. After all, no one joins a cult on purpose. Contrary to popular opinion, the people who join are not always weak-willed people who are easily fooled. Often they are very strong-willed, idealistic people who want to improve something, whether themselves, their neighbors, or the entire world. But as cult groups get wrapped up in their "work," members can lose perspective. Throw in a charismatic leader who is given absolute power, and one can see how things can go wrong. Or not. Many groups that have the qualities that would label them "cults" don't do anything illegal or that sinister. Most of them won't kill anyone or harm themselves. They may reject the comforts of modern society or take up beliefs that seem weird to the rest of society, but many would say the fulfillment they get out of being in the group more than makes up for that. So how does one know if a cult is truly bad?

Being able to tell that difference was what I wanted to explore with *The Church in the Darkness*. As a game designer, I'm always thinking of settings that would be interesting to explore in game form. Looking at a cult and deciding if they were apocalyptic sounded like an intriguing mystery to base a game around. Mystery stories are essentially stories as puzzles (can you figure out whodunit before the end of the book?) and work very well as game narratives, which are often full of more literal puzzles for players to deal with. The downside of puzzles—whether a crossword or a metal ring puzzle or a mystery novel—is that after one has solved it once, it is significantly less interesting. The joy of "figuring out the solution" will never be repeated. So if the central mystery in our game is "is this group dangerous or not?" it made sense that we would want to make the answer to that mystery different every time someone played. This is in part because it would make the game replayable, but also it would allow the game to explore the difference between a benign cult and a more sinister one, a difference that can be very subtle indeed. To pull all that off, we would need a very specific procedural storytelling system to make this very specific story work. Knowing what story we wanted to tell directly influenced the architecture of our narrative systems.

INSPIRATIONS

For both gameplay and narrative, we took our inspiration from the tumultuous real world of 1970s United States, including several real-world cults from that period. Studying those groups, there are many common threads that are perfect for a game like this. A remote jungle compound is inherently a confined setting—ideal for a game—with a natural boundary around the play space. Almost all cults are fearful of outsiders; this helps explain why most of the people players meet in Freedom Town are fearful of their presence and will either attack or flee. This means we can make a whole simulated community without building everyone into a fully interactive character. But we took certain characters who are more skeptical about the purity of the cult and turned them into fully fleshed out personalities who will talk to players.

We deliver a lot of our narrative via loudspeakers placed around Freedom Town, another tactic employed by real-world cult groups. It's a natural fit for an action game with a narrative, where you can hear the cult leaders preaching their dogma while you simultaneously play the game. Through listening to this dialog, the player learns that no words spoken by the leaders are accidental: everything is propaganda, and it's propaganda that you hear constantly (Figure 14.2.) Also, the voices on the PA in the camp may inaccurately report events related to what the player has done, showing how leaders may use their preaching for disinformation, another common cult tactic. Talking to former members of cults, I learned that members of a group would often remember the same event completely differently, depending on how indoctrinated a particular member was.

My largest takeaway from real-world cults led to me to portray almost everyone involved in the group as having fairly noble motives. Almost every cult group you encounter provides some positive benefit. Whether it's helping people get off drugs or move away from abusive

LIVE AS ONE ★ FIGHT AS ONE

FIGURE 14.2   Propaganda takes many forms throughout the compound.

situations or lifting them out of poverty or promising to take care of them when they're old or promising to fight to make the whole world better. The non-stop propaganda in the game is a way for players to hear some of the cult's beliefs and realize that they may actually agree with many of them. At the same time, there's always something slightly "off" about what's being said, leaving most players with the feeling that no matter how good their intentions, the Collective Justice Mission starts a good idea and takes it at least somewhat too far, and in more sinister outcomes, way too far.

Beyond our real-world inspirations for the game, we had inspirations from other games. Board games are by their nature almost designed to be replayed; indeed, digital games that are meant to be played once can be seen as aberrations from the centuries of board game design that came before them. Naturally, board games that attempt to have a stronger narrative component have to figure out a way to make that narrative replayable. The best mass market example one can think of is the board game *Clue*, which endeavors to model a murder mystery, with different victims and guilty parties each time. But beyond modeling these plot points as game tokens, *Clue* doesn't do much to make the game feel like a story.

An early digital game from 1983, *Murder on the Zinderneuf*, had always intrigued me as a computer version of *Clue*, but using the benefits of a digital game to make it feel more like a story. Instead of just hunting for pure "clues" without a narrative as one does in *Clue*, *Zinderneuf* uses a Madlibs-like system to make the experience feel more like a story. Characters have pre-written scripts with open slots for characters' names, attributes, and qualities. The game employs various "Murder Scenarios" and then slots the passengers on board the *Zinderneuf* (a large blimp) into those different scenarios. The main mechanic of the game was interrogating as one of the several detectives the player could choose, with characters reacting differently to different investigators. The game even included a "red herring" to distract players, but as designer Paul Reiche III told me: "The Red Herring character was there to add a little misdirection. I think we found that the Red Herring had to be pretty dang obviously Red Herringy or the player would just get confused." (For more on the game and the context of its creation, see Chapter 6.)

I took this as an important lesson for procedural mystery games: players are so unaccustomed to experiencing procedural narratives that if you force them to figure out the story in order to win the game, at some point you must make the story pretty obvious to give players a fair shot.

Another game that has long fascinated was the *Blade Runner* adventure game from 1997. The game feels very much like a '90s -era point-and-click adventure game, but under the hood *Blade Runner* is actually a complex simulation in which any character can be killed at any time and the story randomizes which characters are replicants, with obvious plot ramifications. This all leads to over 40 possible endings. As Louis Castle, the game's executive producer and director, told me:

> We did not build a complex branching tree but instead ran a simulation of all the avatars in the world and had the complex data base of inputs drive variables that would surface events and clues … In effect clues were passed from avatar to avatar creating an impression of the player which avatars reacted to. The emergent play allowed players to chase down witnesses to their actions to prevent propagation of the player's indiscretions … It was

actually almost impossible to get the same game experience even if you loaded an old save game.

Castle, Louis, personal communication

Though being delighted by the premise and structure of the game, my biggest takeaway from *Blade Runner* was the curious way players saw it: most players did not even realize *Blade Runner* involved procedural storytelling. On the one hand, this could be seen as a triumph for the game; if it feels just like a completely authored game, the procedural storytelling must be doing its job. As Louis Castle said:

> The choices in *Blade Runner* were intended to drive the narrative to adapt to what the player did naturally ... We certainly saw the world within two extremes but we also made the conscious choice to support either extreme as valid and equally importantly, and support all areas between the extremes ... [This was discussed] in the marketing/PR but the point of the design was to allow each person to feel they were doing the 'correct' thing so we did not push the point of paths or multiple outcomes.

Castle, Louis, personal communication

Though I respect this creative intent, I see an unanticipated downside. Players will play a game differently if they know it is truly reacting to their actions, just as they are more likely to replay it if they know the story will be different.

Although the complexity of the procedural storytelling being done in something like *The Walking Dead* adventure games is much simpler than what *Blade Runner* did ("procedural" is probably the wrong term for what *The Walking Dead* does), the game does an excellent job of telegraphing to the player that choices matter, so everyone who plays the games knows what they're getting into, and this changes the way people play the game.

CORE SYSTEMS

With these games as inspiration and a strong plan to tell a specific story inspired by cults in the real world, we picked the narrative systems we would need to tell the story dynamically, keeping the mystery an unknown each time the player plays. Part of this design was really wanting players to replay the game, so any one playthrough is short enough that playing it again doesn't seem too daunting. Though it may take 2 to 4 hours of total playtime for many players to get to one ending, it usually takes them less than an hour on each subsequent try, allowing them to explore the narrative and where they can take it more once they have the hang of the gameplay. As is the nature of a game that blends narrative with infiltration/stealth gameplay, we get wildly different playtimes for players. Some take it very cautiously and meticulously and it lasts a lot longer, while some charge in headfirst and may move through faster. So too, some players will exhaustively search for every document and scrap of paper they can find, reading them carefully and thinking about how they connect to what else they've learned. Some will of course spend less time digging into the lore, just pushing through to an ending as some players prefer. But for all players, replays get quicker and quicker as players learn the way the game works and know what they're doing when they start another playthrough. Since there are no cut scenes or any activities that require a fixed amount of time to complete, player speed is very much self-driven (Figure 14.3.)

The core of the systems lies with the randomization of the cult leaders' personality from several discrete starting states. We could have gone with a more complex system for generating this narrative starting point. Though more complex character simulations involving lots of personality traits that produce subtle results can be very interesting and have been done well by other games, there's a point at which those changes are too small for players to easily perceive, and one runs the risk of creating a game in which the simulation is rich but players' understanding of it is poor. We wanted to emphasize changes that were substantial enough that they would be keenly noticeable to players. So we built something we felt players could keep a handle on, which allowed us to craft custom dialog and narrative pieces for each potential starting state. Some other factors are thrown in to randomize specific parts of the story separate from the preachers' core personalities—these are done for specific story beats intended for narrative flavor as well as to provide a little noise in the system.

FIGURE 14.3   The player finds themself in a potentially dangerous situation.

On subsequent playthroughs, players are given the option of playing the same story start state as in their previous playthrough, or they may pick one they have never finished before, or they can pick entirely randomly. Though the mystery was a core part of the design, we recognized some players would want to build on knowledge accrued in a previous playthrough (where they may have died before finishing). While playing the game multiple times, players will of course see some content repeating, particularly when they pick to play the same story starting state again. But we authored enough variety of content to allow players to continue to see different parts, even when in the same starting state. And though not every part of the narrative they uncover will be new on those replays, seeing repeating content will reinforce the conclusions players have reached about content seen earlier, which means they are a "leg up" in detective work on figuring out just how dangerous the cult leaders are this time around.

As the narrative start state is randomized, so are a number of game-play factors. The world of Freedom Town is a large, open map, which players can explore in any way they like, from the main roads to side areas or foot trails hidden in the woods (Figure 14.4.) The player starts in a random location around the perimeter of the map, thus forcing

FIGURE 14.4   Freedom Town.

them to see different sections of the map with each playthrough. The physical locations of the core characters in the game are moved around the map each time. Players' required goal is to make contact with their nephew Alex and then lead him out of Freedom Town; exploring the map to gather info that leads to Alex is the player's core activity. An optional though encouraged goal is to find the preachers who lead the Collective Justice Mission, and an algorithm places them elsewhere on the map, far from Alex's location and the player's current location; the preachers are only placed there after players have made one of several chunks of narrative progress. All these locations are pre-authored, and the density of guards is increased around each position to ramp up difficulty for players as they reach these final objectives. In addition to moving players around the map with these moving objectives, we also randomize all resource locations and guard layouts. A more elaborate take on the procedural generation would have involved reconstructing the physical map in a number of different configurations, but this was cut for scope reasons early on.

I mentioned that finding the preachers is optional, and indeed it forms one of players' larger choices: do they just want to save their nephews and get them out of the cult? Or do they want to prevent something bad that might happen to everyone in the cult in the future, after getting Alex out. The ending summarizes not only their actions and Alex's outcome, but also what happens to the cult group as a whole. How much detective work players want to do is up to them. It may be that players rescue Alex and find out what happened after they left. Players who choose to sleuth around longer will find more information and can make a more informed decision about what to do. When the ultimate ending shocks players who may have been completely focused on getting Alex out, it is my hope that players will rethink how they approach a situation like that, in a game or otherwise. I hope players realize that gathering data and evidence is important before jumping to conclusions or taking irreversible actions. Ultimately, this is the player's choice, and there are very few limitations put on players doing what they want to do once they get to Alex.

The narrative is delivered during gameplay using a few key techniques. The cult leaders Isaac and Rebecca Walker address their followers over the PA system spread throughout Freedom Town (Figure 14.5). As players maneuver between guards and searches for Alex, they will unavoidably hear about the leader's dogma and instructions to followers.

FIGURE 14.5   A part of the PA system used by the cult leaders.

There are several banks of lines played purely randomly, with certain lines of dialog in each set that will change based on the leaders' personalities on that playthrough. There are multiple stages of the cult leaders moods, so after players have been playing for a certain amount of time or done specific actions, the dialog banks will advance in sequence. Mixed in with the random lines of dialog is a series of dialog that always plays in the same order, with lines that change depending on the leaders' personality. This non-randomized dialog gives a spine to what players will hear and gives the PA dialog more structure than it would have were it entirely random. It is also set apart by being the only dialog in which the cult leaders talk back and forth to each other.

Running in parallel, players search trunks to find resources like medicine and food (both for quick health recovery), gadgets, weapons, and other equipment that will help them get through Freedom Town. Players will also search in desks, which give players documents that serve both practical and purely narrative functions. One route to Alex is to with increasingly detailed maps that ultimately reveal his location. These maps are only found in the desks, and players are encouraged to search the desks to help them find the maps and find Alex. However, mixed in with the maps are letters, paperwork, diary entries, and other documents that help tell the story of Freedom Town (Figure 14.6).

The game uses a system to place the items in the desks in a very specific order. Regardless of which desks they search, players will always find the maps in an order of increasing detail. Purely narrative documents are sorted into several categories: a) some tell the story of Alex in the camp; these are always found in the same order with variations depending on which starting scenario players have, b) other notes tell the story of other characters in Freedom Town—each of these sets is also found in order with that set, but the orders of the sets are randomized, and not all sets will be present in a given game, and c) still other documents that are randomly sprinkled in for further bits of narrative color. The system used for propagating the desks with documents ended up being one of the most complex systems in the game, with a series of weightings used for the different sets to create notes sequences that felt different to the player each time but still told the story of that playthrough of the game.

FIGURE 14.6   A postcard from Alex.

A final element of the narrative is comprised of side characters, added to make sure player hear the point of view of members of the cult, not just the leaders. These vary their location and change their dialog based on what they think of the cult leaders' dispositions that playthrough, as well as reacting to some of the players' actions in Freedom Town thus far. They too provide a route to Alex, as they will share what they know of his location if players request it. Though there is substantial variation to what they can say, these characters are some of the most heavily authored content in the game, functioning much like characters in many RPGs.

PLAYER CHOICES

With just those systems in place, on each playthrough the player would get one of several specific stories, with some randomized variation providing different slices of those stories. But when one adds in the players' own choices, there's a combinatorial effect creating many, many more variations in the overall story of one given playthrough.

At a very basic level, this is a narrative that changes with how much players choose to explore it. Do they try to find all the friendly characters and hear their stories? Do they risk their lives to talk to

Isaac and Rebecca and hear their point of view? Do they try to collect all the documents in the game to see what they contain? And since all the characters and all the documents will never be in one or even five playthroughs of the game, how many times do they play the game to try to experience all of the story content? How much time the player spends digging out narrative content is a choice in itself.

Players make bigger choices expressed through infiltration gameplay as well as more narrative related choices. For the core fast-paced stealth gameplay (Figure 14.7), players have the option of playing lethally or non-lethally, with further options to try to avoid detection completely (which can be quite difficult) or merely flee when danger presents itself and allow the gameplay systems to reset once they have escaped detection long enough.

There are gameplay consequences to playing lethally—more aggressive guards and leaders who are more likely to execute the player when they are captured. But there are also narrative changes, both in terms of the dialog players are likely to hear and certain characters who will refuse to speak to players or help them if they have been too murderous. The amount of times players have been detected will lead to some light narrative changes, where the characters will comment on players'

FIGURE 14.7 Stealth gameplay as the player approaches two guards.

more brazen infiltration. The gameplay consequences of being spotted are limited to the moment, with alarms going off and guards running in, but this resets, allowing players to progress and not get stuck in a negative feedback loop merely from being detected.

Players also makes choices in what they do with key story situations. The game's only required objective is that players find and at least start a conversation with Alex. What Alex says in that encounter changes depending on the starting scenario and the players' gameplay choices up to that point. From there on, the players' main choices are to let Alex stay in Freedom Town, to ask him to follow them out, or force him to come with them. Players also have choices about whether they next try to confront or ultimately assassinate the cult leaders themselves. The whole premise of the game is that players don't know if the cult leaders are fully apocalyptic/dangerous or merely radical in their beliefs, and once players come to their own understanding of the situation, it's up to them to decide what to do with that information. Since the game features continuous gameplay, it's possible for unintended consequences to start to unfold. For instance, players may try to rescue Alex but get him killed during a shootout with guards. Or players' presence in the camp may upset leaders and cause them to move up their plans for apocalypse.

All of these player choices lead to more branching dialog, using systems developers of RPGs and interactive fiction have been using for decades. This too involves a heavy amount of authorship and script-writing, with all of the game's dialog voice acted. Though it could have been interesting to sink time into a text generation system to provide more variation to the notes players find, this was not something we chose to pursue. Though the systems for handling these branches may not be particularly innovative, because the starting state changes every game, there are many more possibilities and possible endings than one would normally find in a choice-based narrative game.

With all this choice, it's easy for players to lose track of the overall arc of the story they are creating with the game. A system we added to the game to better anchor players' experience involved "Chapter Titles." This is text laid over the screen when key events happen, coupled with a Roman numeral (Figure 14.8.) Starting the game gets players "I. Down in the Jungle"; when they get captured by the cult leaders they might get "II. They Know You"; when they find Alex and lead him out of the game they could get "III.

I. Down in the Jungle

11

FIGURE 14.8 The game begins.

Exodus." Lots of other game events are tracked, providing a large variety of potential chapter sequences for players. The goal of the chapter system is to let players know the choices they are making have real weight and make them feel that they have truly told their own story when their sequence of chapter titles is displayed at the game's end.

For the ending, in addition to that story summary and final chapter heading, players receive a longer piece of text that wraps up how the cult reacted to the player's presence in their town, as well as what happened after the player left. Endings are built out of three text chunks, written to be combined in a wide variety of ways. First is what happened to Alex, or rather what players chose to do with him. Next is how Freedom Town reacts to what players did with Alex, Isaac and Rebecca, or other elements of the town, depending on what players chose to take on. A third sentence says what happened to Freedom Town based on players' choices, an epilogue of a sort. The system for handling all these permutations became complex enough that it had to be written in code instead of being hooked up with level logic.

Indeed, the system is complex enough that I don't actually know how many permutations are possible, so I often say "more than 20." I look forward to seeing players talk about all the unique endings they have achieved.

CONCLUSION: WHY BUILD IT?

I must confess to some amount of self-consciousness around writing a chapter on *The Church in the Darkness* for a book on procedural narrative. The level of technological complexity in this game is easily dwarfed by games that have much larger procedural narrative ambitions. Our choice to focus on our relatively simple version of procedural narrative was partly due to scope. This project took a long time to make, given our team size and our wanting to make a 3D infiltration game with a decent feature set to go along with our strictly narrative ambitions.

Another part has to do with our intent. We chose to architect our dynamic story systems in a very specific way because of the story we were trying to tell and the way we wanted to involve the player. I wanted to show the many sides of looking from the outside at a cult group by literally letting the player play games in which multiple cults might exist (Figure 14.9), where players would make different choices not because they were "trying to see all the content" but because the

FIGURE 14.9   Signs of distress among members of the Collective Justice Mission.

context of those choices were changing. The narrative systems we chose to focus on were the best way I knew to accomplish that.

The Church in the Darkness ends up being a highly authored exercise in procedural narrative. I was sculpting a very specific experience for players, despite giving them plenty of space to change and finish that story in their own way. When we take on procedural narrative projects, I think it's important that designers, programmers, and writers think about their intent. What is their game trying to accomplish in terms of narrative? What is most important in getting that story across? The goal shouldn't be to create procedural narrative just to make an impressive tech demo but to create it because it is the best way to tell the stories we want to tell.

3

Worlds and Context

R ich settings, compelling backstories, and evocative descriptions are all tools of a competent writer. A carefully constructed world can bring out the full potential of the narrative, and the right descriptive text by itself can pull the reader into the story, ready to set forth on the promised journey with the author. Most video games depend from their inception on their objects and spaces; even game designers focused on procedural narrative are confronted immediately by the need for the elements of world-building. In this section, we will examine several projects that have engaged creatively with this aspect of the craft, ranging from planetary descriptions to historical accounts.

Even with the power to construct an entire universe, a storyteller does not operate in a vacuum, separate from the real world. The broader social, moral, and political context finds its way into every piece, and the piece itself can reflect and transform this context for the benefit of the reader. Games with procedural stories can operate at this level as well, and we'll analyze some cases in the chapters that follow.

This page intentionally left blank

CHAPTER 15

Generating Histories

Jason Grinblat

Freehold Games

P rocedurally generating history is a daunting task. The process of proceduralization requires codifying relationships into rules, and real-life histories are tangled webs of people, places, and events whose complexities obscure their relational mechanics. The task is further complicated by the fact that history serves a rhetorical function. That is, historical accounts are used to promote certain cultural narratives that can belie the facts they purport to narrativize (this function is routinely neglected in video games' treatment of history, even in primarily hand-authored games). History generation is a new practice—part of the burgeoning subfield of *qualitative* procedural generation—so these problems don't yet have canonical solutions.

This chapter offers one formulation of history that we developed while doing research for our far-future roguelike game *Caves of Qud*. We use this model to discuss how a few other games generate their histories. Then we delve into the details of *Caves of Qud* and the generative history system we implemented for it. We cover the constraints and aesthetics that guided our design, how we generated and engaged with histories, and how the system produces coherent narratives through a process we call historical rationalization.

To proceduralize, we must start to untangle the web. This means unpacking the biases encoded in our intuitions, examining our subject in detail, and articulating a vision for its simulation. If we can make headway on this task for history—a subject with as much systemic richness as any—we'll have opened up our art to a new class of possibilities.

ENTITIES AND EVENTS

Over the course of our development cycle, we started to untangle the web ourselves and think deeply about both the mechanics of history and our vision for a generative history system. Part of this process involved researching other games that experiment with generated histories. The model described in this chapter came about by sussing out the patterns across our own design and the designs we encountered. By no means is it the definitive formulation. It's meant only as a first step toward a systemic reasoning about history and a bootstrap for those looking to design their own generative history system.

Our model sees history as the interplay between historical *entities* and historical *events*. Entities are people, places, and objects—the subjects of history. Events act on entities and change them. Think of entities as history's nouns and events as its verbs. In algorithmic terms, entities are data structures—essentially, bags of properties—and events are functions that change those properties. A history, then, is composed of a set of initial entities and a sequence of events. The process a generative system uses to determine its sequence of events we call its *historical logic*. What the system chooses to report about a particular event's resolution we call a *historical account*. Accounts are exposed to players, often via text that's generated according to the details of the event. Systems that implement this model do the following four things.

1. Model historical entities

2. Model historical events

3. Relate events together via an underlying logic

4. Expose historical accounts—the (alleged) results of events—to players, often via text generation.

What events look like depends on the style of history being generated. Events are where a lot of the feel of our generated histories get encoded. In *Caves of Qud*, we were shooting for an ancient world aesthetic, so our events include things like "#*character*# sieges a city" and "#*character*# builds a monument," the kind of events you might expect to read about in the biography of an ancient king or queen. But if you were generating the history of, say, a high school class, your events might look more like "#character# takes a test" and "#character1# and #character2# go on a first date."

How might a system relate its events via an underlying logic? There are several ways. In *Epitaph*, an idle game by Max Kreminski where players direct the course of a civilization's history by choosing which technologies it acquires, an event's occurrence affects how likely future events are to occur. For example, if players grant their civilization mastery over fire, breakouts of foodborne illnesses become less likely but forest fires become more likely. These likelihoods are implemented via a set of weighted tables.[1]

In *Dwarf Fortress*, events are related via the logic of a deeper simulation. Dwarves and other sentient creatures—examples of the game's historical entities—act according to the rules of the game's physical and social systems. When these rules cause a dwarf to do something the system judges newsworthy, that action gets logged as a historic event and its account recorded (these accounts are the annals you read in "Legends" mode). Incidentally, this is how real-life histories are manufactured: an authority creates a narrative from a subset of a larger pool of events, though in the case of real-life histories the authority may distort or fabricate events.

Later in the chapter, we'll explore another approach to historical logic, the one we used for the generated histories in *Caves of Qud*.

SUBJECTIVITY IN HISTORY

I mentioned that historical accounts describe only the *alleged* results of events. Before we go further, it's worth unpacking this qualification and elaborating on the point about history's rhetorical function. The aim of history as commonly understood is to recount past events *accurately* so as to approach some objective reality (i.e., what *actually* occurred). But historical accounts are always subjective, told from biased perspectives and used to promote certain cultural narratives. By and large, games don't reckon with this richer picture of history, preferring instead to adopt the reductive frame of objectivity.

There are of course exceptions. *The Elder Scrolls* series—particularly *Morrowind*—explores the intersection of history and power through heresies, narratives that are at odds with historical doctrine.

Opera Omnia—a beautiful gem of a game by Stephen Lavelle—takes on the subjectivity of history as its major theme. You play as a historian who specializes in migration patterns. Your politician boss has political motives, and you must cynically construct historical models to justify them. These games make explicit arguments about history, but *all* games that incorporate history make arguments about it, explicitly or implicitly. As we start to proceduralize history, we should be mindful of what arguments we're encoding in our algorithms, especially as the reductive framing of history has been used to justify so much harm.

In tackling this problem for *Caves of Qud*, we articulated two kinds of history: history as a *process* and history as an *artifact*. The former can be thought of as the playing out of rules and relationships that continually produce the present. To simulate this process, we might seek to reproduce its logic. On the other hand, the latter is a constituent of the present, something we engage with through a contemporary lens and whose complexities may be obscured by that flattening of perspective. Only historical accounts are accessible to us in the present, and, as mentioned, those accounts are always biased and incomplete. To generate this type of history—that is, to generate historical accounts—we might seek to recreate the logic that produced it, or we might invent a new logic that reproduces it altogether. This is what we did for *Caves of Qud*.

HISTORY GENERATION IN PRACTICE: CAVES OF QUD

Primer

Caves of Qud is set thousands of years in the future among the geologically reclaimed ruins of a vast arcology. It draws inspiration from a variety of historically minded sources, including pen & paper RPG *Gamma World*, "Dying Earth" genre fiction like Clark Ashton Smith's *Zothique* and Gene Wolfe's *The Book of the New Sun*, the subversive works of New Wave sci-fi authors like Ursula K. Le Guin, historical texts like Edward Gibbon's *The Decline and Fall of the Roman Empire*, and roguelike predecessors *Dwarf Fortress* and *Ancient Domains of Mystery* (ADOM).

We use several techniques to construct the world of *Caves of Qud*. In many ways, the game is a hybrid of handcrafted and procedural systems. In contrast to most roguelikes, it features the kind of over-arching, handcrafted narrative you might find in a traditional open-world RPG. The world map is also static, but individual areas are highly procedural and vary in detail from game to game. Many physical systems are simulated, environments and bodies are mutable, and there's a rich social and political landscape for players to navigate.

Humanity's relationship with history is one of the major themes of *Caves of Qud*. By embedding players in a layered labyrinth of lost and contemporary civilizations, it argues that our insights into the past are always filtered through the lens of the present.

Constraints and Aesthetics

Because our design only makes sense in the context of the forces that shaped it, let's first discuss some of the constraints and aesthetic principles that guided our choices of entities, events, and the historical logic that relates them. In *Caves of Qud*, players engage with the past only from the diegetic present, so we centered the perspective of history as an *artifact* and focused on simulating historical accounts, things like monuments, artwork, and historical texts. This meant we could cheat on simulating authentic historical logic as long as the accounts it produced were themselves authentic.

Two major constraints limited the scope of our design. First, because the generated histories were being added as a tertiary system to a game far along in its development, we were constrained on the resources we could devote to its breadth and complexity. Second, the generated histories had to mesh with the voice of the handcrafted lore and narrative that had already been developed. To comply with these constraints, we focused the generated histories around the mythic lives of five significant rulers—called *sultans*—from a diegetic age known as the sultanate, in which one of *Qud*'s early advanced cultures thrived and before which much of the handwritten lore took place.

We also wanted to give the sultans characteristic personalities that blurred the line between history and myth. To this end, we assigned each sultan an archetypal unit of culture we called a *domain*. Domains include culturally resonant, physical objects and phenomena such as glass, jewels, ice, and stars, as well as abstract ideas such as might, scholarship, and chance. They function similarly to epithets in epic poetry, associating a character with a memorable trait.

Finally, an aesthetic principle that guides much of *Caves of Qud*'s procedural generation is the high valuation of novelty in its output. We like to let our generators run wild. To this end, we avoided prescribing a narrative arc for the sultans' lives. That is, we didn't include story beats like "the sultan has a formative experience" or "the sultan overcomes an obstacle." Instead, we gave the generator room to trace atypical life paths, relying on our players' *apophenia*, the human tendency to over perceive patterns, to drive their interpretations. This point is especially important. Players engage with the sultan narratives in a game world full of rich narrative context. The sultans are a part of a cultural tapestry that includes the ruined environments of the diegetic past, the characters and cultures of the present, and the aggregated experiences of their myriad player characters. Each of these acts as a cultural touchstone that colors interpretations of the sultans' lives. This allowed us to aim for evocative biographical narratives—rather than meticulously detailed ones—that leverage our players' apophenia. Because we generate several sultans per instantiation of the game world, and because the details of any individual sultan's life have a limited effect on the player's critical path, we felt comfortable giving the generator this room to thrive.

Cultural Artifacts and History's Impact on the Generated World

Let's look at how histories are generated and engaged with in *Caves of Qud*. When a player starts a new game, the world-creation engine generates a unique history in five periods, each one centered on a generated sultan. Each period is comprised of several historical events per our model, and for each event, a historical account is generated as a descriptive text snippet. Internally, we call these historical accounts *gospels*. Histories are generated one gospel at a time, and so gospels form the basic discrete unit of history in *Caves of Qud*. Currently, each event manifests a single gospel, but we've discussed extending the system to generate multiple gospels for competing interpretations of the same event.

During play, players engage with the generated history via gospels shared by NPCs or appearing in the descriptions of cultural artifacts—

namely, shrines, paintings, and engravings—encountered in the game world. These cultural artifacts are generated dynamically as players explore new areas, and each depicts a single gospel from a sultan's life, chosen randomly from the generated history. Figure 15.1 shows an example of a sultan shrine, including the gospel for the event it depicts. Players can encounter these gospels in any order. As they do, they are inscribed in a journal and sorted chronologically (see Figure 15.2). Players can swap gospels with NPCs through a custom of cultural exchange called the *water ritual,* mediated by a currency of reputation with various in-game factions. Over time, players accrue more and more of the gospels from a sultan's life, and a biographical narrative coheres.

FIGURE 15.1   A shrine depicting a historical event from the life of Uumasp II, a procedurally generated sultan of ancient Qud.

```
────────────────────[ Journal ]──────────── ESC or 5 to exit ─
                      Sultan Histories
>[History of Midukht I]

 $ On the anniversary of a great battle, a babe was found swaddled with a
briny spice root in each hand by a group of bears in House Quarter
Qamrod. They took her into their fold and fostered her, and she became
known as Midukht, Desiccated Heir of Bears.

 $ Deep in House Quarter Qamrod, Midukht discovered Urvalep Mesh. There she
befriended winged mammals and fixed a satisfying meal.

 $ Throughout the entirety of 25, Midukht laid waste to all of Qanetara,
sowing with salt the fields of mysterious strangers and mollusks. She
became known as the Terror of Qanetara.

 $ After treating with fungi, Midukht convinced them to help her found a
college in House Quarter Qamrod for the purpose of deciphering the
meaning of brine. They named it the College of the Salt-Spangled.

 $ While traveling through Qanetara, Midukht stopped at a market in the
Hamlet of Nibytara. At an obscure shop, she purchased a desiccated
                                          ─< 7 Quests | Tinkering 9 >─
```

FIGURE 15.2   Several gospels from a sultan's life appear in the player's journal.

Historical events also shape the generated game world. The sultans visit places that are designed as historical entities and instantiated as historic sites during world generation (see Figure 15.3). Items named during the course of life events are also modeled as entities. If a sultan leaves a named item at a location as the result of a life event, that item is instantiated according to its historical properties at the appropriate historic site. Players engage with the histories through cultural artifacts that tell the sultans' stories, and this historical knowledge acts as a vector for players to find and engage with the material remnants of the sultans' lives.

The Model in Action

To reiterate, our system models history as the interplay among historical entities—places, items, and sultans represented as data structures—and historical events that modify the properties of those entities. In order to engender coherence in the generated historical narratives, the events themselves are parameterized by the properties of existing historical entities, including the very ones they modify.

Let's examine how the system generates an individual sultan's history (illustrated in Figure 15.4). First, it instantiates a historical entity that represents the sultan in an initial state with a few core properties: name, pronouns, birth year, birth region, location in birth region, and domain. Then, it resolves a birth event for the sultan, one

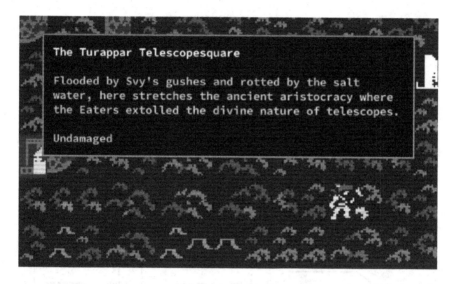

FIGURE 15.3 A historic site generated in the world history, instantiated in the game world and procedurally described.

of the few events of a sultan's life that are actually prescribed, along with becoming the sultan and dying. Next, it *randomly* chooses a life event—for example, *sieges a city*—from the event pool. Based in part on the sultan's state and in part on random branching, the event resolves an outcome, and then it modifies the sultan's properties and the properties of any non-sultan historical entities that are consequently affected. A gospel for the event is generated via a Tracery-like[2] replacement grammar whose rules map sultan properties to text fragments for a variety of narrative circumstances. As a result of the event, some global properties of the history are also updated, such as the current year. The system then serially chooses and processes about twelve more events in the same fashion, each one parameterized by the sultan's state at the start of the event, and each one transitioning the sultan to a new state by the end of the event. Finally, if the sultan is still alive, the system selects a generic event that results in the sultan's death. Taken in aggregate, the gospels for the events in the sultans' lives form their biographies.

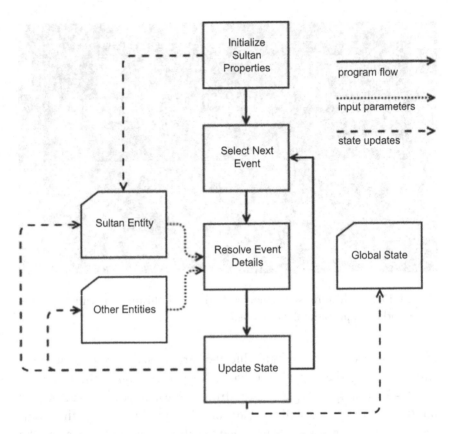

FIGURE 15.4 Flow diagram for the generation of a sultan's history.

Causality

Note what the random selection of events implies about our system's historical logic: strictly speaking, there isn't any. Historical cause and effect aren't intrinsic. Events themselves are chosen at random, but their gospels often profess causes. These *rationalizations* are generated inside the events and are mediated by the sultan's state. As an example, consider the sieges a city event, whose gospel starts with the following pattern:

Acting against *#injustice#*, *#sultanName#* led an army to the gates of *#location#*.

When determining how to replace *#injustice#*, the event examines the sultan's properties for meaningful state. If, for instance, the sultan has any allied animal factions—say, frogs—#injustice# may be replaced with "the persecution of frogs." In this way, the event's effect precedes its cause. When the sultan's state fails to produce a suitable cause, the event can even create one by, say, altering the sultan's allied factions property to include frogs and performing the aforementioned substitution. In these cases, there's a full reversal of the expected causality: the effect causes the cause.

Narrative Coherence

Though there's no intrinsic causality to the series of events in a sultan's life, the event parameterization promotes player-interpreted causalities that give rise to coherent biographical narratives. The sultan's shared state acts as a glue that holds the accounts of the disjointed events together. Domains play an especially important role in the parameterization of events. In the context of the replacement grammar, almost all gospel patterns include symbols that represent domains, meaning that once the replacement is complete, the generated text frequently includes narrative references to the sultan's domains. The effect is the production of a narrative coupling between these domains and the sultan's personality. The domains act as narrative threads that tie together the events of a sultan's life.

Table 15.1 includes the full set of gospels for the life of Antixerpur, a generated sultan, with text fragments marked up according to how they were generated. Let's look at how rationalization causes a micro-narrative to cohere. In gospel 5, Antixerpur treats with cats and convinces them to help her found an excavation site. Then, in gospel 6, she liberates cats at the Battle of Old Teggash. Though Antixerpur's rendezvous with cats played no role in the system's decision to have her initiate the Battle of Old Teggash, the gospel claims otherwise. When put to the task of rationalizing the battle, the event logic repurposed Antixerpur's affiliation with cats, which had just been created as a result of gospel 5. With the aid of apophenia, players can draw narrative conclusions for why Antixerpur might have chosen to fight on the cats' behalf. Maybe she struck a deal with them; they help organize her digging operation, and in turn she fights to liberate them. Because of the limited number of sultan properties shared across many events, emergent micro-narratives like this one are quite common.

TABLE 15.1 an example full set of gospels for a generated Sultan in *Caves of Qud*.

Number	Gospel
0	(sultan initialization; name set to **Antixerpur**, pronouns set to **she/her**, birth region set to **the Philosophers' Quarter of Shaneruk**, and domain set to **ice**)
1	*At daybreak on the first day of summer*, a **geologist** found a babe with a freezing icicle in each hand outside her dig site. She and her fellow geologists adopted the babe and named her Antixerpur.
2	In 230, Antixerpur assassinated the sultan of Qud over an ordinance prohibiting the practice of encasing things in ice. She won and **ascended to the throne**. She was 21 years old.
3	Acting against the prohibition on the practice of taking a spiritual trek through the tundra, Antixerpur led an army to the gates of **Minekesh**. She *sacked Minekesh and persecuted its citizens, forcing them to change its name to* **Antixerpurplatz**.
4	Acting against the prohibition on the practice of encasing things in ice, Antixerpur led an army to the gates of **Darchesh**. She *sacked Darchesh and slaughtered its citizens, forcing them to change its name to* **Antixerpurabad**.
5	After *treating with* **cats**, Antixerpur convinced them to help her found a **dig site** in the Philosophers' Quarter of Shaneruk for the purpose of excavating ancient blocks of ice. They named it the **Freezing Dig Site**.
6	At the Battle of **Old Teggash**, Antixerpur fought to liberate cats. She wielded a frosty **hammer** with such prowess that it became forever known as **Frostycus Catsfriend**.
7	*Deep in the wilds* of the Philosophers' Quarter of Shaneruk, Antixerpur stumbled upon a clan of **bears** performing a secret ritual. Because of her reputation for murdering someone with a dagger made of rime, the bears *furiously rebuked her and* **declared her a villain to their kind**.
8	*While traveling near* Old Teggash in the Philosophers' Quarter of Shaneruk, Antixerpur was captured by bandits. She *languished in captivity for 7 years, eventually escaping to* **Urashur**.
9	*While wandering around* the Philosophers' Quarter of Shaneruk, Antixerpur discovered the **Shrine at Mailimrod**. There she befriended **highly entropic beings** and calculated the distance to a nearby star.
10	In 300, Antixerpur won a decisive victory against the combined forces of **the Jewelers' Quarter of Biilitum** at the bloody Battle of **Tappa Cave**, though she lost her prized **Frostycus Catsfriend** during the course of the conflict. As a result of the battle, Tappa Cave was so devastated by icy winds that it was renamed the **Freezing Marsh**.

(Continued)

TABLE 15.1 (Cont.)

Number	Gospel
11	In 302, Antixerpur won a decisive victory against the combined forces of *Suppir* at the bloody Battle of *Miarravah*. As a result of the battle, Miarravah was so devastated by <u>icy winds</u> that it was renamed **Freezingmoor**.
12	Deep in *the Historians' Quarter of Tunepad*, Antixerpur discovered *Tarchenna*. There <u>she</u> befriended *mysterious strangers* and <u>dug into the earth's strata</u>.
13	In 306, Antixerpur, the Untitled, died of natural causes. <u>She</u> was <u>97</u> years old.

Text representing a change in state is **bolded**. Text generated according to existing state is <u>underlined</u>. Text generated via random branching or synonymization is *italicized*.

Antixerpur's domain of ice, chosen during the pre-historic initialization step (gospel 0), was also repeatedly incarnated in the gospels, coupling her with the archetypal phenomenon. Miraculously, she's found as a babe with icicles in her hands (gospel 1). Early in her life, she fights against the prohibition on ice-associated practices: encasing things in ice (gospels 2 and 4) and taking spiritual treks through the tundra (gospel 3). Later, she founds a dig site to excavate blocks of ice (gospel 5), wields a frosty hammer during a momentous battle (gospel 6), and historically devastates two sites with icy winds in her wake (gospels 10 and 11). These ice-flavored text fragments are manifested by the replacement grammar according to Antixerpur's initialized domain, and collectively they act as a narrative force that pushes through the aggregated events of her life.

The subversion of historical logic is a strange choice, but it dovetails with *Caves of Qud*'s themes and far-future, science-fantasy setting. The game is about engaging with the artifacts of the past without the context that produced them. It strives to render the present in high definition and evoke curiosity at how we got here from an obscure past. By subverting historical logic, the game encodes its own ignorance about its world history and the full spectrum of its complexities.

CONCLUSION

We now have a framework for thinking about history generation and an example of its application. Let's enumerate some questions we can use to interrogate our intuitions and guide the designs of our future generative history systems.

- In what narrative context will our histories be engaged? Are we interested in centering history as a process or as an artifact that's viewed through a present lens?

- Who's telling our histories? What are their biases?

- How can we break our prospective histories up into entities and events?

- What logic do we want to use to relate our events? What arguments does that logic make about history?

I see procedural generation as a way to explore the mechanics of our world and the meaning we make out of engaging with them. History's importance to our social world is megalithic. It's threaded everywhere through our cultural fabric. Turning our procedural eye toward history is a new beginning in meaning making.

NOTES

1 I highly recommend browsing *Epitaph*'s publicly available source code for a simple, accessible example of a generative history system: https://github.com/mkremins/epitaph

2 Kate Compton. 2015. Tracery. (2015). https://github.com/galaxykate/tracery

CHAPTER 16

Procedural Descriptions in *Voyageur*

Bruno Dias

V oyageur was born pretty much the exact wrong way for a video game. It was designed around a technique that I'd become enamored with and wanted to use and around a tool I developed to build it.

In late 2015, Emily Short published a piece of generative writing called *The Annals of the Parrigues*. A guidebook to a fictional medieval country, it's mostly a travelogue of towns and villages, their geography and culture. Around that time, I started thinking about (and discussing in conversations with Emily and others) a rough idea of a game that would use a similar text-generation technique, a sort of interactive *Parrigues*. What if you could travel from town to town, reading a description of the local scenery in each place, trading stories and bartering with the locals?

Parrigues, along with Kate Compton's Tracery library, informed the design of the tool I'd call Improv: a text-generation library specifically suited to *Parrigues*-like goals, and the backbone of this *Parrigues* game I wanted to make. That game would become *Voyageur*.

Here's the brief for how Improv had to work:

- I wanted to generate text from a grammar. I knew from Tracery that this was a very good way of authoring generative text because it's much easier to reason about and structure. It also more or less guarantees that any glaring syntactical errors in the generated text are the product of a faulty corpus and not some inscrutable ghost in the machine.

- Those grammars had to be straightforward human-and-machine readable, probably formatted as JSON. In Voyageur's actual codebase, the corpora are all written in YAML for ease of reading, but they get translated to JSON (which Improv consumes) at compile time.

- Improv needed to be able to keep track of a world state and generate text that conforms to that world state. That is, if it describes a village in a desert, it must then not talk about the river that runs through the center of town. This would enable it to generate complete coherent descriptions of a place.

This last point is what drove me to build a library specifically for the purpose; Tracery didn't really support that kind of functionality. The techniques that Emily outlined in the appendices to *Parrigues* would act as a template, but I'd eventually deviate a lot from her methods.

SETTING THE STAGE

From the start of the project, the idea of one-way travel was at the forefront of my mind. Mechanically, this was shaping up to be an explore-and-trade game in the vein of *Elite*, and the dominant strategy in these games is to find a profitable trade route and grind it. I didn't want that player behavior; I wanted to encourage the vagabond-like behavior of moving from one port to another, never looking back, picking cargo up on the way; to me this was always the most *fun* way to play those games, and my favorite examples of the genre had ways of encouraging it. Sid Meier's *Pirates!* used wind direction to guide the player along the trade lanes of the Caribbean, encouraging long loops around the map, for example.

I also knew that the procedural locales wouldn't stand up to repeated visits. Planets in *Voyageur* are fundamentally static, which works as you're only staying on them for a brief moment.

Given that procedural generation gave me "unlimited" worlds to put in front of the player, I could just cut off the possibility of backtracking entirely. You're on an immense river delta, carried down by the current; maybe you can choose which fork in the water's path to take, and thus what port to visit next, but you can never go back. Each place you visit is a moment in time, congealed by your memory of it; you never get to see it change, because you can never return. Finding the emotional and narrative complement to this mechanical construction was at the heart of designing a setting and a story for *Voyageur*. This image of being on a canoe drifting downriver is also where the name comes from, referencing the 19th-century subculture of French Canadian canoe men who would ferry furs across North America, a working title that stuck.

Space travel was natural. Hopping from planet to planet, rather than trudging from village to village, would allow the game to explore wildly different environments and settings. It also naturally complemented the procedural nature of it, and the disposability of individual ports; players would visit many places throughout a play session, and the idea of exploring the galaxy seemed more resonant than an improbably meandering river system.

In *Voyageur*, the little vagabond spaceship is equipped with a *descent device*, a piece of mysterious alien technology that works in unexplained ways and to unexplained ends. You pump electricity into it and it displaces your ship, faster than light, roughly toward the galaxy's center of mass. You can steer a little, by accelerating this way or that while you "descend," to ensure you "hit" a particular star system on your way "down." But all trips are one way.

The devices enable a nomadic lifestyle for a class of voyageurs that can travel through space much faster than other humans can. Everyone else travels on warp drives that are huge, expensive, and take months to traverse a few light years; the descent device will take you to a neighboring star system in instants. This is a setting in which humanity has traveled the stars for a long time, having colonized a large section of the galaxy over the generations. Human expansion, going outward in all directions, has outpaced how fast humans can normally travel within a single lifetime; human societies are out of regular contact with the vast majority of humanity, which they know of only through outdated information that has been carried down on ships over decades or even centuries. This description, taken from the game, exemplifies what you might encounter:

> This city is a network of squat domes connected underground, each one containing a hint of green visible through its translucent exterior. After dark, the residents vanish from the streets as if summoned away by some unheard curfew warning. All around, the signs of ongoing terraforming are evident; every habitat window is fitted with an AR view of how Earth-like this world will be in a hundred years. You find the locals here to be mistrustful of travellers like you, and life is uncomfortably burdened by many regulations on the use of resources and disposal of waste.
>
> *(Voyageur)*

Traveling as a voyageur is inherently lonely and melancholy; every place you see is a place you'll never see again, as a few weeks of descent travel are fast enough to take you past the horizon of how far you could travel in a lifetime by other means. Everyone you meet regards you as an exotic curiosity but also as suspicious; after all, what could possibly lead someone to abandon home forever and choose this lifestyle?

IMPROV: THE TOOL

I built Improv before I started work on *Voyageur*, partly because I wanted a proof of concept that was robust enough that I felt comfortable embarking on the full project but also because I felt the tool would be useful as an open-source resource for others, and because it was ultimately based on someone else's methodology.

Tracery and Improv are both *grammar* approaches to generating text (or, any content that can be expressed as a string of characters, like SVG images). They both use *grammars*, sets of *rules* that define how text can be constructed. Each rule consists of a name, or key, and a set of possible completions for that rule, *phrases*. Say we're generating descriptions of cats; a rule called **color** would then include several phrases for possible cat coat colors: "brown," "orange," "black," "tabby," "calico," and so on.

In Tracery (see Figure 16.1), rules contain simple lists of phrases. In Improv, the phrases under a given rule are split into *groups*; each group carries some metadata that describes its contents and then one or more phrases.

Improv (see Figure 16.2) works essentially like Tracery does. The generator works on a loop; it's given the name of a rule to follow as a starting point. It then chooses randomly from the grammar a possible completion for that rule (a *phrase*). It then performs some simple template expansion on the phrase; the most important functionality is including other rules, which the generator then fulfills recursively until the entire "tree" of a chunk of text has been traversed. So we might start from a rule called "cat_desc" and randomly select the phrase "This is a #coat_color# cat … ." Tracery then interprets "#coat_color#" as markup to be replaced by following the **coat_color** rule, so that you end up with "This is a calico cat …."

Improv differs from Tracery in *choosing what snippet to use*. Tracery has a single "source of truth," the grammar. Improv has two: the grammar and the *world model*. A world model is just a computer-friendly description of an underlying reality by which the text is bound. Text meant for humans is messy in a way that's not amenable to computation. Take this sentence from a Wikipedia article:

HMS *Agamemnon* was a 64-gun third-rate ship of the line of the British Royal Navy.

This sentence implies a ton of domain-specific information that isn't organized in any particular way or even present in the text itself. We could list these as explicit facts:

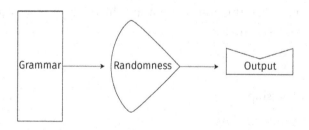

FIGURE 16.1 How Tracery works, using randomness to choose from possible values hierarchized in a grammar.

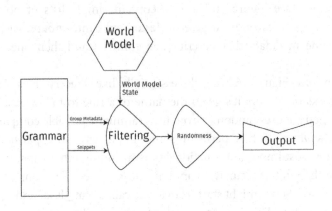

FIGURE 16.2   An idealized view of how Improv works.

- It flies the flag of the UK.

- It's a warship.

- It's a ship of the line.

- It's a third-rate ship of the line.

- It's belongs to the *Ardent* class.

- It's an 18th-century ship.

- It's a wind-powered sailing vessel.

- It's a square-rigged ship.

- It's armed with muzzle-loading cannons.

We can standardize this information and hierarchize it into ontologies and create a world model:

- Flag: UK
- Role: Warship
  - Ship of the line
    - Third-rate

- Class: *Ardent*

- Era: C18

- Propulsion: Sail

  - Square-rigged

- Armament: Cannons

Before choosing which specific phrase to use to fulfill a rule, Improv performs a *filtering* step. Filters, in Improv terms, are functions that take two arguments: a world model and the metadata from a given group. They compare the two, returning either a number or a null value. A null value means "discard this group entirely." A number added to that group's *score*, or "salience," is an indication of how appropriate or inappropriate the group is to the current world model.

This filtering step gives a subset of the grammar that has been selected with the filtering criteria; normally, that means conformity to the world model. From this subset, Improv then chooses randomly what specific phrases to use.

Improv itself has no knowledge of how to perform this filtering, though. An Improv generator is defined with a purpose-specific set of filters supplied by the developer. While some filters mark phrases as inappropriate for use outright, Improv is designed to mostly rely on "soft" filtering: assigning phrases a score, then using only those phrases that score high enough.

"High enough" is variable; Improv utilizes a user-defined formula to choose what that means based on the highest score in the sample. Given m, the maximum salience score in the sample, the culling formula is supposed to return c, the culling threshold; phrases with lower salience than c are discarded. This seems like a detail but makes a huge difference to how a generator behaves. A formula of $c = m$ makes for a generator that is always choosing from the most salient phrases available to it and is therefore not very *random*. *Voyageur* uses a formula of $c = m - 10$. 10, here, is a value arrived at experimentally by tweaking the generator. When using *Voyageur*'s filters and corpus, m tends to hover around 30; this formula is similar, but *not identical*, to discarding phrases that didn't reach 70% of the maximum salience score. Experimentation has shown this to be a good balance of unpredictability and coherence.

FILTERING, REINCORPORATION, AND SOURCES OF TRUTH

The heart of the generator is the filter stack. The filter stack started out as an attempt at generating text that was *coherent*, stopping self-contradiction. It evolved into a sort of expression of what I think makes for a good procedural description.

Voyageur's planet generator, the most important Improv generator in the game, eventually shipped using a "secret sauce" of seven filters, four of which are part of the Improv library, and three of which are custom-built for *Voyageur*. Those filters are:

- **Mismatch filter**: Compares a phrase's tags to the world model's tags and returns null if the phrase's tags aren't identical or a subset of the model's tags. That is, this filter culls outright contradictions like incorporating tags marked "tundra" into the description of a desert world.

- **Dryness**: Dry as in "don't repeat yourself." This is one of the oddest Improv filters; it outright culls phrases that have already been used. This is where it starts to get more complicated than the idealized model in Figure 16.3. As it happens, Improv needs a memory to do its job properly.

- **Full bonus**: Gives a salience score bonus to phrases with tags that perfectly match a tag in the world model. So if a planet is marked as a desert world, it's more likely to get desert world phrases in its description.

- **Unmentioned**: Gives a salience score bonus to phrases with tags that aren't present in phrases that have been used. That is, bias the generator toward bringing up facets of the planet that haven't been mentioned yet. The goal here is to create well-rounded descriptions that cover as much ground as possible.

- **Tweak filter**: Custom-built for *Voyageur*, the "tweak filter" simply gives phrases salience score bonuses that are hard-coded into the corpus; some phrases are just arbitrarily more salient no matter what. More on this hack later in this chapter.

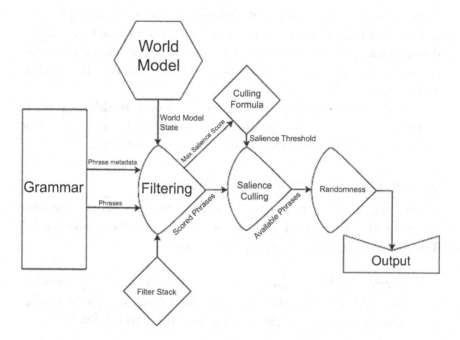

FIGURE 16.3   Improv in more detail: culling and filter stacks.

- **Lensing filter**: Another trick arrived at after a lot of trial and error. Every planet in *Voyageur* is "seen through a lens," which might be its culture, biome, or some other important facet. Phrases that have the corresponding tag (that is, phrases that mention/reflect this aspect of the world) have a higher salience. This helps differentiate the *descriptions* of similar models; the generator is concerned with different aspects of a planet each time.

- **Bias filter**: The bias filter tilts the generator toward discussing important aspects of the planet being described. It gives a salience bonus to phrases that mention a planet's special features, prevailing ideology, or biome; the goal is to make sure that every description touches on those core aspects.

Compared to this complex mix of filters, the actual grammar is pretty simple; every planet description is just an optional intro statement ("Your ship alights …") followed by some loose phrases about the planet. This structure is purposefully loose; I didn't want descriptions to be long, and I didn't want too much structure. I think a way of building descriptions in which sentences have more of a relationship to one another is possible, but it requires an approach other than this kind of grammar.

To cull the grammar according to the world model, Improv is performing a complex negotiation, balancing multiple factors. But I haven't discussed where the world model comes from yet.

WHERE WORLD MODELS COME FROM

When I first started planning out *Voyageur*, I was really concerned with the issue of where world models come from, the "source of truth." There were, to my mind, two approaches here:

- *A priori* truth: You generate the world model separately, probably through some approach that's just like rolling on a random table. Then you use the world model to feed the world generator.

- *A posteriori* truth: You tell the generator to generate a phrase. Then, that phrase's tags get added back into the world model, a process I called *reincorporation*. Subsequent phrases abide by this altered world model.

The second approach really appealed to me; it was what Emily used in *Parrigues*, and it allowed the corpus to guide the frequency of everything in the game. If I wrote a lot of text for desert worlds, I would end up with more desert worlds but that would be fine as I'd have a lot of content for them. I started building *Voyageur* with the assumption that this was how I wanted it to work, and reincorporation is a core feature of Improv (Figure 16.4). All you have to do is turn it on with a switch as you instantiate a generator.

This plan fell apart almost immediately. For one thing, planets in *Voyageur* don't stand completely alone; they are part of a region, and the region has its own features (e.g., government, culture). Those features form a sort of substratum that the planet descriptions would build on. As I explored the possibilities by actually coding *Voyageur*, I quickly arrived at a hybrid model that the shipped game actually uses.

Voyageur planets are initially seeded with some basic features—the planet's class (desert, tundra, metallic, Venusian, etc.) and some reflections of the planet's overarching region. This allows me to sidestep one of Improv's weaknesses, the difficulty of expressing more complex logic about how different parts of the world model relate to one another. For example, a city world must have a developed, non-agrarian economy; this kind of logic is handled by the code that "seeds" planets with initial metadata and not at all by the Improv generator.

It also quickly became apparent that letting the corpus dictate the frequency of everything didn't work so well in an actual game. To balance the game's economy, I needed to be able to tune knobs directly. It would be problematic if, to make a certain type of good or event less available, I had to either delete some lines from the corpora or add more writing for all other kinds of planets.

A huge chunk of development time was spent writing the corpora of *Voyageur*'s planet generator. Procedural generation is, effectively, a way of getting 200% of the content with 400% of the work. Some elements of *Voyageur*'s corpora are scraped from public-access data (mainly, lists of names), but those lists had to be vetted and reviewed by a human (viz., myself) before they could be conscionably used. For the most part, the corpus consists of many snippets of hand-written descriptions, little individual turns of phrase that I put in place so that the machine could recombine them. Writing in this style is difficult; you can't rely on the natural flow of a paragraph to guide you as you write, and you have to conform to the way the text is going to end up being used.

Toward the end of the development cycle, a lot of time was spent tuning the generator. The planet generator just wasn't producing good output; similar planets read too similarly. Building some ancillary testing tools helped reveal that some phrases were seriously under-utilized. An Improv generator is, ultimately, very hard to reason about. Improv taught me that you can write out an algorithm by hand, using traditional non-ML methods, and still not fully understand why it's producing a particular output.

Tuning those systems is slow going. You change the specific mix of filters and scoring values being used, then generate some planets to see if the descriptions feel good. Then you run the system

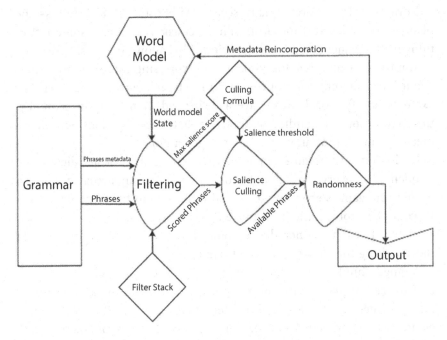

FIGURE 16.4   How Improv works, with reincorporation.

thousands of times and collect statistics to try and corroborate your feel. It's maddening. It took me a long time to really understand what my problem was.

Voyageur's filters were designed to replicate some good ideas about how to write a description: have an angle (lensing); bring up the important stuff (bias); don't dwell too much on one thing (unmentioned). All of that was working well, but invariably some phrases would fall by the wayside regardless of the specific balance of factors I put in place. This was particularly true of phrases that are rarely appropriate to a planet, phrases that were in effect little gems meant to show up with low frequency. I spent a long time trying to tweak the system to achieve a "good" distribution of phrase usage and realized I couldn't. Different groups of phrases were being left behind no matter what I did.

This was the great last realization I had working on *Voyageur*: You need to put in some guardrails. I eventually just added hardcoded salience score "tweaks" to several of the game's phrases. This in effect gave phrases that were showing up too rarely, or not at all, an artificial bump. Yes, I could have done that programmatically. But that would have required another step at compile time or a long and slow "self-analysis" at game launch, and ultimately it would have been another automated system that I would need to tune. Manual tweaks worked *very* well. If you think the procedural descriptions in *Voyageur* are good at all (Figure 16.5), thank them.

Voyageur's planet generator is a lot more complicated than I initially thought I'd need. It maintains a history of what phrases it used and uses that history to make valuations about whether a given phrase is repetitive. It relies on "guardrails" put in place to tweak the overall distribution of phrases.

Output that's too random quickly turns into bowls of oatmeal; there's a lot of variability, but that variability doesn't *mean* anything. *Voyageur* looks to a world model, to an underlying reality that touches on the game's other systems to make that randomness mean something.

I ended up bumping into the opposite problem from bowls of oatmeal; what I'm calling the "brutalist building problem." When the generator is too slavishly dedicated to using phrases with good salience, when there's not enough randomness, you quickly start getting descriptions that are too good at surfacing the underlying model; form follows function a little too well. Planets start to look kind of naked, to lack ambiguity or flourish; once you've seen one farm world, you've seen them all.

CONCLUSIONS

This kind of text generator balances on this razor's edge: too random, and there's no meaning; too much meaning, and there's no room for emotional attachment beyond simple recognition of game state. Whether the output in *Voyageur* successfully walks that tightrope, I'll leave for you to judge. It's certainly the case that it could be improved by doubling or tripling the volume of content in the corpus. I don't think I went in with naive expectations, but I didn't realize how much work would be needed to get the generator in shape.

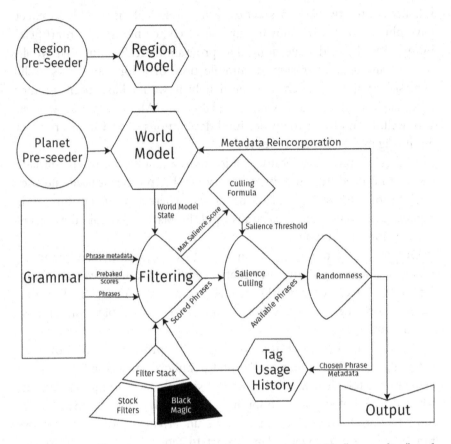

FIGURE 16.5 The *Voyageur* planet generator, complete with "pre-seeding" and tweaks.

I'm also a bit dismayed at how much of this is fluffy trial and error and how little of it seems to be transferrable. I can't really give you a methodology for tuning a generator similar to *Voyageur*'s; I know what worked for mine, but what worked for mine was probably very particular to *Voyageur*'s content and mechanics.

That trial and error did help shape how I think about this kind of procedural generation. And, in turn, the generator shaped the game. *Voyageur* is much more of an ambient, low-agency experience than originally envisioned. The game was originally supposed to have an ongoing subgame where you'd glean information from reading planet descriptions and use that to make savvy trading decisions.

That never really panned out. The only way to make descriptions work as functional gameplay hints was to make them so dry and repetitive that players would actively resist reading them. The planet descriptions are fuzzy and not very informative; that's what gives them flavor. How to square that circle of procedural generation that delivers *beauty* but also *functional information* is left as an exercise for the reader.

This page intentionally left blank

CHAPTER 17

Generating in the Real World

Mx. Lazer-Walker

M ost of this book is concerned with how to use procedural generation for various storytelling purposes: fleshing out a virtual world,
providing a narrative experience for players to interact with, creating
small digital toys that produce comedy and spontaneity and joy.
Implicit in this is that the worlds we're creating are digital ones that
live in our pockets, TVs, or desktops. Increasingly, people are creating
narrative experiences that intersect with the real world. Whether that's
through augmented reality, physical installations such as immersive
theater and escape room games, or traditional transmedia experiences
like ARGs, audiences are hungry for stories told through more embodied means.

This chapter aims to explore what it means to combine computationally driven procedural generation and real-world embodied storytelling. First, we'll explore some techniques used by existing
non-digital physical experiences to create room for emergent player-
driven stories. After that, we'll talk about *Computational Flâneur*,
a site-specific generative poetry walk that came out of my research at
the MIT Media Lab, as a case study for exploring the technical and
design processes behind blending digital generative systems with the
physical world.

HOW DO ANALOG WORKS USE PROCEDURALITY?

Modern discussions of procedural generation and storytelling, by virtue of the emphasis on games and digital procgen, tend to focus on how emergent stories can arise from the intersection of complex interactive systems. But it's worth looking at the ways locative experiences—such as immersive theater and site-specific art—create spaces for emergent player stories without using the systems-heavy approaches we're used to in digital games.

The Connecting Power of Embodied Play

It's remarkable how physical components cause people to feel invested in procedurally generated content. Party games like *Apples to Apples* and *Cards against Humanity* rely on this phenomenon. Given a randomly chosen prompt, each player has a hand of possible proce-durally generated responses and must select the card that makes the best (or funniest) pair. There is strategy in deciding to hold onto a certain card for later and in reading the current judge's sensibilities, but the process feels analogous to curating a Twitterbot's output. In a weird sense, these games are comedy generation systems driven just as much by the algorithm of a shuffled deck as by the creative input of the players. And yet, they work. Players feel real agency, and real ownership over their jokes. People generally feel more connected to the outputs of systems when they feel their inputs are meaningful. That's only ampli-fied when the experience they're having is one in which they are physically embodied in that experience.

Case Study: Sleep No More

Sleep No More is an immersive theater piece by Punchdrunk, currently running in New York City and Shanghai. It's ostensibly a (non-verbal) retelling of Shakespeare's *Macbeth* and Hitchcock's *Rebecca*, but you'd be hard-pressed to glean that if you weren't already familiar with their plots. *Sleep No More* is a freeform experience that takes place in "the McKittrick Hotel," a warehouse in Manhattan more than six stories tall and spanning a full city block. The show is a "hyperdrama," a term meant in the same sense as hypertext: as characters move around the hotel in real-time, you're also free to move around the space. For the 2 to 3 hours you spend in the McKittrick, you choose where to go and what to see.

The appeal of *Sleep No More* is the ability to go anywhere and do anything. If you want to follow Macbeth for two hours, you can do that, hang out at the bar, or even just go to the library and read. All of those, the promise goes, are equally valid *Sleep No More* experiences.

In one sense, *Sleep No More* is a strictly plotted piece of theater. Actors' paths through the McKittrick are pre-planned, their movements and interactions as precise and interconnected as a mechanical clock. But the sheer size of the physical space affords a similarly large narrative possibility space: no two players will have the exact same journey. Since no one player can experience everything, a critical part of the joy of *Sleep No More* is the informal post-show debrief, when you inevitably head to a bar or coffee shop with your friends to discuss the adventures you've been on and to hear stories of what you might have missed.

Such a brute-force approach to emergence fails in an infinitely reproducible videogame—note the sheer volume of spoiler wikis and Let's Play videos that accompany every open world videogame. However, it succeeds wildly in an experience that costs $90+ for a bounded 2–3 hour experience in a specific warehouse in Manhattan.

Case Study: Then She Fell

Even within the world of immersive theater, other paths exist. *Then She Fell*, by Third Rail Productions, is another theater piece in New York. Taking place in a former psych ward in Williamsburg, it intertwines the stories of *Alice's Adventures in Wonderland* with the real-world relationship between Lewis Carroll and the young girl Alice Liddell.

Unlike *Sleep No More*, *Then She Fell* is largely linear. Each performance has room for only a dozen audience members, each of which is taken on an intricately planned guided journey through scenes and set pieces. Each attendee at a given performance will have a different experience, but two audience members at different performances with the same random seed (if you will) experience the same scenes in the same order.

Counterintuitively, this linearity affords a different sort of player story. This mechanical shift means the majority of the audience's experiences can be one-on-one (or close to it) interactions with actors. The result is that the individual moments that stick out in players' minds feel far more vividly personal. A live actor responding to what you say and do in the context of a single scene and set of interactions doesn't meaningfully shape the overall story arc but does stick out far more clearly in your memory. If a big part of immersive theater is the post-show debrief with friends, this optimizes meaningful shareable moments.

Case Study: Janet Cardiff

Part of how Punchdrunk is able to pull off what it does with *Sleep No More* is the complete control they have over the space. Much like game designers creating digital worlds, the players have control over every individual sound, sight, and even smell of the environment you're experiencing. Similarly, even though *Sleep No More* is heavily plotted, the use of live actors means there's room for give and take as actors respond naturally to the audience.

The sound artist Janet Cardiff has neither of these luxuries in her work. In the 2000s, she built a series of audio walks, half-hour experiences that intermingle the artist speaking to you with a complex binaural soundscape over an actual real-world space. Her 2004 piece *Her Long-Black Hair*—available online (https://phiffer.org/hlbh/) thanks to the archival work of Dan Phiffer—has you walk through part of Central Park in New York City while she tells you stories.

More than being about the words she says, her pieces are about the binaural soundscape that surrounds you. Early on, you hear police sirens blare behind you on 59th Street and aren't sure whether the sirens are there in real life or just in the recording. You hear a couple arguing or a child laughing and similarly question what is real and what isn't. This isn't a living, breathing piece of theater like *Sleep No More*. It's a static piece of recorded audio, exactly the same for every participant, whether today or a decade ago.

Yet her audio walks feel special and deeply personal. My time with Cardiff's work felt like it was an experience meant just for me and meaningfully changed my relationship with that specific corner of Central Park. There's something ineffable about an experience designed for a specific space, more so than a location-based game like *Pokémon Go*; this is fiction specifically built to shape your relationship with a specific place. I can't visit that corner of Central Park without my own memories entwining with those of the Cardiff walk.

This largely works because of her phenomenal use of psychology. I mentioned earlier the otherworldliness of hearing a couple arguing behind you and not knowing whether they are physically present. Because the positional audio is pre-baked in, if you turned your head, the audio would turn with you, and the illusion would be broken. But, miraculously, nobody turns.

How does she do this? At the most basic level, she explicitly tells the player to not turn around. More than that, the authored narrative she tells is one of regret for the past, with a core emotional theme of not looking back. At one point, she even tells the story of Lot's wife. The result is an experience where players are pre-disposed against doing the thing that would break the illusion of the technology. It feels like a magic trick, but it works stunningly well. Similarly, it would be easy for Cardiff's wayfinding instructions to fail and leave you lost if you were walking at the wrong speed. That doesn't happen, though, because she uses similar framing techniques to ensure you're walking at precisely the intended pace.

For the most part, these are design tools used to provide a consistent experience. They logistically ensure that players are in the right place at the right time, and they emotionally provide a set of "special" experiences that feel tailored to you despite being static. Within this framework, Cardiff is able to play on the randomness and unpredictability of the public physical space to create room for emergent synchrony with her static recorded audio. Specifically, she is able to play off three types of elements:

1. Things that won't change

When Cardiff plays police sirens behind you, she makes a safe assumption. As long as there are cars in Manhattan, there will be police sirens on 59th Street. Even though this should be fairly uninteresting—they're only police sirens!—the fact that you recognize it as being specific and authentic to the space resonates deeply with you. Because you're physically there, you feel like she's responding to the experience you're having.

2. Things that are meaningful whether or not they change

At one point, she has you walk through the Central Park Zoo, and she references a polar bear. By the time I did the walk, there was no polar bear enclosure there; that specific polar bear was likely long dead. It still worked, though, and works either way. If the polar bear had still been there, that would have felt meaningful, as if she knew the space I was inhabiting. Even though the bear wasn't there, it still felt meaningful, a brief meditation on the transience and shaping of public spaces. Either way, it felt like a special experience built for me.

3. Things she can't possibly know about

If the player story of a roguelike is one that emerges out of the intersection of complex systems, and *Sleep No More*'s story comes out of a combinatorial explosion of interlocking authored content, Cardiff's work explores the intersection of a single authored narrative strand and the infinite random noise of public space. This is simultaneously more open ended and more limiting than the other forms we've explored. Of the times I've experienced *Her Long Black Hair*, the unique moments in any given playthrough were often insignificant—the weather or the number of people there. Sometimes they were more drastic, like the time I had to reroute because Keanu Reeves was shooting a film by the Bethesda Fountain. Although Cardiff's dialog doesn't and can't explicitly reference these, carefully chosen open-ended language can provide a framework where even these little details still feel meaningful and intentional, as if they were conscious design decisions.

WHY BOTHER TO BRING THE DIGITAL INTO THE PHYSICAL?

If existing embodied experiences are already able to do interesting things with procedurality, why would we bother mucking around bringing software into the mix? Dealing with the intersection of the digital and the physical is a pain to deal with and debug. I'm certainly not one to claim that there's something inherently superior about digital works or that bringing technology into embodied experiences is something to do merely because we can.

The experiences we've discussed are all fairly baroque. *Sleep No More* and *Then She Fell* are large-scale theatrical endeavors requiring custom built-out spaces and dozens of live actors and as a result command extremely expensive ticket prices. The relative impermanence of immersive theater also means that, unless you're lucky enough to build something as wildly successful as *Sleep No More*, a few years in the future your work will largely live on in the form of static documentation. This is regrettable for individual creators, but even worse it inhibits larger design discussion around this sort of work.

Design communities emerge when people have a shared body of work to discuss. Traditional theater relies on strong local communities; digital art and games communities are more distributed, but infinitely reproducible works mean that conversations can happen across time and space. Finding ways to create more automatable forms of immersive theater is one way to create works that can be longer-lasting.

Works like Cardiff's don't have these problems, but Cardiff's work is singular. The amount of effort to make a static audio piece like hers function is staggering; mixing in already-well-understood digital elements to create more interactive works that capture what's beautiful about hers can lower the barrier of entry to making more things like that, without requiring people to become experts in binaural audio production and psychology.

AN ATTEMPT

My research at the MIT Media Lab focused on how we could blend these existing situated storytelling techniques with the sort of procedural storytelling used in modern digital games. How could Cardiff's audio walks be improved by weaving in a sensorial awareness of the world via the player's smartphone? How can techniques taken from interactive fiction be used to provide experiences as transformative as *Sleep No More*, but for free in a public space instead of requiring hordes of live actors and a custom built-out set? How can all of these experiences more meaningfully shape our experiences with public spaces? In broad strokes, I was interested in building site-specific interactive radio plays that used smartphone sensors as a means of input. Rather than focusing on discrete player choices, I was particularly interested in the effect more subtle morphing of a story could have.

Early discussions focused on a short play set in a major art museum. One dynamic we wanted to explore was having a linear, authored play respond to the player's environment; the arc of the story you were listening to would be the same no matter where you were in the museum, but the specific dialog would be subtly shaped by where you chose to be, peppered with references to the specific art around you and influenced by the dynamics of that space.

More interesting than that dialog layer would have been the background layer of other overheard conversations, a la Cardiff's binaural soundscape, playing on the voyeuristic joy of listening to strangers at museums. These would be tailored for you based on whatever sensor data we could gather: you'd hear different stories if you were there on a weekday or a weekend, winter or summer. There'd be audio snippets you might only hear if it was raining outside or on a particularly busy day in the museum. The goal wasn't to create something where completionists felt the need to (or even the possibility to) "collect" every possible story but rather to create an experience where the procedurally surfaced authored content felt so in sync with the physical space that, like Cardiff's work at its best, you weren't sure what was real and what was fiction.

In principle, none of this seems too far afield of what's already been done in the digital world. Conceptually, the procedural generation techniques for modifying story flow are similar to others described in this book. On a technical level, the scripting language I built for prototyping was similar to other modern choice-based interactive fiction tools. But the hypothesis was that building these sorts of interactive experiences in a physical space, based on sensor data, would create a substantively different experience.

Designing for New Platforms: Start Simple

Creating experiences for novel interfaces usually requires a bottom-up approach rather than a top-down one. Instead of defining what the end experience should be and working backwards, the best way to deal with "alt control" games is generally to start by prototyping around low-level interactions to see what works, eventually building up larger systems and interaction patterns to support what's intrinsically satisfying about the moment-to-moment experience. Even though we had a high-level vision for a piece, we began with low-level experimentation about what was possible and, more importantly, what was legible to players.

What's Possible?

In some cases, a technology will likely be viable in the future but isn't quite there today. My work specifically eschewed traditional screen-based augmented reality (think *Pokémon Go*) for this reason. The idea of overlaying visual content on top of the world is interesting; in practice, until we have dedicated AR glasses (and maybe not even then!), the awkwardness of staring at the world through a handheld slab of glass was at odds with the desired goal of connecting people to, rather than isolating them from, the world around them.

As another example, I was initially very interested in using head-tracking positional audio, but experiments using the phone's motion sensors proved overly finicky. If a phone is sitting in a purse or a pocket, you can pretty reliably determine body orientation, but people will naturally shift their heads, not their entire bodies, to listen for new things. Screen-based AR prototypes could get players to subconsciously move their phones in sync with their head movements, but as described above, visual AR has its own set of problems. It seemed like positional audio was a problem best tackled via Janet Cardiff-style design solutions rather than technical ones.

These examples are all based on users providing their own smart-phones, since that's what we were designing for. Head-tracking, for example, is pretty easy if your setup allows you to adopt a computer vision solution or if you can somehow place motion sensors on your players' heads (like, say, a VR or AR headset). In our case, though, other design constraints meant that technical solutions that could work in other situations were off the table to us.

What's Understandable by Players?

A modern smartphone has a dizzying array of sensors. For most of them, the question is less what we can do with them and more what players can understand about them. An iPhone's altimeter, for example, can tell relative vertical distances well enough to distinguish what specific step of a staircase you're on. One prototype I built was for a park that's essentially a giant vertical set of stairs, with the hope that

I could use that data to pace a relatively non-interactive story to the player's speed. On a technical level, it was very easy to use altimeter data to position the player along the track of climbing the stairs. Since it was one dimension instead of two, in many ways it was easier to deal with than GPS or other forms of location.

In practice, the data was too finely grained. Players didn't really have a mental model for a computer system responding to their movements at a per-step level, rather than, say, just reacting when they finished climbing a specific set of stairs. Similarly, it was far more legible when I used the altimeter for a prototype built for a multi-story building, telling the player when to get on or off the elevator. The technology worked great, but we didn't have the design vocabulary necessary to take full advantage of the granularity of the data we had.

This is a general theme in a lot of my experiments. The prototype that turned into *Computational Flâneur* (described later in the chapter) began with the assumption that how quickly the player was moving through a space would be an interesting input into a procgen system, for example, but it became quickly apparent that players had no mental model for their moment-to-moment movement speed meaningfully affecting a system at any level of complexity beyond "the music gets more intense when you're running than when you're walking." As a result, I ended up throwing out "movement speed" as an input for that piece, despite its being easy to track accurately with consumer smartphone GPS.

CASE STUDY: COMPUTATIONAL FLÂNEUR

After all of those early prototypes and design lessons, it became clear that the next immediate step wasn't jumping straight to a narrative piece, but rather creating something more textural to play around with how procedural generation felt in a space. The result was a generative poetry walk, called *Computational Flâneur*, built for Fort Mason in San Francisco. As you wander through Fort Mason, your phone makes up poems based on where you walk and reads them to you. Walk by the cannons and you'll hear poems of war; walk by the waterfront and you'll hear poems of the sea.

Crucially, *Computational Flâneur* doesn't aim to produce actual good poetry. It's designed to create simulacrum of the poetry listening experience, putting you in the sort of contemplative state that fine art appreciation often can. But it's also designed to serve a similar role to doodling: it's interesting enough to pull you out of your own thoughts but not interesting enough to hold your attention. Half-attentive, your mind gets distracted by the environment, allowing you to appreciate the present moment in a beautiful physical space more than you would if you were distracted by your own thoughts. It's guided meditation by way of nonsense.

Actually Developing in the Real World

Digital procedural generation is great because of how incredibly tight software feedback loops can be. Prototyping a system and getting immediate feedback on whether it's doing what you intended is usually orders of magnitude shorter with digital systems than with physical ones.

Making digital/physical hybrids like *Computational Flâneur* is a more complex problem. Even though you're writing software, there's no avoiding prototyping and playtesting in the actual world. But while some types of playtesting categorically need to happen in the flesh, others can be done digitally. It's worth taking the time to design your design system so that you can test any given part of the system with as minimal fuss as possible.

For *Computational Flâneur*, that meant a few different things:

1. Being able to run the neural net-powered generator on a computer without GPS. For the poetry walk, there was a series of map regions, each of which had a set of keywords. Each snippet of poetry was generated using a randomly chosen keyword as the starting text. I abstracted this to being able to generate output for a given keyword, so I could manually generate poetry on demand for any given snippet.

2. Being able to walk around anywhere and have poetry play. If I wasn't in the physical park, the app would generate random regions and act as if they were real regions. This let me hear the poetry in context: as I walked, I'd hear poetry snippets that were

thematically coherent, and then I'd hear the shift as I moved to a different region, without having to physically be in San Francisco.

3. Finally, it was important that, at any given time, the game was deployable to an actual iOS device that could physically run in the park itself. I could more quickly test whether the poetry seemed sensible in a vacuum, sure, but it was impossible to gauge the experience of hearing the poetry in the park itself without physically being there.

Staging playtesting and prototyping like this meant that I could do most of the work without being in the physical space, which was vitally important for maximizing the amount of work and the number of discrete iterations the piece was able to go through before its premiere.

The Boundaries between GPS Regions

A concrete example of a design consideration that could only be prototyped in-person is the way we transition the player between GPS regions. As described earlier, the heart of the piece's technical implementation is a series of geofences. When you're inside a geofence, you hear snippets of poetry that relate to that geofence. Some geofences are nested or have overlapping, and in those situations the output is a blend of the two with some weighting applied. But what is the subjective player experience of crossing the boundary from one region to another? At first I assumed this was a homogeneous problem, but the solution ended up needing to be different for different boundaries.

In Fort Mason, there is in fact a "fort" area. It's home to the largest parking lot in the park, so I assumed a lot of players would begin the piece there. One of the most straightforward ways to get from there to the main grassy area is to climb a set of stairs, but the staircase is fairly long and not that visually interesting; in early playtests, getting players to go up it was difficult, which made for a frustrating experience for them. Creating a distinct geofence region for the staircase turned out to be an effective way to convince players they were going the right way, and that exploration was a rewarding experience.

Conversely, there are a bunch of sub-regions within the fort that I didn't want players to even consciously notice. I wanted to generate poems, for example, that referenced when players were standing by the waterfront, but I wanted that transition to be a subtle one rather than an explicit threshold crossing. This meant doing nothing other than just letting the abutting regions each generate its own content.

As a final example, that grassy area above the fort neighbors a walled community garden. I didn't necessarily want to explicitly shepherd players into the garden, but I did want to amplify the feedback systems in place: players should be aware that something new awaited them if they kept walking, whether or not they did. This was especially important since the garden only has one entrance, so getting in requires conscious effort. The garden has a distinct soundscape: aside from the poetry, I swap out the subtle background audio of children playing for birds chirping, so that shift happening would be obvious. All I needed to do here was make the geofence for the garden slightly larger, so players would hear that shift before being properly within the garden walls; that proved enough.

A Side-Note: Neural Networks

Most of the procedural generation methods used in games and generative art tend to involve a human author providing opinionated scaffolding within which a computer can generate content. Whether you're writing a Tracery grammar or a procedural level generator, you're usually trying to find the right balance between hand-authored and computer-authored content.

Computational Flâneur instead generates all of its poetry via other means: an algorithm is trained on a large corpus of existing text (mid-20th century poetry in our case) and told to generate new text that looks like the existing text.

This sort of approach is common. Even if you're not formally familiar with Markov chains, you've likely seen "ebooks"-style Twitterbots that generate new tweets in the style of another account via a Markov chain. At a high level, a Markov chain probabilistically samples an existing corpus of text to generate new text. Given an input of a 2- or 3-word sequence, it tells you what word is statistically likely to come next. Repeat this a dozen times, with previous outputs as new inputs, and you have an original sentence that statistically resembles the original text.

Computational Flâneur doesn't use a Markov chain, but rather a character-based neural network (so-called "deep learning"). At a high level, this approach isn't that different from a Markov chain. The lower-level math of how to train a neural network differs, but from an aesthetic standpoint, you can think of these sorts of neural networks as essentially Markov chains on steroids.

Most importantly, a neural network is capable of having a broader sense of context. You can give a Markov chain more context by looking at longer sequences of previous words, but when you do so it tends to produce less-interesting output: if you ask a Markov chain with a relatively small data set "what word is most likely to come after this sequence of 5 or 6 words?," there are far fewer potential answers than if you only give it the previous 2 or 3 words.

A neural network, on the other hand, excels at looking holistically at the whole context of your corpus while also more heavily weighting the most recent generated text. This results in being able to produce text that seems superficially more "real," without degenerating into simply parroting back exact phrases from the training set. It's possible to, say, train up a char-rnn on a corpus of C source code and watch it spit out code that, while still nonsense, is syntactically valid to the point that a C compiler will accept it.

Text generated this way, via either Markov chain or neural net, tends to reveal itself as fake almost immediately and gets repetitive rather quickly. This style of procgen is a fairly poor fit for situations other than when you desire a "bot-like" aesthetic, which is why you tend to see this approach most often limited to things like Twitterbots.

In the case of *Computational Flâneur*, though, this is exactly what we're looking for. My goal was to create not something believable as actual poetry, but rather a series of words to paint the broad brush-strokes of "you are listening to poetry."

A System to Create Moments of Synchrony

This neural net-based poetry generator is a lot like a Twitterbot in that both are, in a sense, slot machines. They're variable reward systems that usually spew out relatively uninteresting content but every so often produce something deeply interesting and meaningful. What makes that work in the context of *Computational Flâneur* is twofold.

On a logistical level, when joyful moments of synchrony work, they really work. Seeing a Twitterbot make an unexpectedly coherent joke is one thing; hearing a poetry robot recite a couplet that directly references what you're seeing in the real world feels like magic, and all of the sensor research we'd done beforehand is focused on increasing that number of hits.

On a thematic level, the structure of *Computational Flâneur* means that those moments of synchrony serve to do more than just delight. Structurally, they're akin to a meditation gong: that surprise and delight pulls you out of your thoughts and deepens the connection you have to whatever physical elements of the park triggered that joy.

Cadence

Yet another useful lens for analyzing procedural generation systems is what sorts of larger emotional arcs you can create with them. People using procedural generation for more traditionally narrative experiences are typically placing their generated content within larger framing structures and thus have a large range of possibilities. Twitterbots, on the other hand, are endless streams of content. There's the occasional rare meta-arc of a bot, as in the case of the public discovering the human authorship behind @horse_ebooks, but the way Twitterbot content is consumed means that it's very difficult to do anything other than have each piece of generated content be its own isolated unit See also: Chapter 27, "Things You Can Do with Twitterbots."

With narrative games, there's an expectation that if users have been playing for a while, they'll save, quit, and return later. We as creators need to make sure that any individual play session is satisfying, but we can design an overarching narrative arc without caring about whether it'll take an individual player one sitting or 10. That doesn't work in the real world, where it's pretty essential that one "session" is a complete experience. You can design an experience that lasts over multiple visits to the same space, sure, but the effort required to physically return will generally make each visit feel much more like a distinct experience.

I wanted *Computational Flâneur* to be an experience where people could show up in the park, start anywhere, walk anywhere, and spend as much time as they wanted on it. As a result, the arc of a single session of *Computational Flâneur* felt far more like a Twitterbot than that of a narrative experience. Early attempts to overlay in background music to try to guide players toward some sort of emotional arc or conclusion felt so clumsily misguided that it wasn't even worth thinking about, say, whether there were ways to analyze player focus and interest in order to subtly nudge players to wrap up their walk.

The Effect of Cadence on Repeat Visitors

In theory, this Twitterbot-like flexibility gives the piece far more longevity and replayability for any individual player. Much as you can dip into a Twitterbot's feed whenever you want to see something new and delightful, this design makes it easier for players to come back to the park again and again and get something new and valuable out of the experience every time.

In practice, though, this didn't really happen. Most players' experience with *Computational Flâneur* was limited to visiting Fort Mason once and having a single journey. Encouraging repeat visits is (presumably) a combination of making it low-friction to come back (as is the case with a Twitterbot) and giving players active reasons to do so.

For the former, Fort Mason itself was likely part of the problem. For the people I know in San Francisco who enjoy this sort of experience, Fort Mason just isn't part of their daily life. It's not particularly out of the way, but it's just not a place the target audience visits unless there's an event actively bringing them there.

Another concern is that there wasn't anything about *Computational Flâneur* that actively rewarded repeat visits. I could imagine a version of the piece that encourages players to come back, especially since Fort Mason is so relatively easy to get to within San Francisco, but the version of the project that shipped didn't really have anything drawing people back other than the promise of more of the same.

BUT I JUST WANT TO KEEP MAKING DIGITAL THINGS!

Even if you have no interest in designing physical experiences, most procedural generation systems—particularly those that exist to aid storytelling!—don't exist in a vacuum. The challenges of integrating digital procedural generation systems with physical systems are in many ways extreme versions of the sorts of challenges you normally face with digital procedural generation.

We've discussed how to ensure that the weird inputs feeding your algorithm are understandable by players, rather than making the system feel purely random and how to manage other elements of the world that players may perceive as inputs but can't control and can't even be fully aware of. We've talked about the importance of breaking down your design problems into smaller composable sub-problems that can be built and tested more easily in isolation. We've even talked about ways we can eschew digital algorithmic systems entirely, creating the same sort of interesting emergent storytelling behavior we're after purely through static analog means.

Of course, there isn't a strict binary split between "digital" and "physical." Many of the approaches we've discussed are essential for building work on one extreme of the spectrum, just as they're not strictly necessary for purely digital works. But designing procedural generation systems that use sensor data or other forms of non-traditional inputs and output can be a lot subtler than experiences like *Computational Flâneur* built for walking around gigantic physical spaces. With anything like that, it's useful to keep thinking about how we can use all of the tools in our tool belt to provide delightful new experiences for players!

This page intentionally left blank

CHAPTER 18

Dirty Procedural Narrative in *We Happy Few*

Alex Epstein

Compulsion Games

W e Happy Few is a survival adventure game set in a 1964 England that lost World War II and was occupied for four years by the Germans. Now, everyone is taking happy pills—Joy—to forget the terrible things they did back then. You, the player, are not. So you have to flee. The world of *We Happy Few* is a small archipelago, of which the biggest islands are procedurally generated (Figure 18.1). In the playthrough of the first player character, Arthur, the ruined Garden District is two islands, and Hamlyn Village, where happiness is obligatory, is two more islands. (These numbers vary in the other playthroughs; it's a conceit of the game that big things change between playthroughs because the characters remember things differently.)

What's so challenging about telling stories in a procedural sandbox?

On one level, it's not. As in most single-player story-driven games, our three playable characters' stories make their major emotional turns in cinematics that play in a set order in a set sequence of locations. The train station may be north or south of the military camp, but we always send you to meet Ollie in the train station first; you can't even get into the Victory Memorial Camp until after that. Encounters are

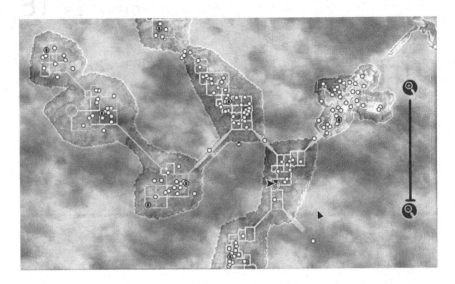

FIGURE 18.1   An example generated island of *We Happy Few*.

linear, too, controlled in Unreal by blueprints and map triggers that are enabled in a certain order.

So what am I even doing in this book?

Encounters and player character stories carry the most meaning when they are part of a rich, dense, immersive world.

We create a world through art, of course, and game mechanics, and through environmental narrative—letters, journals, graffiti, signs, and other building blocks of story—as well as systemic dialog—greetings, taunts, passive (overheard) conversations. When the people and places that populate the world have their own stories, the world feels particularly rich, dense, and immersive.

In a procedurally generated world, we don't know which bits of narrative the players are going to experience in which order. We don't know where they'll go or when. This is partly true of a handcrafted sandbox. We can guess that players will hit the near stuff first, but really, we have no idea what they'll do (except break the game if they possibly can).

Okay, we could try to force each story in the world to unfold linearly, using those pesky maps and blueprints. But it would be impossibly restrictive for everyone and an implausible amount of work. More interestingly, the world wouldn't feel real. In life, we get stories in anything but chronological order. Their bits are out of order; some bits are missing. The information we get may be anywhere from contradictory to entirely false. To make sense of them, we have to interpret.

YOU HAVE A SUPERPOWER

Fortunately, people are *extremely* good at making stories out of faulty information. Too good: many cognitive fallacies exist because our brains are hardwired to make stories out of the various things we see, whether or not they have anything to do with each other. The Gambler's Fallacy, for example, makes us think that a series of wins means the next throw of the dice will also likely be a win. Or that a series of losses means we're "due" for a lucky break. See also the Conjunction Fallacy, survivorship bias, the No True Scotsman assertion, *post hoc ergo propter hoc*, and so forth.

I believe that human beings are hardwired to make stories out of facts, just as we're hardwired to learn language. I wouldn't be surprised to learn that there's the equivalent of Broca's area for stories in the human brain. We are built to interpret the real world through stories. We are built to know how to feel through stories. A good story makes you feel something emotionally. I would even say that in a game it is very hard to make the player feel something other than frustration, boredom, flow, and satisfaction without a story.

Music and art can carry emotion on their own, of course. Music even seems to have its own part of the brain: some people who lose their ability to speak because of certain brain injuries can still sing songs with lyrics. Generally games use music to underscore emotions rather than to do the heavy lifting on its own, but a game without a story could rely on music to carry the emotions. Unfortunately, games are not used to asking players to make stories for themselves. Let's face it, these days, players are not often asked think very hard about stories. They are used to puzzling out the best approach to a devious puzzle or honing their combat reflexes, but they have come to expect that any bit of narrative they don't completely get will be laid out for them and explained.

Fortunately, we can rely on the superpower all human beings have of making stories out of disjointed facts. To populate our world with NPC stories, all we need to do is make a bunch of pieces of narrative and count on the players to put them together. Obviously, the pieces of narrative need to *be* part of a story, and we need to provide enough of that story to allow the players to find it, even if they missed some bits of it.

Obviously, they need to be *good* stories. A good story has

a character we care about,

with an opportunity, problem or goal,

who faces obstacles and/or an antagonist and/or character flaws,

who has something to lose (jeopardy), and

something to gain (stakes).

Obviously, they need to be stories that *can* be told out of order, meaning that their emotional value isn't destroyed by the wrong order. They can't depend on pacing, suspense, or surprise. We need to train the players of our game that we're not going to make all of the stories for them, and they should feel free to create.

MENTAL WORK MAKES EMOTIONAL ENGAGEMENT

We use what I call "dirty narrative," which demands interpretation from players. You give players pieces of narrative and let *them* figure out what story they belong to and how to put everything together. Dirty narrative is a handy approach even in a handcrafted game world with an enforced linear progression. But in a procedural sandbox, it is particularly *necessary*. When you let the player fill in the gaps between your bits of narrative, you make the player an active consumer of narrative, an investigator rather than a passive viewer. Paradoxically, the more mental work they do, they more emotionally engaged they become. Good dirty narrative stories have the same elements as all good stories. What distinguishes them is that, instead of trying to make as clear as possible what happened to whom, where, when and how, they intentionally demand interpretation.

PULL VS. PUSH

Some of the elements of dirty narrative are:

a. translucent lies

b. absences

c. mysteries

d. inconsistencies

e. tangents

All of these are "pull" story telling. I learned as a screenwriter that the least effective way of telling the audience anything is to just tell them. Pushing information at the audience pushes them away. But if you can get the audience to ask the questions before we answer them, then the audience pulls themselves into the story.

How did we use these in *We Happy Few*?

a. Translucent Lies

A translucent lie is a lie you can see through to the truth. What makes it translucent instead of transparent is that it tells you something about the liar, as well. For example, in *We Happy Few*, every proper decent citizen takes a happy drug, Joy (Figure 18.2), and wears a happy face mask to seem to be smiling. There's a jolly television announcer who always smiles and has nothing but good news.

You easily see through the lie to the truth. A society that insists that everyone is happy is probably not terrifically happy. (Is there anything creepier than being in a group of people who are all smiling all the time?) You also know something about the liar. This society must be hiding something terrible, or it wouldn't need to pretend happiness. (Funnily enough, in our development of the game, the masks and drugs came first. Our studio head wanted a game where everyone wore masks and took drugs. The lost war, the occupation, the fake "victory," the themes of memory and denial, all came up as we retro-engineered the world and its story from those two game mechanics.)

FIGURE 18.2   Jack with Joy, in *We Happy Few*.

b. Absences

There are no children in *We Happy Few*. That's not strange by itself: most video games don't have children. Children come in all different sizes, which makes them a pain to model, and people in real life get terribly upset when a game allows players to kill them. We didn't want to just not have children; we wanted a palpable *absence* of children. In our backstory, all the children of Hamlyn Village were sent away during the German occupation (Figure 18.3). So, in the Village, adults jump in puddles. They play Simon Says. The TV announcer encourages you to join in, because "if you don't, who will?"

In the burned-out Garden District, there are graffiti drawings of children with their faces scratched out. A crazy woman mutters, "What am I going to do with all the little shoes?" Someone has tucked spoons and plates into bed with children's toys. Maybe that abstraction is not powerful enough. "One death is a tragedy; a million is a statistic," as Stalin said. You quickly find the secret hidey-hole of one child, Sebastian Dainty, whose parents kept him off the train, along with their increasingly anguished letters after he failed to eat the birthday cake they left.

You can't see a black hole. But if there's enough stuff around it, you can't miss that it is there. Stars cannot orbit around nothing. Likewise,

FIGURE 18.3   A drawing in *We Happy Few.*

we can make the player spot the absence in our fictional world by showing how it distorts the things we can see.

c. Mysteries

Some mysteries are best left unsolved.

Our TV announcer jokes about Foggy Jack. Of course he doesn't exist. Women have certainly not been found dead in the street in the morning, with certain organs surgically removed. People warn each other not to be out after dark or Foggy Jack will get you! You might find an interrogation report in police headquarters about someone who hears someone in the fog saying Foggy Jack's catchphrase ("I'm afraid you've come to the end of your time.") You might find a suitcase full of engraved cards that say the same thing. Is he real? What is he? Who is he? I could tell you, but where's the fun in that? Remember the old horror movie rule: the monster in the shadows is scarier than the same monster in sunlight. The monster in the shadows is 10% special effects and 90% whatever each audience member fears most.

Where are the children now? Are they alive? Where did Sebastian go? That would be telling.

d. Inconsistencies

Our game tells three player character stories that overlap in time. Each of the three appears in the other two's stories. Three Arthur-Sally scenes, for example, happen in both Arthur's and Sally's playthrough. Oddly, in Arthur's story, the last two take place at Sally's lab. In Sally's story, they take place in an abandoned playground. In Arthur's story, he asks her, "How could you?" (Figure 18.4)

FIGURE 18.4   A man in *We Happy Few*.

She answers, "Because I liked him? Because he had that adorable beard? I don't know. There isn't a reason for everything." Which does not, let's face it, sound like an excellent reason, even if you don't know what he's talking about.

In Sally's story, she answers, "Because he took me in when my mum died? Because he was so generous? Because he said he loved me? I don't know, some things just happen, whether you want them to or not." (Figure 18.5)This is another kettle of fish entirely.

In Arthur's playthrough, his old crush Sally is adorable but flakey and maybe a little bit toxic. But in Sally's playthrough, it's Arthur who's the jerk.

Which is the truth? Who knows? How would anyone know? You can't measure both the velocity and the location of a particle. Everyone has their own version of events. It's not just an interpretation or explanation;

FIGURE 18.5 A woman in *We Happy Few.*

it's not just different answers to "why." It's an actual sequence of facts that contradicts someone else's sequence or someone else's facts.

Anyone who's been in a relationship long enough has had this argument:

"I told you [x]."

"You *never* told me [x]!"

In real life, most people's version of events makes them the good guy. "What is truth?" asked Pontius Pilate. It's an odd conceit of games that you can depend on what NPCs are telling you. That certainly is economical: you only need to get the information out once. But it is unnatural, and what is unnatural in a work of fiction is alienating. What's valuable about inconsistencies, when properly handled, is they are like translucent lies: the players not only figure out what they need to know, they also learn something about the various people telling them the various versions of the truth.

e. Tangents

In real life, people are the heroes of their own stories. They do not exist to tell you things. They do not exist to ask you to do things for them and then they will give you quest rewards. Of course, in a video game, quests need to be given somehow, and NPCs are a particularly fun way to get them. But the player can learn a lot more about other characters if those NPCs appear to be actively pursuing goals that have nothing to do with you and only *tangentially* relate to your goals. For example, you are trying to find the brilliant Dr. Faraday, and the two bobbies (Figure 18.6) working reception at headquarters know where she is. They refuse to tell you, but you overhear one of them telling the other that Bobby Hickinbotham, who's supposed to look after Dr. Faraday, feels so guilty about what's been done to her that he's gone to the Reform Club "to get his arse spanked."

This becomes important to you because you'll need to steal his ID (the quest item), but it is important to our world story because it shows how this society has people who feel so guilty they literally seek out punishment. How far we can go with tangents depends on the game's design philosophy. In a completely immersive, naturalistic game, that offhand comment, preserved in your journal, might be the only tip you

FIGURE 18.6   Two policemen in *We Happy Few*.

get about how to get to Dr. Faraday. You'd have to interpret the tangent for yourself.

More likely, "Find Bobby Hickinbotham at the Reform Club" becomes your next objective, complete with a map marker for the Reform Club and a tick box in the upper right of your HUD, so you do not, after all, need to interpret what you heard. The writer should be able to negotiate a compromise with the level designers so that the player who wants immersion can avoid some of the gaminess of quest giving, while the player who just wants to get to the next mission can avoid the verbal puzzle.

What these five techniques have in common, again, is that they require interpretation. We don't tell you, "There are no kids and here's why." We want you to notice the absence and ask why before we start feeding you clues. We don't tell you, "Here is a society where everyone takes a happy drug, and here's why." We start with characters accusing you of not taking your Joy, and then you start to uncover the reasons they're taking it. The best time to answer players' question is after they've asked it. If you answer it earlier, you're pushing it at them, and that pushes them out of the story.

There aren't really five distinct techniques. There are no hard boundaries between them. All dirty narrative could be boiled down to "something should be there but isn't" and "something's there that shouldn't be." The list is intended more to get you thinking about how we can challenge players to make their own stories out of the bits of narrative we've strewn around for them to find or rather, that we've put into the game for the procedural generation engine to strew around. If they do, they will pull themselves into our story.

DIRTY NARRATIVE IS DANGEROUS

Now, dirty narrative is dangerous. It's about breaking the rules of clear storytelling. What if people don't get it? Clear narrative is fairly bulletproof. If you have a character we care about, with something to do and challenges, who can win something and lose something, you can usually tell it all in order and people will be satisfied, if not necessarily blown away. Dirty narrative is "execution dependent," a screenwriting bugaboo that means "if this is done superbly, it could be brilliant, but if it's done less than superbly, it will be supremely awful." The Quality Assurance people periodically send me bugs about the inconsistencies and holes in NPC's stories. What if players just think we're being sloppy? But the upside is big. In procedurally generated worlds, we really need dirty narrative to encourage the player to make connections between the bits of lore we've made, but whose placement we can't control. However, training the player to make those connections is critical in any narrative game.

Video games have thousands of assets, but the real world has uncountably many, and we are aware of at least, say, billions of them. In any naturalistic game, we *need* the players to fill in the spaces between our paltry thousands of items (Figure 18.7). If they're waiting for the game to hand them everything they need to know, our world will not persuade them it's real. If we use dirty narrative, forcing them to interrogate and interpret our world, they may.

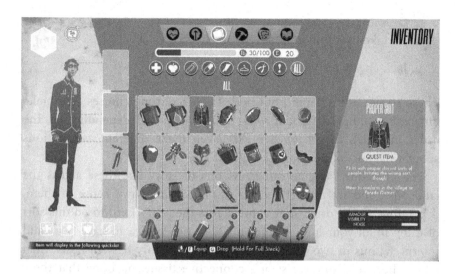

FIGURE 18.7 Inventory menu of *We Happy Few*.

THE HOLY GRAIL

Could there be procedurally generated story? That would be the Holy Grail, wouldn't it? Game narrative does not scale. Every bit has to be handcrafted. The player may experience a game with 31 possible endings as a choose-your-own-adventure. But the writer still has to write all 31, and making 31 stories that work is non-trivial. (Trust me on that one.) Faction-based narrative—where befriending a dwarf in the Iron Hills earns you a duel in Rivendell—can feel open and surprising and sandboxy. But someone still has to write all the branching forks of the story. If only we could procedurally generate story! Well, we can (e.g. *Dwarf Fortress*). We can generate a lore item that says that [select name of hero from a list of hero names] slew the terrible [type of monster] named [generated monster name], but that doesn't automatically make an emotionally engaging backstory. Only some choices are fun. If Dorothy stays safely in her storm cellar, she doesn't go to Oz. But a writer *could* craft story elements that have strong, but different, meanings in different orders. For example: Story 1:

a. Jack cheats on Jill,

b. Jill takes a job in another city,

Story 2:

    a. Jill takes a job in another city, and

    b. Jack cheats on Jill.

These stories are different, but both feel like strong choices. We make different assumptions about why things happened depending on the order in which they happened. We even make different assumptions about what sort of people Jack and Jill are.

The procedural engine can strew bits of story like these across the landscape, and we can let the players make their own sense of them, depending on the order they come across them. It's hard to do this sort of thing in all your lore. A story made of two beats can have two valid interpretations in two different orders. If your story has ten beats, then either they need to have strong connective tissue, meaning that there really is only one natural way to put the beats together, or it's going to become incoherent when you shuffle it. You can't just throw multivalent story elements out there for the player to play with, and expect each shuffle to give you *Oedipus Rex*.

We're not necessarily trying to create great non-player-character stories. We're trying to create an immersive environment. Each individual story doesn't have to be brilliant; it has to reveal things about the nature of the world. Whether or not Jill dumps Jack, the players are still in a world in which guys cheating is a problem. And we are trying to give value to replaying the game. For that we don't need every beat to be moveable. We just need a few permutations that allow the players to reconstruct different past events when, in later playthroughs, they hit a different assortment of story beats, or even hit the same beats in a different order.

The most important thing we gain is that we really are never sure if we have all the facts, if they're in the right order, or if we really understood what's going on. In a game, everything is theoretically knowable. In the real world, you can never be too sure. Just knowing you can't look up the ultimate answer on the Internet, because there is no ultimate answer, helps the players suspend their disbelief that they're looking in on a world, rather than just pushing electrons around.

CHAPTER 19

Beyond Fun in *Frostpunk*

Marta Fijak and Jakub Stokalski

11 Bit Studios

I hope it's safe to say that we're beyond arguing about whether games are just for fun. *That Dragon Cancer, This War of Mine, Train* and now *Frostpunk* are just a few examples of titles that eschew traditional boundaries of games-as-entertainment; these titles focus on themes (and mechanics) examining various aspects of human condition, traditionally unseen in mainstream titles.

Of course, games *are* entertainment. There is nothing wrong with focusing on the "mere pleasure" of juicy interaction, puzzles entertaining the mind or pure orgy of the senses as the main sources of value in games. Those can be worthwhile—letting us relax, faze-out, feel wonder or pleasure. Thankfully though, we're reaching the point at which we can be more nuanced. I sincerely hope that, as a medium, we're reaching the point where content of the game is more important than back-of-the-box feature sets and genre conventions. But what *makes* game content important, really?

MAKING SENSE OF THE WORLD

Humans see the world in stories. In fact, the ability to link events into coherent narratives is an automatic psychological process, one we can't shut off even if we wanted to. This allows us to make sense of events and our place in them. It allows personal growth and learning from experience. It allows for many cognitive mistakes too, but that's a discussion for another time (see Daniel Kahnemans' *Thinking, Fast and Slow* (2011, Farrar, Straus, and Giroux) for some chilling examples of cognitive automations and bias).

Would it be a problem to draw personal experience from different kinds of media? After all, poems, paintings, books, movies are all very different in form. We all use the same set of cognitive skills to experience them. Our brain always tries to search for meaning and coherent narrative in perceived phenomena, and the stories that touch us most deeply are those that revolve around human values.

There are many models for how stories are told, from the classic *Hero of a Thousand Faces* by Joseph Campbell to more modern takes like *Into the Woods* by John Yorke or *Story* by Robert McKee. In the West, these tend to revolve around central tenets of conflict and universal human values that are tested, from *Romeo and Juliet* to *Lord of the Rings*.

Think games are any different? Think again. Games' structure is cyclical, compared to linear media: where stories in books or movies are constructed through beats to scenes to sequences, to acts, games work in loops. Games have the immediate action-feedback loop; the tactical, short-term goal loop; the strategic long-term loop and even further, the social or emotional feedback loop and cultural meaning loop.[1] But whether we're thinking in story beats or looping structures, the *content* can still be about what makes classic stories so powerful: human values.

In fact, they already are. Games routinely place us in situations of life versus death. Victory or defeat. Progress or setback. It's just that these particular human values are extremely overused in games today. There is nothing wrong with them *per se*, just like there's nothing wrong with enjoying yet another summer blockbuster extravaganza. However, if we are to progress as a medium, we could and should, look further.

Take *This War of Mine*. While core loops were built on survival genre staples of resources (having versus not-having), and the long-term goal loop was about life versus death, there were many more nuanced situations that asked more subtle questions. Will you steal medications for your injured party member from an elderly couple, sentencing them to certain death? That's a multi-faceted conflict of mercy versus selfishness without a clear answer. Let's see how we tried to leverage less obvious human values and their conflicts to emotional effect in *Frostpunk*.

DEVELOPING FROSTPUNK

So all of this theory is great and exciting, but in the end we had to make a game, *Frostpunk,* to be precise. *Frostpunk* is a strange beast. The most succinct way to describe its vision would be something like: "a survival-city builder about what society is capable of when pushed to the limit." This statement proved fundamental to orienting ourselves in the tumultuous process of development.

From the very beginning we knew that *Frostpunk* would be a society-survival city building game, but what does that actually mean? We weren't sure. We had some vague ideas about tough choices, people in grim situations, personal sacrifices, etc. We read a lot of books on surviving in extreme conditions and watched movies and documentaries, so we knew what emotions we would like to invoke but not much beyond that. So, the frustration began.

Thankfully, we were in a comfortable situation and had something to rely on! We had previously made *This War of Mine,* which had a design people liked. They empathized with the dwellers, and it was really well received, so we thought it'd be easy to just do it again … and we were so, so wrong.

We knew that there would be tensions between different player motivations, when trying to mix the feelings of *This War of Mine* into the city-building genre. The city-building genre is, by definition, focused on soulless optimization and treating the city as a single entity to play with.[2] You see, most players don't have a problem bulldozing districts in *Cities: Skylines* in order to place a new highway. Yet we needed to help players engage with their populations as people and perhaps engage with becoming dictators; we knew this wouldn't be an easy task.

PROTOTYPE 1: SOCIETY

We started with the basics: the game is about a society. Great. But… what even *is* society? After tons of reading and discussions, we took Oscar Wilde's definition, which is that society does not exist at all: "Society exists only as a mental concept; in the real world there are only individuals".

This was actually a good starting point. We realized we didn't want to have society function as an abstract system; rather we wanted something derived from a group of individuals. We already had some basic city buildings and AI agents, so we started to describe them in more human terms.

Applying the Maslovian hierarchy of needs, we implemented a new system of basic psychological and safety needs. From that moment, every human AI agent had a set of needs that it would try to satisfy, or its frustration would grow and drive the agent to different behaviours. For example, if an agent had an assignment to a home then its shelter need would be met, but if not, then its frustration from lack of shelter would grow.

From time to time, we would have the system check on frustration levels, essentially asking all AI agents if they were "frustrated enough" with a given need to start protesting. If enough agents said yes, we would notify players with a question pop-up, asking something along the lines of, "Your people are angry and want homes. What will you do?"

Thus, a basic society was born. Food was similar in mechanics, but the system itself suggested a new, more profound question: "Should we eat the dead?" If players agreed, then a new food source would be available. Child labour was handled in a similar fashion. From time to time, the system would check if the children were tired and working and, if so, apply a chance for an accident to occur. If this happened, players could decide if they wanted to continue employing children or banish child labour.

If you've played *Frostpunk*, these questions should be familiar, but the form we used in the final game was quite different, as we hadn't yet invented the *Book of Laws*. They were simply little questions that would pop up now and then. This was our first prototype of society, and with great expectations, we started playtesting it. It didn't go well, but we gained some insight and feedback. There were two major problems:

1. There was absolutely no player agency. Those questions seemed to pop up at "random" times from players' perspective, so players could not plan their next move.

2. There was no overarching narrative. The questions were pulled from a random set with no beginning, middle or end, and players felt it.

Importantly, people liked the questions themselves, and it was already interesting to choose peoples' fate in such grim situations.

Prototype 1: Values Analysis

We implemented the foundations for solid city-building genre game-play: resource loops, sinks and faucets, etc., allowing us to build the economy by the book, with nothing particularly ground breaking. Of course, like all gameplay, this too was fundamentally about human values—but these values are pretty standard, as far as these two genres as concerned.

Survival-builder gameplay	
Reflective layer (emotional, cultural loops)	???
Long-term cognitive layer (strategic loops)	Life vs. death (winning vs. losing)
Short-term cognitive layer (tactical loops)	Having vs. not having (resource/building loop) Life vs. death (basic needs)
Visceral layer (action-feedback loops)	Safety vs. danger (cold) Having vs. not having (resource/building loop)

As you can see, there was nothing shocking; in fact, the reflective layer (the one that we had ambitions to fill with non-trivial content) was still largely empty. We wanted the society layer to provide thematic heft that would make *Frostpunk* stand apart. But how did the situation look at the end of Prototype 1?

Society gameplay	
Reflective layer (emotional, cultural loops)	???
Long-term cognitive layer (strategic loops)	???
Short-term cognitive layer (tactical loops)	???
Visceral layer (action-feedback loops)	Compassion vs. efficiency

Again, nothing spectacular. A lack of player agency and more nuanced content prevented this part of the game from playing any major role—yet. But the first hopeful signs were there: making decisions about burying people was interesting!

PROTOTYPE 2: PROPHET

Enriched with this knowledge, we started to make a new prototype. We left the problem of player agency for another time and decided to tackle the lack of narrative. But we didn't want to leave our systemic society-based approach, so to drive the narrative, a new need was introduced: "meaning of life". Yes, no joke, that was an actual systemic need, and, as you can expect, explaining it to players was a huge pain, but let's not get ahead of ourselves.

First, to make the feel of the questions better, we introduced a new interface approach. Rather than popping up on the screen, breaking the immersion and the city building experience, now the questions would be an integral part of the world (more or less). If certain conditions were met, a UI tracker would pop up over a building or an AI agent, and the player could click it to see the question.

So now we had a two-step flow: the call to action (CTA) and then the dilemma (the question). Technical edge-cases aside, the main problem was that people didn't feel the mood of the society as a whole. Sure, every citizen had frustrations, but there was no easy way to check how the whole society was doing. So we created a new element—the discontent. It was nothing sophisticated, just an average of frustrations of all citizens with some weights attached. We put a big red bar of that calculation on the screen so players knew how mad people were. A long red bar meant people were really mad, while a short red bar meant things were good. Simple as that.

With our new toys at hand, we started to construct a narrative arc, mostly based on the new need/frustration (meaning of life, aka fear or angst). Your people would lose their faith, and a new leader would show up to try to give them a purpose and lead them. We called this arc the Prophet.

The Prophet was a series of dilemmas connected loosely to the city building aspect of the game, but that could act mostly independently as a simple series of events on timers related to the meaning of life need. The story told players that people were afraid that they were not going to survive, and out of that fear, a movement was borne, focused around a mysterious guy called the Prophet. He promised them a chance for survival if they followed him. The player had some options for dealing with that problem, such as building guard stations and starting an investigation. On success, the player was presented with the choice of what to do with the Prophet. Public execution was one of the choices, but letting him go was also on the table.

So again, we started the playtesting. Everyone in the company was asked to play and to fill out a survey. This way we knew if there was even a slight chance of narrative building in their heads. Remember that between those scripted events, there were long stretches of city building play, so we weren't actually sure that the narrative part was happening in players' heads.

The feedback was mixed. We found that the narrative was in fact building in the players' heads, but it was completely separate from the city building part. People felt as if they were playing two separate games: a city builder and a pick-your-own-adventure book. We decided that for the next attempt, we should make stories shorter than Prophet and more connected to base game loops.

There was another discovery, mostly from hearing people discuss it over coffee. They wondered if it was a good thing to kill the Prophet. There was no uniform answer. Some people said that in such a dire situation this decision is a no brainer and that the survival of the society is most important. Others argued the total opposite, saying that of course survival is important but not at the cost of humanity and that killing, even in that situation, is not acceptable.

Those discussions were fascinating to witness. We knew we had found something important. So learning from Machiavelli, a new core question for the game was born: "The end justifies the means. ... Or does it?"

Translating to game design, how far should players go to ensure survival, and how many of their morals should they sacrifice in the process? We knew that it should be an open-ended question and that we should not give a straight answer, especially since on that topic, even this chapter's co-authors could not agree.

Prototype 2 Values Analysis

At this point, we knew that making decisions about our people was interesting; we knew that the question of whether ends justify the means is interesting, and we knew that short narratives were interesting. However, we still lacked player agency.

Let's take a look at the values side of things again. We developed the survival-builder alongside the procedural storytelling engine as well. There was much more content, the basic gameplay was more solid, providing more developed decision spaces, but as far as values went, nothing major had changed. We wanted the society to provide the meat.

Society gameplay loops—Prototype 2	
Reflective layer (emotional, cultural loops)	???
Long-term cognitive layer (strategic loops)	???
Short-term cognitive layer (tactical loops)	???
Visceral layer (action-feedback loops)	Compassion vs. efficiency Crossing the line vs. keeping to your morals Good of one vs. good of the many

There was still hardly any long-term gameplay, since all decision-making focused on the visceral layer of interaction. But we had more content to prove that we could mine themes of the game for non-trivial subject matter, provided we could treat it with respect and appropriate tone (more on that later). We felt we could deliver good content, but we were still missing tools to create *actual gameplay* out of the human values conflict that we gravitated toward. This was to be addressed by Prototype 3.

PROTOTYPE 3: PLAYER AGENCY

We had a pretty solid city building game that was growing, so to do some things in parallel and not to burden the rest of the team, this prototype had some steps developed outside the main game.

We wanted to give agency to players, so they could decide what decisions to make and, crucially, when. So we knew we needed a new part of the game that would allow such decisions, which would eventually become the *Book of Laws*. But at this stage we only had those CTAs popping up from time to time.

We started with a mental division between decisions about:

- individuals, which would still pop up in game space (as CTAs) and

- huge issues like child labour or corpse disposal, which would be enacted as laws with a different flow.

How should such an "issues" system work? We wanted every law to have an impact on the core gameplay (new buildings, new abilities, new employment options, etc.) but also to interact with the society part. We already had discontent, so we added a new part, called "agreement for reforms". If players made a controversial decision, the discontent would rise, while if the decision was desired by everyone, the discontent would fall.

After preparing a list of laws we would like to implement in the first pass, we found that this lacked nuance. Our people were in two states: mad or not mad. It seemed that this was not enough for more complex situations in our society. So we started to iterate.

First we created a simple list of laws (child labour, cemeteries, sawdust in food, moonshine and so on) and a set of new parameters for our individuals, so our people were described by fear, hope and discontent. Enacting different laws would change those parameters. If discontent or fear reached maximum level or hope reached zero, the player would lose. This gave us more space for the cost of different laws and integrated the society into the core gameplay loop, because of the chance of failure.

We played around a little more and found that it was hard to decide which things had an impact on fear, especially since it seemed that we all treated fear as counter to hope. So we dropped fear and started to play instead with this 2D space described by hope and discontent. We weren't sure at first how to approach agents on the extreme ends of our 2D space. People with full discontent but also full of hope? People with no discontent but with also no hope? Questions like this allowed us to fully understand what we mean when we say hope and discontent. This was an important step, because we felt these definitions should be coherent along the whole game. If we didn't know 100% what we meant by them, we should not expect the player to know.

So we asked ourselves and finally came to the conclusion that hope is a "will to live", or "how much agent believes in survival". Meanwhile, discontent is more or less being angry with the ruler. Under these definitions, agents with threshold values became clearer. People with high hope and high discontent strongly believe that they will survive, but not with that ruler. People with no hope but no discontent have all of their needs met but don't see a purpose in surviving, as they know that tragedy and/or death will come soon enough.

This concept stayed with us through to the end of development. We added one more mechanic: if the discontent is really high, then eventually people start losing hope, but it's balanced to be subtle, not a core loop. So hope and discontent are more or less independent.

At this point we had laws and some basics of the system, but laws were just a big pile of things to pick from, without any structure or sense of progression. It was hard to tell if you were leading your people in a direction. So we started to build a second prototype of laws. This time we focused more on flow and enacting laws than on the systems working underneath. To be honest, we reinvented the wheel here and tried some weird book-inspired interfaces and flows, including a big dynamic system for the interactions, but we ended up scrapping them for a simpler structure similar to a standard tech tree. It was nothing fancy, just a tree-like structure with a cooldown (so you couldn't enact all of the laws at once) and a rule that every law that introduced was permanent.[3]

These iterated prototypes taught us that we needed a hope bar underneath the discontent and a new tech-tree like structure—the "Book of Laws". After an art treatment, we were ready for another set of playtests! Again, everyone in the company was asked to play, and a survey was attached. We sent it out and waited. And after a while, the feedback gates were opened again.

People liked it! Players felt they had agency, and they started to think about their next moves with the society. They knew what they needed and planned accordingly, managing discontent and hope in the process. Of course, there were things they did not like, especially the way laws were connected to each other. That was a strange observation for us. We knew that we needed to have progression between the laws, so that players knew they were building something, but we didn't understand how important that was for them. So we started to dig around that subject, and keeping in mind the key question (does the end justify the means?), we found something. Going through some sociological books, we found the boiling frog story, and it was perfect!

The boiling frog is a cautionary metaphor of gradual, creeping normalization. It goes like this: if you take a frog and put it in boiling water, it will jump out to save its life, but if you put the frog in cold water and gradually increase the temperature, the frog will not sense it, and you will have a great frog soup. From a biological perspective, this is nonsense, because the frog will run away during both methods, but the metaphor illustrates how humans can accept radical changes to their political and social situations. Have you never wondered how a totalitarian state is born? A few things need to happen, but "boiling the frog" is one of them. You cannot wake up in the morning and decide that everyone who likes pineapple pizza should be incarcerated, but things of similar absurdity have happened many times in history. You just have to do it slowly, with every law pushing the boundary of morality a little bit more. You stretch it and stretch it, and suddenly this law is not as ridiculous as it seems. It's just a logical conclusion of laws that came before.

This is why it is so important to look at our governments when they are making those small changes that are just outside our comfort zone, because they will eventually add up to a bigger change, and then it can be too late to react. This concept perfectly supported the questions already in our game. We started to construct laws around this, especially a second group of laws, which we called the purpose laws. We wanted every step to be a little bit more than the previous one. If players do not stop and think about what they are doing, they can end up in a very bad place, and the same goes for their society. People in the game would revolt if players started with executions of prisoners, but if it's a logical step after many other smaller steps, then it's a different story.

We also had to decide which laws to put in the game. We had an initial list from the first prototypes, but that wasn't enough to fill the trees (first three, then finally merged to two). We did extensive research to fill in the gaps and add substance to support the narrative we wanted to create. The final set of laws is relatively self-contained but certainly not complete. It's not, by any stretch, every possible decision in the situations depicted in the game, but we determined that this set of laws gave players a scope of decisions broad enough for player agency but narrow enough to tell the stories we wanted to tell.

At this point, we had a key question of ends justifying the means, the concept of boiling the frog, a new system of player agency and the knowledge that short stories were interesting.

Prototype 3 Values Analysis

The Book of Laws allowed us to finally push a lot of decision-making into short- and long-term strategic loops. Players were able to strategise around decisions, but their consequences weren't just economical in nature; they touched much more subtle and less obvious human values. This is what we wanted all along.

Society gameplay loops—Prototype 3	
Reflective layer (emotional, cultural loops)	???
Long-term cognitive layer (strategic loops)	Crossing the line vs. keeping to your morals
Short-term cognitive layer (tactical loops)	Extortion vs. balance
Visceral layer (action-feedback loops)	Compassion vs. efficiency
	Good of one vs. good of the many

By now development was pretty advanced, yet we still didn't feel we had nailed the reflective layer. Sure, there was a lot of unusual content for a city-builder-survival hybrid, and it was fun to navigate it, but at the end of the day, some achievement-focused players didn't really "get it". There were few dilemmas focused on the (again, further developed and by now pretty deep) economic gameplay. We doubled down on the types of decisions players made and their consequences to try to create a more permanent, pervasive change in the society. We wanted to make players notice the subtle cues that their choices were not *just* about gathering coal.

FINAL STRETCH

At last, we had a solid foundation, but we started to realize that it was important to show a permanent change to our people. We wanted players to see the consequences of the laws they made, so they could ask themselves if this was the society that they wanted to create, and if this was a society worthy of survival. So, we added consequences to every single law.

We had a neat system for showing stories on a personal level, using those CTAs and small dilemmas. Building on that, we created short narrative arcs, to show how different laws affected the lives of the individuals. We especially wanted to show that some laws were good for the survival of the group but at a great cost for a single person. For example, radical treatment might be good for medical efficiency but could leave someone disabled for life unnecessarily.

As always, with new content comes a new problem: tone. It would have been easy for us to write the most dark, brutal and absurd consequences for every law. But why? And for what? We didn't want to be sad and dark for the sake of being sad and dark. We wanted to show complex humans in complex times. So we tried to write on the other end of the spectrum, with delicate and subtle consequences. Most of these still had depressing undertones, but then the problem was that usually only the person who wrote them understood them. So we found ourselves in quite a pickle. We had a spectrum of tone for our consequences. One end was dark, grim and cartoonish, so every time one of those would pop up it broke the immersion; on the other end we had consequences so subtle that no one could understand them. We decided the key was to find the perfect spot for our game on that spectrum.

I would be happy to tell you that we then used advanced math and estimated the perfect tone on the first try, but that is simply not true. We used brute force. We rewrote it and rewrote it and rewrote it, and finally after weeks we found something we all felt comfortable with. We finally felt the consequences showed something important, not in an obvious way but also not as dark comedy.

We felt pretty good with the place at which our systems and content arrived. But at the beginning of this chapter, I wrote about the empathy for individuals that was in *This War of Mine*. Did we manage to create that in *Frostpunk*? We weren't sure. We started intensive playtesting with external playtesters and … no. There was not much empathy for those little people, but there was something much more interesting happening with our players' post-playthrough reflection. I know, it doesn't sound sexy, but hear me out.

Players did not feel the *in the moment empathy,* but after they finished playing, they started to reflect on the decisions they made. They questioned their own morals and asked themselves if there even was a right choice in such times. That post-playthrough reflection was very interesting for us, so we wanted to support it even more.

The endlog was designed to support this feeling. We didn't want to give answers; we just wanted to support the question, so we did the only thing that we could: we showed players what they'd done, their whole playthrough, and we asked them, "Was it worth it?"

Society gameplay loops	
Reflective layer (emotional, cultural loops)	**What does crossing the line mean?**
Long-term cognitive layer (strategic loops)	Crossing the line vs. keeping to your morals
Short-term cognitive layer (tactical loops)	Extortion vs. balance
	Compassion vs. efficiency
Visceral layer (action-feedback loops)	Good of one vs. good of the many

This proved to us that, at least for some players, we had finally found the reflective layer of interaction.

We were pretty happy with the result. Along the way it had become obvious that *Frostpunk* would be a much more "brainy" game than *This War of Mine,* relying on reflection rather than simple empathy for its emotional impact. It seems that we succeeded, at least to a degree.

Did we nail it 100%? Of course not. There were many reviews and opinions that corroborated our testing: people reflected on what they did to survive, asked themselves big questions about crossing the invisible line: whether that was how authoritarian regimes formed, and whether that means that anyone is a potential dictator under the right circumstances. That's all we could have ever asked from a game aiming to provide more than "just" entertainment.

But there were others that didn't "get it". They focused on the economical gameplay and completely skimmed over the society layer. They didn't notice the people, or they viewed the content of *Book of Laws* and its consequences purely in light of gameplay and goals.

And that's OK, because that means that it's possible to nail it even better next time. The game did tremendously well, both financially and critically, but the fact that some people were not convinced shows that there is more room to provide non-trivial concepts in games. It also shows that players are receptive toward those concepts, praising and enjoying an experience that can hardly be described as just *fun*, an experience that at least to some degree tries to transcend traditional genre and form conventions. Ultimately, for us as creators, it shows that it's worthwhile making worthwhile games.

NOTES

1 See Michael Sellers' excellent book *Advanced Game Design: A Systems Approach* for a coherent taxonomy of game structure.
2 It's worth noting the authors feel this is a deeply satisfying activity.
3 We added permanency of laws for simplicity in the first iteration, but it stayed.

This page intentionally left blank

CHAPTER 20

Procedural Storytelling in *Dungeons & Dragons*

Steven Lumpkin

Guerrilla Games

T abletop role playing games (TTRPGs)—like *Dungeons & Dragons* —are a fascinating design space. In an industry like ours, where product release cycles regularly stretch to the half-decade mark at the high end, and even at the low end rarely compress lower than 6 months, a tabletop role playing game can offer creators the opportunity to rapidly iterate on their creative output. More than that, our table offers us the opportunity to test and explore the very essence of the creative process itself. In the era of Twitch and Critical Role, when the fifth edition of *Dungeons & Dragons* is growing massively in popularity and profitability, if you haven't begun exploring this fascinating tool, let me be the first to encourage you to do so. This chapter will explore some of the tabletop role playing games available to you and show examples for integrating procedural generation as a tool into your creator's toolkit. Finally, we'll tie it all together by discussing what the experience of creating content through a highly procedural, improv-heavy process can teach us about the nature of player stories, player engagement, and procedural generation's goals, risks, and successes.

If you've never played a tabletop role playing game before (henceforth, TTRPG), then very quickly, the simple, overly reductive definition I will give you is that it's a collaborative story-telling experience, commonly in a high-fantasy setting of elves, wizards, and dragons.

One player is cast in the role of the "game master," the primary storyteller (also called a dungeon master, master of ceremonies, or other lofty titles depending on the game being played). The game master is responsible for creating the plot as well as arbitrating the rules, and each of the other three to six players control a single character throughout the story.

Like all good games, the best TTRPG sessions focus heavily on player agency and (in stark contrast to video games, where verbs are tightly defined) the only limits imposed on player capabilities in most TTRPGs are those that make sense in the fiction: "No, you can't climb a tree; there's no tree nearby" or "Well, you can try to climb that tree, but the dragon is raking its claws down your armor right now, so it's gonna be real hard." TTRPGs are a conversation after all, where the game master presents a scenario ("The bartender fixes you with a steely glare, and says 'shame about those murders out in the forest, eh?'"), which the players then promptly ignore in their immediate response ("I tell the bard to play 'Free Bird!'" "I run outside, I wanna steal that fancy horse in the stables!" "Do we have any Cheetos??").

When faced with the challenge of telling a story that incorporates 3 to 6 distractible players with their own interests, game masters can often fall prey to what's called "railroading" the players, forcing them along the intended story experience: "Uhhh, the bartender follows you outside! He's saying something about murders in the forest, when suddenly a shadowy cloaked figure steps up behind him and stabs him! 'You'll never find my forest lair,' the figure snarls, then runs off!" This can be an intensely frustrating experience for everyone involved. So let me assure you: there is a better way, and it shares many features with procedural generation.

If you want to dip your toe into TTRPGs as a story creation mechanism, allow me to suggest that your first stop be a game called *Dungeon World*, by Adam Koebel and Sage LaTorra. Not only are the rules available for free online (google "dungeon world gazetteer"), but also it requires no preparation time before your first session, is set in the commonly popular high-fantasy world of elves/wizards/dragons, and features simple and easy-to-understand rules. You and three friends could sit down and start playing it tonight, if you wanted. More than that, *Dungeon World* introduces game masters to a few pieces of technology that are missing from the classic *Dungeons & Dragons*, and for those of us passionate about procedural storytelling, these pieces of technology are vital. I'd like especially to talk about Moves, Dangers, and failing forward.

MOVES

Moves are the in-game fictional-mechanical actions that both the players and the game master can take. When a player says "I scan the sides of the canyon, looking for any sign of an ambush," that's a Move probably Discern Realities. Moves, you see, are often a bit ambiguous and can be negotiated as to the exact action that's called for by the fiction, in a number of circumstances. Similarly, a player might say, "I thrust my sword into the goblin's chest!", then roll dice, getting a 12, hitting the monster. That's a Move called Hack and Slash.

The game master can also make Moves, which may be entirely narrative or mix narratives and mechanics: "Suddenly, the ground below you groans and shifts, and you hear a hollow roar echo from deep within the earth" would be Show Signs of an Approaching Threat. Alternatively the game master might say, "Okay, you slay the goblin, but remember how the ceiling was shaking and dust filtering down? Chunks of stone break loose crashing down on you, and you take 5 damage," that's Deal Damage (or maybe Use a Location Move).

Notice here that Moves can be entirely narrative, especially on the game master's side, or they can trigger mechanics: dice rolls, threats advancing, and others. A Move can be triggered by:

A mechanical change: "It's been long enough, I'm advancing the clock for the Necromancer Cabal (mechanical change). ... I guess I need to have them make a Move", or

A narrative situation: "Well, showing signs of the approaching threat, the buried dragon, weakened the ceiling. ... I guess I need to make the locations Move to have the rocks fall!".

Both players and game masters have pre-set lists of Moves they can choose to execute—whenever it feels convenient or when the fiction seems to call for it or (especially) in response to players making failed rolls. The game master is given a lot of flexibility in terms of choosing the pacing of the Moves and how much to use "soft Moves" (like warning signs) versus "hard Moves" (like dealing damage), and this is what allows different game masters to develop their own personal and dramatically different styles. The game master is encouraged to make their Move entirely through the in-game fiction and never to name it out loud. The game master's list looks like this:

- Use a monster, danger, or location move

- Reveal an unwelcome truth

- Show signs of an approaching threat

- Deal damage

- Use up their resources

- Turn their Move back on them

- Separate them

- Give an opportunity that fits a class's abilities

- Show a downside to their class, race, or equipment

- Offer an opportunity, with or without cost

- Put someone in a spot

- Tell them the requirements or consequences and ask

What I like about this list of Moves is it provides game masters with a framework, a set of pre-established categories to draw from when building tension in their game. "Use up resources" can mean different things when trying to pick a lock or climb a cliff or find a way through a dark maze, but the consequence is similar in each circumstance. A lock pick breaks, a potion bottle breaks from a fall against a ledge, or a torch snuffs out and a new one is needed.

Especially interesting in the list of game master Moves is the fact that they're all deeply narrative structures. They're not concrete events; they're narrative categories that can inspire us, as game masters, to generate the concrete events that we need on the fly during play. The game rules tend to constrain what seems "fair" in terms of consequences (a goblin's dagger deals a previously designed and specified amount of damage, for example), and the fictional situation often builds to a breaking point that calls for a Move from the game master who, though free to choose from the full and broad categories above, is probably encouraged via what makes sense in the story to choose from a smaller subset of possible actions that just seem to flow from the current fictional point. The amount of narrative information available to the game master intersects with the broad category of possible Moves to inspire the game master's decision-making.

DANGERS

Dungeon World proposes tracking high level pressures against the players' heroism in the form of something it calls fronts (as in "fighting on two fronts"), each of which is composed of a collection of Dangers. Dangers, in *Dungeon World*, are clusters of fictional-mechanical information that powerfully allow for the game master to build a story that grows along with the players, no matter what their actions or inactions may cause in consequence. Let's break down the anatomy of a Danger. Here's the high level:

- Type—what general sort of danger is it?
- Identity—what, specifically, is this danger?
- Impulse—what does this danger ultimately want?
- Moves—how does this danger like to behave toward its enemies?
- Grim portents—how will this danger proceed, if unchecked?
- Impending doom—how will this danger alter the game state, if it gets its way?

Let's drill into each of these parts a bit more.

There are five proposed base types for Dangers: ambitious organizations, planar forces, arcane enemies, hordes, and cursed places. Broadly, choosing the type implies a few things about the fundamental nature of our Danger, and it unlocks further choices.

Each type has a collection of possible identities, each with its own impulse. For example, the identity of an ambitious organizations type of danger could be a misguided good (impulse: to do what is right, no matter the cost), a thieves guild (impulse: to take by subterfuge), a cult (impulse: to infest from within), or more. The identity tells us just what kind of thing this Danger is, and its impulse gives us a fictional motivation for what this thing is trying to accomplish. When we say "Right, our sleepy town is struggling with a cult," we already know the kinds of things that are probably happening behind the scenes.

Each type also has a series of Moves that it can make. Ambitious organizations can make Moves such as attack someone by stealthy means (kidnapping, etc.), attack someone directly (with a gang or single assailant), observe a potential foe in great detail, and more. Consider these Moves the common ways that this type likes to behave toward its enemies. Our cult might have dead carrion crows following our players everywhere or might suddenly orchestrate the disappearance of a key contact with the town guard.

Next, each Danger (or collection of Dangers) has a pre-determined sequence of events, called grim portents. This is a five- or six-step sequence of events that establishes how the situation would progress in a world where the players didn't exist, but it also tells us what will happen if the players are too slow or fail to discover important clues. The Danger in question might even decide to step up its pace, when the players confront the town priest, maybe the cult skips past "Harvest Bones from Old Quarry" and goes straight into "Invoke the Rain of Blood" territory! Finally, the impending doom sets out the end state of the world, from this danger (or collection of Dangers) going unchecked. If the cult gets its way, the end result in the immediate environment is tyranny; our peaceful village has been enslaved, the dead taking the rightful place of the living.

What impresses me about Dangers, as a game master, is that they're almost like a class in a programming language: a pre-defined structure that I can fill however I want, that does similar useful things for me no matter how I fill it. If my players do something unexpected and I'm at a loss for what happens next, I can look at my Dangers and ask myself,

"What's each Danger's instinct? How could that press against the players? Should I advance a Danger's grim portents? What kind of Moves could I make here?" All of the questions that arise during play seem to naturally pull their answers from the information that a Danger organizes, just as procedural algorithms pull from pre-established content blocks to provide to players in a video game.

The interesting thing that we, as game designers, can pull from Dangers in a game like *Dungeon World* is just how narrative some of the Moves can be (especially Danger or game master Moves). "Show signs of an approaching threat" is narratively incredibly broad. It offers no immediate action to the players but serves as a visible notice that things will get bad soon, either due to the players' continued inaction or as a result of their pursuit of their current course of action. This is the real power of playing at a table with a creative game master: the brain's pattern recognition machine can see opportunities on the fly, grab them, and build them into rich narrative experiences. A framework like Dangers makes this process even easier. As game masters, we don't need to pre-define all of the possible "signs" of each danger's "approaching threat," but as game developers, we could build that list!

Signs of Approaching Threats

	Cult Leader Sylvar	The Demon, Vorilex	The Risen Dead
1	An acrid chemical smell, magic broken free from traditional confines.	Sulfur and brimstone on a thick morning fog.	A grief-stricken widower claims his late wife came to visit him last night.
2	A flock of a hundred ravens, all dead, eyes staring from tree branches.	Every dog begins barking at 1:00 am and then runs and hides exactly 13 minutes later.	A hunter swears—SWEARS—his arrow pierced the deer's heart but can't find her body.
3	The sound of nails on a chalkboard, heard in your mind.	A thunderstorm super-cell, its heart glowing a deep magma red.	The tavern keeper refuses to go into the basement, after scraping sounds come from the walls.
4	Every religious symbol in town cleft in two one night.	An exceptionally pious young boy sleepwalks to the quarry's edge.	A woman caring for her deathly ill husband claims he's recovered.

FAILING FORWARD

Though these words aren't strung together in just this way in the *Dungeon World* rulebook, *Dungeon World* is a game that relies on the concept of "failing forward," the idea that when players fail at something, it should advance the story, rather than stop it. (See also: Chapter 7 on "narrative momentum".) This is one of the main ways the game master is allowed to make Moves: when the players fail on their roll or when they roll a success with consequences. In traditional *Dungeons & Dragons*, failing to pick a locked door simply means the players are blocked at that particular juncture and must find another way around, at least, according to the rules as provided by the rulebook. In *Dungeon World*, if players fail on a roll to pick locks, the rules give me responsive options. I could "show signs of an approaching threat" and say "You hear the heavy breathing and thudding footsteps of an ogre coming down the passage behind you."

In addition to the game master making Moves based on player failures, there's another requirement for the game master to follow: the "Moves snowball." The game master's Moves should snowball, starting small and getting bigger and bigger until they smash into the players like an avalanche. What at first was a simple "sign of approaching threat" (e.g., a flock of crows darkening the sky) turned into a soft Move where the cult stole away a key guard contact, which turned into a more threatening Move with the cult keeping tabs on players through carrion crows- which can turn into an ambush by Cult Leader Sylvar himself.

These two tenets tell us when we should make Moves and which Moves come first versus which Moves follow. Essentially, the rules of the game keep ratcheting up the pressure against players at regular intervals, pulling both fictional events and their mechanical consequences from sets of pre-determined lists of possible options, a lot like procedural generation in a video game.

A number of other games are in the same game design family as *Dungeon World*, and each of them plays with these elements in slightly different ways. If you'd rather play in a post-apocalyptic *Mad Max* wasteland, *Apocalypse World* is the progenitor of the powered by the apocalypse system that *Dungeon World* uses. *Blades in the Dark*, in contrast, is a game about playing a gang of thieves in a steampunk city haunted by the ghosts of the past. These two games draw on the same category-based sources of inspiration as *Dungeon World*, empowering the game master to be creative on the fly by providing clear guidance for what categories of events to provide and when.

Stars without Number, by Kevin Crawford, is a TTRPG set in the far future of space travel, laser pistols, and alien species. Not only does it provide a framework for generating an entire star system out of a series of rolls (including multiple planets, with their own cultures, tech levels, alien species, and more), it provides a framework for the game master to "play out" sequences of events between play sessions, allowing the world to change and advance over time. All of these features share DNA with procedural generation, using die rolls to inject randomness into pre-defined sets of possible outcomes.

My own preferred style of *Dungeons & Dragons* is called *the West Marches*, a "hexcrawl" where players explore around an open world commonly drawn onto hexagonal graph paper. As players crawl from hex to hex, exploring for adventure, I make checks against encounter charts. Players might encounter orcs in the plains, vicious living plants in the forest, or undead crocodiles in the swamp. Beyond monsters, players might encounter strange static energy storms or a great murder of crows all cawing the names of the recently dead. As I prepare for play, I pre-seed each of these options onto tables with their own weight that I roll on as players explore, essentially infusing *Dungeons & Dragons* content creation (traditionally highly authored) with procedural techniques. This marriage of the procedural and the authored fills my mind with more interconnected options than I could have thought up on the fly, allowing the pattern recognition machine that is our brain to recognize elements that line up and assemble a compelling experience out of them.

What I love about this style of *Dungeons & Dragons* is how it leaves room for discovery on my side of the table as well as on the players' side. When we all sit down, none of us knows what's going to happen in today's game. My players probably have a loose goal in mind, but on the way there, the game's rules interact with the procedural content generator in ways that create story. Even more, player actions clash with details of the prepared game world and enemy motivations to build narrative connections that our brains can rely on to incorporate random dice rolls as naturally arising events that are tied to the story, rather than as arbitrary mad lib interjections.

Let's talk about a recent example. My players were exploring the forest to find a trio of lizards worshipping a false god, a boast one of them had made after drinking from a magical drinking horn (the boast itself a randomly rolled result!). They made their way into the forest, encountering a quartet of (randomly rolled) Orcs, and then getting ambushed by a (randomly rolled) van-sized burrowing praying mantis called an Ankheg, both fights costing them spells and hitpoints to overcome, resources that are difficult to recover. When they finally made it into the forest and got ambushed by a (randomly rolled) set of living plants, one of my players correctly judged that his dwindling resources would benefit from avoiding this fight and set out with negotiations.

To my amused surprise, the *Monster Manual* rulebook I pulled these from assigns these plant creatures as speaking the common tongue. On the fly, I had to come up with a motivation for these living plants to be attacking interlopers into their territory. I decided, somewhat arbitrarily, that they wanted to secure the primacy of plant life and thus wanted to slay flesh-bound creatures, but they weren't picky about what, exactly, was killed. With that, some clever bargaining on my players' side, and some lucky dice rolls, my party negotiated safe passage through the forest; players would do some killing for these plant creatures, in exchange for safe passage. This was all a surprising turn of events that was made possible only by the roll of the dice (THIS many of THAT monster type) crossed with my players' dwindling resources pressuring them to play smarter and find outside-of-the-box solutions that would retain more of them.

From here, however, my knowledge of the world I had built was enough to let my creativity step in; what these plant creatures wanted specifically was the death of a basilisk that I had placed in an adjacent zone during preparation. As my players slowly made their way past old, crumbling statues of previous adventurers, and the knowledge of their foe slowly dawned on them, they began to hatch a plan to dig a pit trap and lure the basilisk into it with a handful of well-placed illusions, slaying it while they had it at a disadvantage. The battle was fierce, and one of them succumbed to its gaze and turned to stone—definitely a source of future adventure—but at the end of the day, the party was victorious. What they don't know yet, though, is that this basilisk was itself the false god that the aforementioned trio of lizards was worshipping ... And now I have something interesting to build future events on.

Even in this story, we can see the kinds of frameworks that allow procedural content generation to be valuable. Procedural content, whether for computer games or tabletop role playing games, relies on our brains as pattern recognition machines and storytelling machines. The most powerful procedural content in computer games comes from content that seems to imply a story: a dwarf mourning the loss of her spouse in the recent elephant attack gains sudden inspiration, carving a beautiful elephant-tusk spear, engraved with a dwarf weeping before an elephant; the dwarf is supplicating; the elephant has a fearsome gaze.

Likewise, at the table, the best use of procedural content is to inject randomness into the pattern recognition and storytelling machines of our brains. Of course, these plant creatures want something; they hate something nearby. Of course these wolves are following you; you've been smoking bear meat for rations from your recent fights. At the table, the most unexpected events can become fodder for our creative minds to open up to the possibilities at play and tell stories that we never would have come up with on our own, such as:

Yes. When your Speak with Animals spell finishes, the wolf fixes you with a knowing glare. He tells you a tale of sorrow, how the woman he had befriended years before was slain by the rat king. You carry her signet ring now, found in the detritus of the lost temple you plundered; he and his pack will guard your return to town if you consent to give him the ring at the end of the journey.

TTRPGs give us the opportunity to look at this process of creation-through-discovery, pattern recognition, and the sorting of those patterns into stories in real time. Many TTRPGs (*Dungeon World, Apocalypse World, Blades in the Dark, Stars without Number,* even certain styles of *Dungeons & Dragons*) can provide us with additional tools for sorting events into a story-friendly structure, naturally pushing the action forward and driving tension higher. Using these tools can make this process clearer and help us see what our brains latch onto, both on the player's and the game master's sides.

For me, procedural generation at the table is strongest when it drives against the game's mechanics, encouraging players to make interesting decisions. It's also best when it inspires everyone at the table to have eureka moments of spontaneous justification—the storytelling that naturally justifies this event as a logical one that fits into the world and story, rather than as the pure random happenstance of dice rolls that it is. It's easiest to guarantee that when the procedural content has strong ties to the rest of the world: plant creatures with motivations linked to a nearby monster, wolves that follow the players because of their freshly smoked bear meat. Motivations, instincts, and goals can help the entities in your game world feel more deeply integrated, as well as intentionally doing the work to tie content to content, building a web of connections to justify even the results of the smallest roll. The more narrative connections there are, the more players and game master alike will be willing to accept the arbitrary results of the dice as intuitive and apply their own interpretations and stories on top of this framework.

Give it a try sometime. If you're passionate about storytelling and procedural generation, then cracking open any of the TTRPGs I've mentioned will give you a window into your own mind and the minds of your players. From there, it's easy to begin exploring what creates compelling stories at your table and some possible avenues for integrating the links and structures necessary for compelling procedural storytelling into your work as a digital game designer. At worst, I guarantee you'll end up surprising yourself with what you come up with, and there are far worse ways to spend a Sunday afternoon.

4

Characters

Robust characterization is a key element of storytelling. We are people, and fictional people that share our dreams, struggles, and fears provide a connection between the story and us and ultimately between each other as we navigate life's mystery together. Whether through action, description or dialog, the author can skillfully distinguish characters, make them relatable, drive the narrative, or teach us something about ourselves.

The challenge of generating even a portion of these elements to the end of creating believable or memorable characters can feel almost insurmountable. As luck would have it, some have withstood the crucible and returned with wisdom for you, dear reader! In the chapters to follow, we'll focus on personalities, action, and dialog, keeping in mind that the lessons and techniques of the other sections can be applied to character descriptions, development, and narrative arcs specifically.

Pitfalls are numerous, and in the sphere of video games, traditional writing intuition may not apply. Do characters with sparse detail feel repetitive? How much detail is too much? Which archetypes work best in practice? Can the generated characters perform their mechanical functions in the game world? As with all game design, proceed with care, and always keep the experience of the player in mind.

This page intentionally left blank

CHAPTER 21

Maximizing the Impact of Generated Personalities

Tanya X. Short

Kitfox Games

P ersonalities, in real life or in algorithms, can be summed up as "what we do and why we do it". I would argue that personalities, their causes and their expression are made up of four major components: motivations, relationships, ability and knowledge, which can be separated into reasoning and behaviour (Figure 21.1):

So, if you pick a reasoning and a behaviour for your generated character, theoretically you're done. You generated a personality. Congratulations. But is it an interesting personality? Does the player understand what it is? Are the connections between the reasoning and behaviour satisfying? In this chapter, I will hope to share a few ways you can help your characters' personalities (or other generated narrative elements) feel "more interesting", and have a stronger impact on the player's experience of your game. For these purposes, I'll be skipping over the actual methods of generation for the most part and instead focus on design methods.

TIP 1: DEFINE THE PLAYER'S INTERPRETATION PROCESS

Which came first, the motivation or the behaviour?

Even if we think someone's reasoning occurs before actions, we are likely to say "Arron usually tells the truth, therefore he is honest"

REASONING

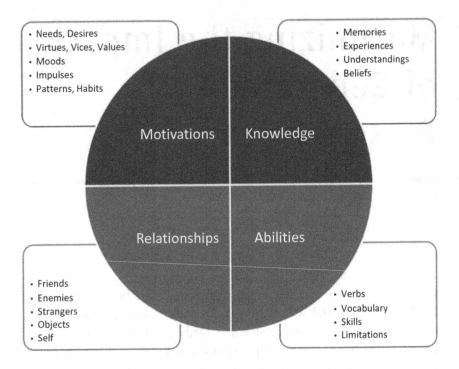

- Needs, Desires
- Virtues, Vices, Values
- Moods
- Impulses
- Patterns, Habits

- Memories
- Experiences
- Understandings
- Beliefs

Motivations

Knowledge

Relationships

Abilities

- Friends
- Enemies
- Strangers
- Objects
- Self

- Verbs
- Vocabulary
- Skills
- Limitations

BEHAVIOUR

FIGURE 21.1 A pie chart of reasoning and behaviour.

(character judgment) and also say "Arron is honest, therefore he usually tells the truth" (logical statement). But for your game, you need something stronger than correlation; the player needs to understand which is causing which.

It might be natural to encourage the player to use the "character judgment" method: if the player observes that Arron tells the truth, the player can see that therefore he is honest. Passive media favours this "show don't tell" approach to storytelling—interpreting others' actions mirrors our real life experiences. Personality-interpretation gameplay is usually found in authored media, such as *Uncharted* or just about any novel.

However, currently in the procedural generation space, the opposite experience is offered. Generated personalities tend to be explained up-front, closer to a "tell then show" approach, with the player taking information about personality traits and comparing it to character behaviour to form a mental model of the underlying algorithm, such as *Crusader Kings II, Black and White,* or *Dwarf Fortress.*

This is likely because in system-driven simulations; an appeal of the genre itself is the gameplay of learning those systems and coming to understand them deeply. Since causality is key to understanding the meaning of a simulation, hiding it behind character judgments or other "fuzzy" interpretations is likely to frustrate your players. Players enjoy defining a cause and an effect, even if (as is likely) the effect becomes another cause, which creates another effect, and so on.

In *The Shrouded Isle* (Figure 21.2), as discussed in Chapter 21, villagers generate with names, portraits, gender, family affiliation and 1 random virtue and 1 random vice. These traits change their ability to contribute to the village and allow special events to occur.

For example, the virtue accusatory (seen on Nadya in the upper right of Figure 21.2) mostly means that characters are skilled at penitence tasks but also means that the engine may select them to populate certain random encounters, such as those involving wild accusations.

Importantly, in this screenshot, Nadya's "accusatory" virtue happens to have been previously discovered and revealed to the players. In this case,

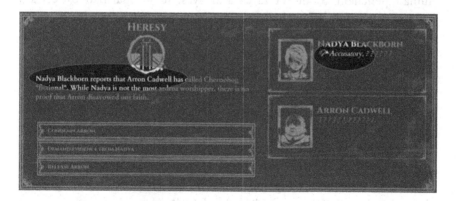

FIGURE 21.2 *The Shrouded Isle* (2017)

the players can use their knowledge of Nadya's personality as a factor in how to react to the situation. Knowing that Nadya is accusatory, they may be more sceptical of this report—they use their knowledge of her personality to decide whether or not she is telling the truth.

If Nadya's virtue were only displayed as "??????" in a *Shrouded Isle* event, the accusation event would then provide a clue—maybe Nadya is accusatory, or maybe Arron really is a blasphemer, or maybe both. Later, when the truth is discovered, this is a learning/discovery moment for players.

In *Moon Hunters*, we made the traits a reactive system entirely—the game tried to interpret the players' behaviours and choices into mythic hero traits (cunning, foolish, etc.). The behaviours were experienced by players and used to calculate the "reasoning" and then displayed as the players' personality traits. It's possible this might have been more satisfying for players if they had been able to input on the reasoning itself or further explore the influences of one on the other.

In order to employ the other tips that follow, you must first decide which your system and player experience depends on first—does behaviour determine personality, or does personality determine behaviour? And how does it appear to players?

TIP 2: PERSONALITIES ARE ALREADY SUBTLE

When it comes to physicality, there are many highly effective cues you can use to tap into human biases, assumptions and instincts, such as the human penchant to detect faces and eyes, to be alarmed by certain colours, etc. Connections between reasoning and behaviour (i.e. personality) are difficult to "see" and are based more in culture than biology. Personalities are 4th dimensional qualities, proving themselves over time and are subject to interpretation.

It's tempting to hide some reasoning elements (needs, desires, virtues, etc.) because it's clearly more natural. Behaviour-first messaging makes your characters more lifelike and puts behaviour at centre stage, allowing for gameplay closer to authored content. But why are you generating personalities in the first place if you could just generate the behaviours directly? In a game without exposed reasoning or personality-related gameplay, maybe "random" really is good enough.

In the current game landscape, it's fair for players to assume that personality elements that are invisible are, in fact, missing. Players don't have a good reason to expect game characters to have psychological depth. You might need to be fairly blunt about your systems if you want your generated behaviour to be noticed at all, never mind understood correctly. This means there are at least 3 ways in which normally advisable subtlety can backfire when implementing personality generation systems.

"Secret" Systems Are a Risk

When I joined the *Age of Conan: Hyborian Adventures* (2008) team as an AI designer, I had been an ardent supporter pre-launch and fairly engaged player in those first weeks, almost reaching the maximum level.

I must have played 40 or so hours, just for the fun of it. I visited a dozen areas, observed the quest system and interacted with or killed thousands of monsters and evil non-player characters (NPCs) on my road to heroism. In my interview, I wouldn't have been surprised if they had asked me questions about the AI behaviours. If they had, I would have said the scripting in the camps of soldiers had many nice flourishes: soldiers would sometimes eat, drink, sleep or chat together, and it made for varied tactical situations.

However, I was stunned in my first few days at work to find that, actually, almost all NPCs had a deeply modelled motivational system based on the Maslovian hierarchy of needs. Even characters whose only purpose was to populate "grinding" zones (masses of creatures spawned only to be killed *en masse* for currency or experience points) would first try to seek safety, then if their hunger meters were high enough, they would try to eat food, to sleep if tired, to socialize and finally to self-actualize. Those soldiers had been chatting not because a designer told them to do so; it was part of their internal, deeply simulated systems. It was sophisticated, expressive, modular and completely invisible. A fair approximation of a "living, breathing" world had been given to me, and I'd missed it!

If *Age of Conan* AI had been structured differently or expressed its reasoning (hunger, sleepiness, etc.), maybe I could have detected causality. But the NPCs' needs grew invisibly, and the core gameplay (combat, combat, combat) gave me no incentive to watch for those expressions, even if they had them.

So, learning from *Age of Conan*, I understand why *Dwarf Fortress* exposes as much as it does. It's the safest route to making sure your effort actually influences player perception. It might be overkill in some instances, but causality is easier to determine. For those elements we hide from the player, it seems safest to hint that they are there somehow. *Civilization* rulers may have become increasingly complex over the years, but they've also started being more coy about hidden elements, hinting at them overtly. This piques curiosity and prepares the player for emotional satisfaction when those elements are eventually revealed.

Non-subtle obscuring allows the player to engage in both sides of the causality chain, with a bit of personality-interpretation gameplay up front and then personality-prediction gameplay after.

Subtle Behaviour Patterns Are a Risk

Extreme personalities are rare in real life. If you choose to become inspired by findings from real-life psychology, such as the Big 5, you'll see the most common traits are something like "mildly confident" or "mostly cooperative"—you know, relatively average. Out of 5 axes, only 1 or 2 tend to be somewhat extreme at most. So you might be tempted to model your game similarly and make most of your characters mostly average. Even for characters that are quite extreme (again, realistically), you might be tempted to make your character act on the one "extreme" trait only 1 out of 5 times.

This "realistic" subtlety is a trap for the same reason that hidden systems are: players might never actually see a character act in an interesting manner. Instead, if you focus your characters' behaviour on the limited ways in which characters are extreme, and push it even a little further than realistic, it's more likely that their traits will be observable for players. In the previous example of the accusatory character in *The Shrouded Isle*, imagine the character went around a game world mostly *not* accusing people. It would be unfair to expect players to intuit the invisible.

I wasn't a designer on *Crusader Kings II*, but I would bet this is a major reason characters in *Crusader Kings II* are "Wroth", rather than "sometimes irritable". With more extreme personality types, the systems are genuinely easier and more available to understand and detect. It can help to lean on archetypes, as they already tend towards extremes—we're used to it even in traditional authored storytelling. Ravenclaws in the *Harry Potter* universe aren't just "kinda smart"; they are defined by being the smartest.

Beware Passivity and Non-action

One final note on subtlety: pro-active behaviour is generally less risky to base a personality on than passive or avoidant behaviours. A character that *wants* to do something is more easily perceived and understood than a character that wants to *not* do something. This can be a problem for some character types that are natural in storytelling: those who are mostly passive, shy, avoidant, or easy-going. Many classic virtues (such as chastity or temperance) were primarily defined by their preference to avoid popular activities. These unfortunately make for the least compelling personalities in a generated setting, as they may appear identical to simply average or disinterested characters.

Arguably, the most successful personality type in *King of Dragon Pass* was the trickster, who was the most flamboyant and notable of the characters, while the rest were mostly measured and balanced in their approaches. In personal correspondence, David Dunham has said he felt it worked well and uses similar archetypes in *Six Ages*.[1]

There are ways to highlight more passive characters' patterns, but generally, the more you can re-orient your design to provide opportunities for characters to express their trait *actively*, the better.

For example, rather than merely abstaining from sexual activity, which might take many years to observe, a chaste character could recoil in horror from sexual content, shame others who engage in flirting, randomly rant against sexual indecency or actively try to avoid temptation. All of this is closer to a detectable pattern for the player, even if a bit silly.

TIP 3: COMEDY IS CLOSE AT HAND

Writers go back and forth about whether satisfying narratives are more challenging to create in comedies or dramas. For system-driven "stories", I think it is clear that good comedy is easier to pull off than good drama. Why? I'm going to assume briefly that you aren't trying to fool the player into thinking your characters are authored content, and I will assume your players know that your characters are generated. Trying to produce Turing-test-passing procedural storytelling is a bit like trying to sell roller skates to someone who wants a bicycle—it's a waste of everyone's time and throws away whatever advantage you might have had. Machine collaborators can produce many unique, fascinating flavours of narrative, but if you want to create and sell an authored story, get an author. If you disagree, simply skip this tip.

So, whether it was part of your marketing or core to your gameplay, your players are engaging directly with the fact that these characters are system-driven. Nobody is under the illusion that your characters are people, or even human-authored people! Once players are mentally in the intellectual space of engaging with AI pro-actively, they are emotionally far from the submissive position of suspended disbelief or "immersion".

In order to reach the kind of emotional investment in these little characters that we get from authored stories, players have to internalize your systems completely. Only then can they map humanity onto the characters. That means there are (potentially dozens of) hours between when the game starts and when drama can begin. I suspect that *Dwarf Fortress* might never have become popular if its core gameplay hadn't started out less personality-driven and more accessibly survivalist. By the time someone created an interesting user story involving dwarves' personalities and culture, they were 40+ hours in.

In the hours of gameplay leading up to the players' moment of "grokking", it's much easier to make funny situations than riveting drama. Not only are the outcomes often surprising, but your characters are the symbols of people, which gives them an awful lot in common with the setup for a joke. Jokes typically use symbolic theoretical people and situations anyway. A/an (insertnoun) and a/an (insertnoun) walk into a bar. ...

TIP 4: ALLOW AFTER-THE-FACT INVESTIGATION

In an ideal world, players understand everything that is going on and are filled with anticipation for an important, complex event. However, when exploring interactive simulations, especially of the human psyche, it's totally reasonable for players to ask "Wait, what just happened?"

Assuming there are multiple characters in your systems (presumably with different personalities and needs and behaviours), players may not be focusing on the right place at the right time. It can then be helpful to provide some kind of tool for the players to play detective, and opting into a deeper level of systems can help diffuse what happened and why. A few example tools:

- Logs or journals of character actions/behaviours

- Rewind time to re-play and watch events with different actors

- Actual in-character investigations (ask characters questions, etc.)

This can easily add scope to your gameplay features, but as long as you're creating gameplay about personalities, maybe it's what your game needs anyway.

TIP 5: REACTIONS ≥ ACTIONS

"It's not what happens to you, but how you react to it that matters."— Epictetus

Normally, in order to observe multiple characters' personalities, you observe them in sequence following their proactive "natural" inclinations and compare them to other characters. A tells the truth a lot and B lies a lot, so maybe A is more honest than B. However, you can process more information per second if you can compare simultaneous character reactions, especially if they're extreme, say to someone's injury or misfortune, as in Figure 21.3.

Or you can even quickly gauge a whole crowd's feelings, when the change is sweeping (Figure 21.4).

It's worth a quick warning that part of the reason reactions are so effective and economical is that we have so many expectations surrounding them. Reaction-based personality expressions can become complicated much more quickly than proactive solo actions. The more factors in your system, the harder it is for a character to pick a consistent or even somewhat appropriate reaction. Human priorities are not particularly elegant or obvious.

For example, when a character dies, does your AI care more that

A) he/she hated the person who died, or

B) that he/she is a kind person, or

FIGURE 21.3   *The Sims 4: Kids Room Stuff* (2016). Courtesy of Electronic Arts.

C) the judgmental friend is in the room, or

D) the person who died did so in an embarrassing way, or

E) the murderer was his/her lover, etc.

But whatever you do to organize your characters' priorities, if they often use these in *reacting* to others' actions, this can help constantly communicate their personality, even when they don't have as many chances to act.

TIP 6: CHANGE IS POWERFUL

People (or at least their needs and desires) tend to change over the course of their lives, due to experiences, learnings, traumas, and/or nature.

Although it might seem counter-intuitive, having someone's personality change at key moments can actually be more compelling than the personality itself. In the face of adversity (or the ravages of time), some people get weaker/more flawed, some get stronger/less flawed, and some get weirder. That's how life goes.[2]

Darkest Dungeon hinges some of its most compelling gameplay moments (the gain and loss of quirks) on moments of crisis and character

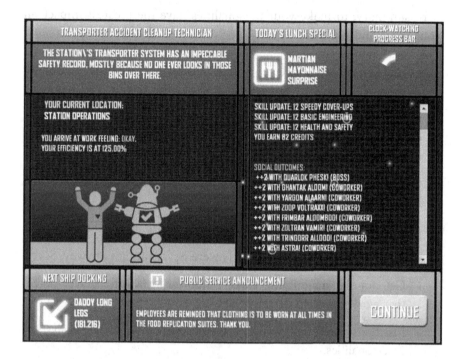

FIGURE 21.4   A group of co-workers react to the player's status. *Redshirt* (2013).

personality changes. Designer Tyler Sigman confirmed to me that quirk gains are relatively arbitrary, with some broad exclusions or inclusions based on mission content. Crucially, transformation is fascinating on its own as a learning moment with the character and doesn't need deep explaining of factors and motivations, assuming players are given enough information (state 1, trigger, state 2) to invent their own reasoning. Whether the formerly Brave character becomes Cowardly, or a formerly Unyielding character becomes a Warrior of Light, the player can come up with their own meaningful narrative explanation for the transformation.

SUMMARY

Although the RTS and strategy genres have been dabbling in generating character personality types for decades, personality as a distinct game-play system is a relatively new subject, without the decades of exploration and discussion of terrain or text generation.

In summary, to make your personalities have the greatest impact on your game and players:

- Chicken or egg?: Have a clear vision for whether reasoning powers motivation or vice-versa, from the engine and from the player perspective.

- Beware hiding too much: Be as clear as possible about what's under the hood.

- Beware "normal" personalities: Extremes are easier to see and understand.

- Beware passivity: Actions are easier to see than non-actions.

- Embrace the comedy: Your AIs were never human anyway. Sorry.

- Get out the magnifying glass: Empowering a little player detective-work can help defray chaos.

- Reactions are high-value: Two characters + one catalyst = 2 personalities.

- Transformations are gold: Even if your traits or behaviours are subtle, a strong and clear change can be compelling on its own.

NOTES

1 *King of Dragon Pass* is an excellent game with procedural personalities that doesn't use many of my tips. David Dunham explicitly warned me that subtlety can be helpful when trying to tell a convincing story. He makes a very good point. I would say to choose your design risks carefully; if you are willing to risk players missing out on your systems, what other risks will you mitigate?

2 Though at least one study shows that we tend to become slightly more confident, conscientious and emotionally stable throughout adulthood but decrease in sociability and openness to experience in older age. Roberts, Brent & E Walton, Kate & Viechtbauer, Wolfgang. (2006). Patterns of Mean-Level Change in Personality Traits Across the Life Course: A Meta-Analysis of Longitudinal Studies.

CHAPTER 22

Procedural Characters in *State of Decay 2*

Geoffrey Card, Jørgen Tjernø, and Matthew Bozarth
Undead Labs

O ne of the core features of *State of Decay* is permadeath. You are trying to survive in the zombie apocalypse, and your decisions matter because when characters die, they are gone forever, and you will never see them again. That isn't exactly true. While watching people play the original game, we learned that pretty often players started the game over from scratch when they lost one of their bespoke starting characters. As the new game began, players found the characters they had lost alive and well.

That is certainly a valid way to play, but as we were designing the sequel, we realized that we wanted to double down on that original vision. We wanted to create a world where it meant *more* when characters died, because players would literally never see them again. That meant we needed to generate a near-infinite series of characters for players to feed into the meat grinder, one by one.

While many of the characters in the original game *felt* random, that was actually an illusion. They had random names, but all of their *traits* (their life history, their skills, their personality quirks, their physical appearance) were handcrafted, with a specific set granted to each character. There were actually only a couple hundred possible characters in the game. To jump from a few hundred possible characters up to a number that is effectively infinite meant we needed a system that could generate new ones on the fly.

It couldn't just be *any* system. Remember, one of the main purposes of the system was to make the deaths of our characters more meaningful to players. That meant not only making them unique, but also making them authentic and relatable. These characters needed to be random without *feeling* random, or players wouldn't be able to connect with them, and their deaths would be empty and meaningless. So what can go wrong with a procedural character generator to make the characters seem fake and unconvincing? The problems fall into two broad categories: Blandness and Contradictions.

BLANDNESS

If it feels like every character is Generic Human Number Five, then why should a player care which one runs headlong into danger? (See also: Chapter 1).

At first, there seems to be a sort of tension between these two. After all, the easiest way to avoid contradictions is to make characters more bland. Give them fewer distinctive features that could possibly conflict, and you're safe from contradictions—but no one cares. Add more distinctive features, and your characters get more interesting—but you also start generating weirdos now and then that nobody believes.

Real people are distinctive and complex, and so are all the best characters in the stories we read. If we wanted our system to create characters that *seemed* like they might have been authored by a real human being, we needed to build one that could make distinctive choices without making a mess.

Avoiding blandness was the first problem. We knew that no matter how well we did, every long-term player would eventually start looking at all our characters with glazed-over eyes. Our challenge wasn't to ensure that every single character stood out like a movie star. That's impossible. Instead, our challenge was to make sure that *some* characters stood out like movie stars, and when players looked more closely at those characters, they were built in such a way that players could easily uncover a story about who they were as distinct individuals.

So we designed the system from the inside out to be about telling that story. All of the gameplay-relevant aspects of a character (their health, stamina, skills, etc.) were derived from one central set of *traits*. While the numerical stats were bland and boring, the traits all had colorful player-facing story descriptions that could say a lot about who each character was.

We made some rules about how those traits were expressed:

1. Traits were always written in the first person. There wouldn't be an omniscient narrator telling you about each character. The characters would describe *themselves*, in their own voices.

2. Most traits offered a story from the past or a specific opinion about an issue, rather than just a description of the trait. This gave characters something to talk about in the description and a chance to make an impression on players.

Then the goal was to structure the characters so that the features that were most interesting to players on a *mechanical* level would lead them back to the traits, which were designed to tell a *story*.

A character's *name* is the first aspect a player learns and is the focus of a lot of attention. So we created a nickname system that would occasionally override a character's more traditional name with an unusual nickname derived from the traits. A character who used to sleep in a tree to avoid zombies might be named "Squirrel," for instance. A player seeing the name might ask, "Why are they called *that*?" and go exploring on the character sheet to find the answer from the traits.

Characters also had *skill specializations* and *hero bonuses*, which were highly visible benefits that players put focus and effort into unlocking. We set up both to try and catch players' eyes and make them wonder, "*Why* does this character have this feature?" The process of searching for the answer would lead them straight to the backstory contained in the traits. The hope was that players would only need to do this a few times to get the overall impression that *all* of their characters were interesting and unique—even the ones they never bothered to take a deeper look at.

CONTRADICTIONS

If characters seem to have sets of traits that would never occur in actual people, then players are put off by them and can't suspend their disbelief.

A good author is often able to create a character that is full of apparent contradictions and then tell you a story that helps you accept and understand that character. But we weren't telling a unique authored story about each character, so we didn't have that luxury.

Players of *State of Decay 2* know that their characters are procedurally generated. When they see characters with traits that seem to conflict, they don't think, "What an interesting character; I can't wait to see what the author makes of these contradictions!" Instead, they think, "Whoops, the random character generator made something dumb." So the standard for what counted as an unbelievable contradiction was going to be more stringent for us than it would have been for a more traditional storyteller. That meant we needed rules.

CONTRADICTION WINNOWING

We needed a system that would choose one trait, and then as it chose the next trait would winnow out all of those that might conflict with the first. As it continued to select trait after trait, the list of potential options would get smaller and smaller. We set it up so that each trait could be associated with an arbitrary number of tags. A trait tag would be outfitted with rules for how often it could appear on the same character and what other tags it could appear alongside.

For example, the career tag had a rule that it could only appear on a character *once*. Once the game applied a career trait (like firefighter, gas station attendant, or lichenologist), *all* other traits with the career tag would be eliminated from consideration. No character could have more than one career in the game.

In real life, of course, many people have multiple careers. But on randomly generated characters, seeing two different pre-apocalypse jobs doesn't make characters seem interesting and complex. It makes them seem like mistakes.

Tags could also explicitly single out other tags to eliminate. For example, at one point, a tester reported that they got a character who ran marathons but was also a couch potato. Now, in an authored story, you might be able to make that work. But in our game, it felt wrong. So we created a new pair of tags, called active and inactive. We applied the active tag to any trait that indicated that the character loved to move around and do physically challenging things, and we applied the inactive tag to traits that made the character sound physically sedentary. Then we made those tags mutually exclusive. So, once a character received a trait with the active tag, all the traits with the inactive tag were eliminated and vice-versa.

This system ended up being even more versatile and useful than we imagined. At one point, for instance, a designer requested that we make it so that all starting characters were limited to low-level skills, so that players had plenty of room to improve and customize them at the beginning of the game. All we had to do was create an invisible trait with a beginner tag, and apply it to all the starting characters, then create an advanced tag and apply it to all the traits that offered advanced skills. If those two were mutually exclusive, then no starting characters would ever have advanced skills. It didn't have anything to do with how convincing the characters were on a story level (which was the reason we created the system), but we could still pull it off.

Adding new tags to a thousand different traits can be tedious, though. Anticipating that, we chose to structure our trait list as a hierarchical tree, with groups and subgroups of traits nested inside each other. Then we could apply a tag to an entire *group* of traits at once, rather than needing to repeat the effort for each individual trait. So, when we got the request to eliminate advanced skills from starting characters, rather than drilling into each trait and applying the advanced tag where necessary, we dragged and dropped all the relevant traits into a handful of new advanced subgroups, then applied the new tag to the subgroups instead.

This winnowing system was ideal because we didn't need to think of everything up front. Throughout development, testers or developers would report new pairs of contradictory traits (or other concerns), and each time, it was a simple matter to create a few new tags and eliminate those issues from the game.

IDENTITY CONTRADICTIONS

Another type of contradiction that we knew we needed to handle carefully had to do with character identities. A character's name, appearance, gender, and voice always needed to line up in a way that felt like they could belong to a real person. Again, the standard for believability here was much more stringent than it is in reality. Life circumstances can create all kinds of interesting people who challenge expectations and stereotypes, and we wanted to represent those people however we could. But if *every* character was a jumbled mix of ethnicities because we poured all the elements of identity into one giant pool and chose them at random, it wouldn't look like we had created interesting, unique people. It would look like we weren't aware of real-world cultural identities or that we didn't care.

Our goal was for players who came from different backgrounds to have a chance to run across characters who felt genuinely familiar to them: "This is one of *my* people," which was especially important to get right for players who rarely had that experience at all. So we created a similar winnowing system, in which each name, appearance, gender, and voice had rules that could focus future choices on options that would feel correct and appropriate to players. But we also built in rules for weighting those choices so that we could focus *most* characters on common combinations of features (such as a male voice peppered with Spanish words lining up with a Latino appearance, a Spanish first and last name, and a Mexican nickname), while still allowing rare characters that step across those lines (like giving that same character a more African appearance and a common English last name). One rule we developed while working with cultural backgrounds was to go highly specific, rather than going broad.

It is very easy for a developer with one specific cultural background to view other cultures and places as monoliths, where everyone is the same. This is a massive mistake, which could result in some very awkward experiences for players who are intimately familiar with the cultures we are trying to depict.

For instance, the nation of India is internally as diverse as the entire continent of Europe, with a rich variety of different cultures, languages, religions, and naming traditions within its borders. That meant that if we created an "Indian" cultural background with "Indian" name lists, there was a good chance that most of our characters would come across to Indian players as though they were awkward mishmashes of different backgrounds and not truly Indian at all. So instead, we started with *one* region of India, and themed all our names to come from that one place. We did research on the most common names in that area and ran our selections by people whose families came from that region, to help us catch errors and to come up with appropriate nicknames and diminutives that would feel authentic to players.

We always tried to err on the side of caution and avoided including something if we had any doubts about whether it would sound appropriate in context. That means there are some very common Indian names (like Patel) that do not yet appear in the game, but the characters that *do* appear should feel more authentic as a result.

Because of the era of game development that we live in, we are free to continue to add new cultural backgrounds to flesh out our representation of Indian Americans, as well as any number of other cultures and add them to the game in free content updates after release.

As a side note, it was fascinating to explore some of the distinctions that different cultures brought in for naming characters. At one point, we were vetting our name lists past members of the Microsoft localization team, to make sure we had done everything we could to catch potential mistakes. The translator from Spain went through our Spanish nickname list with a metaphorical red Sharpie, eliminating almost everything we had included and making incredulous notes about these nicknames not being real. At first, we were taken aback. How did we get everything so wrong? Then we ran the same name list by a member of the team who grew up in Mexico and got the opposite feedback. These nicknames were absolutely real, and *not* including them would make Mexican characters seem unrealistic. So we realized our mistake. We had collected nicknames from Mexican sources on the Internet but put them on a nickname list that was universal to *all* Spanish-speaking backgrounds. They were distinctively Mexican names, to the point that a player from Spain or the Philippines or the Dominican Republic would find them completely foreign. What we needed to do was copy those nicknames, paste them into our Mexico-specific list, and eliminate them from the general population. Luckily, we had the infrastructure already in place to do just that. That infrastructure also allowed us to support other unique naming practices that members of other cultures brought to us.

Our Lao advisor told us about *seu lin*—informal nicknames that have nothing to do with a Lao character's given name but are used almost exclusively in place of a first name. Those took advantage of an independent nickname list in our data structure that few other cultures used. (Unfortunately, we couldn't include our advisor's own *seu lin*, which was Poo. There were several cases where a legitimate and awesome name from another language had to be eliminated because in the context of a game made by English speakers, it would come across as parody instead of representation, even with the best of intentions.)

In another case, our Ethiopian advisor reacted poorly to the first mix of English and Ethiopian names we tried, until we came up with the idea of including the Old Testament name list (e.g., Abraham, Isaac, Ishmael) over the common English list. Suddenly, the characters began to feel more like his friends and family. That highlighted the importance of letting our cultural backgrounds flexibly mix and match a variety of weighted name lists, so that we could respond to that kind of feedback in minutes by simply referencing an additional list, rather than spending hours writing new custom name list that incorporated both Ethiopian and Old Testament names.

That feature also made it possible to include the list of common English given names as an option on nearly every cultural background, to reflect the reality that people whose families come from all over the world tend to converge on the same list of names after a generation or two in the States, while their last names remain a distinctive record of their ancestry.

We received feedback soon after release from some game critics who said that the amount of cultural variety among our characters was unusual and refreshing, which actually highlights one of the great values of using procedural generation in the first place. A developer from a specific cultural background is always going to show some unconscious bias in one direction or another when making and placing bespoke characters one at a time. It's nearly impossible to keep track of everything you've done, and everything you think you *should* do, and avoid making mistakes.

By setting some initial goals, and then assigning an automated system to stick to those goals *for* you, it is much easier to avoid stumbling into biased representation—though, of course, there are still plenty of opportunities to introduce content that is just wrong. When you do, the system isn't going to know any better and will naively present your mistakes to the player.

ORDER OF OPERATIONS

So far, this chapter is mostly about all the awesome things that went right with our system, but there is one major place it broke down, and we would love a chance to try again with the benefit of hindsight. The process of generating a character has a specific order in *State of Decay 2*. Certain decisions are always made first, and others are made later.

While the trait tag system is set up so that the character generator can select traits in any order, and the list will always be winnowed appropriately, most other character features are far less flexible. For instance, the generator needs to know the age, gender, and cultural background of a character *before* selecting the voice. We had a bug at one point, and the generator was selecting the voice too early, before the age was determined; we ended up with characters who looked barely out of high school speaking in cracked, gravelly voices, while weathered old veterans were speaking like fresh spring chickens. We needed to push back the voice to be one of the very *last* choices that the character generator made, but that led to problems of its own.

One of the challenges of *State of Decay 2* is the fact that its characters are so flexible. In the original game, we had *one* voice assigned to deliver news over the radio, and after years of playing the game, our players were so tired of Lily Ritter's voice (despite the performance being wonderful) that they wanted the character to die. She could not, because her role was so critical to the game. In the sequel, we decided to eliminate that role (the ubiquitous, immortal radio character) from the game and decided that *every* character should be able to play *every* role in the community.

That was a *very* expensive decision. We ended up with 14 playable voices (more than double the number in the original game), each of which needed to be able to serve almost every purpose, which meant that any time we wanted to add a few lines to the game, we needed to book sessions with 14 different actors. Late in development, it became clear that we needed more voiceover to support our missions than we could possibly afford to record 14 times. So our lead writer suggested that we split the lines up and guarantee that certain roles in our missions were *always* played by certain voices. Then he could record each of those lines only three or four times, rather than 14, and we could get a lot more voice into our story.

We knew that this was not what our system was built to do. It was built to generate enormous variety not enforce tight constraints, but it could technically be pressed into service to make this work, so we decided to go for it. It was the right call—but it came at a cost.

Because voice is one of the *last* choices that the character generator makes, it is the absolute *worst* place to enforce tight constraints. If you constrain the first or second choice that the generator makes, that's no big deal. The generator is already built to commit to early choices and use them to winnow down later choices, and everything runs as it should. But if you constrain the *last* choice, and the generator doesn't *know* you've done that until it gets to the end, then it is very likely that earlier choices will eliminate *all possible options* for that last choice. For instance, if we decided that the only voices that a character was allowed to have were voices A, D, R, and Q, it turns out that there are no young-sounding female voices on that list. So if the character generator randomly decides to make that character female and young, when it gets to the voice-selection stage, it will go, "Whoops, there aren't any valid voices. Guess I'll pick a random one and hope for the best." For most characters, this fallback would be tolerable. The character might sound a little weird, but it's not an enormous deal. But if we're spawning that character *specifically to speak certain lines in a mission*, and *those lines were only recorded for four specific voices*, it's a disaster. The line isn't spoken at all, and there's an error. And because of the way the process was built, we could never even be sure *which* constraint was the most instrumental in creating the problem.

ORDER OF OPERATIONS, REDESIGNED

We spent so much time chasing down specific bugs where a character would show up to a mission with the wrong voice that it made us wish we could rethink our entire approach. If we had the chance to build a system like this from scratch, we would make two major changes to the way it is structured. First, we would build *every* feature of a character the way we built the traits. All features would share the same set of tags and the same rules for limiting and excluding them as a character was assembled. The fact that different character features had different rules, and needed dedicated code to make them winnow each other appropriately, ended up burning unnecessary time and adding unnecessary complexity. For instance, when we wanted to make traits that were specific to old or young characters (like *arthritis* or *college freshman*), we couldn't just include an old or young tag and leave it at that. We had to create an entire subcategory of traits that only applied to each of those age groups, because in our game, age is a fundamentally different type of feature from other traits.

Unifying all character features under a single exclusion system would have simplified this immensely, and we probably would have taken much better advantage of it, offering more traits that sounded like they spoke from a younger or older perspective. Second, because we can't always predict which features of a character will be constrained, and how that will play out in the step-by-step generation process (leading to bugs like the ones with all the mismatched voices), we need to build into our system a means of "backtracking" when it hits a dead end. This means that when the system has exhausted all the possible options for a particular character feature, we should let it undo a previous choice and try another. So if it runs into a situation where there are no valid voices, it can step back and select a different age, gender, or cultural background and try again, as many times as it needs to.

This way, the rules are guaranteed to *eventually* find a match if one exists at all, eliminating most of those cases of mismatched characters coming out of the system because they were forced to ignore constraints. If there are *still* cases left where characters can't generate properly, it will be because their constraints are mismatched on an obvious, fundamental level that should be much easier to diagnose and fix in content.

SUMMARY

So in the end, we learned that the best decisions we made were the ones that allowed early choices about a character to freely constrain later choices in a way that was unhindered by locked-in decisions about structure and order.

People, by their nature, are weird and complex, and we each start from different places when fashioning the stories that we tell ourselves to make our identities feel rational and consistent. Procedurally generated people can feel more like us when they put themselves through a similar process and use their own voices to tell us who they are.

CHAPTER 23

Plot Generators

Adam Saltsman

Finji

> If a writer of prose knows enough of what he is writing about he may omit things that he knows and the reader ... will have a feeling of those things as strongly as though the writer had stated them.
>
> Ernest Hemingway, *Death in the Afternoon*

> One may tell the reader that the character went to a private school, or one may tell the reader that the character hates spaghetti; but with rare exceptions the character's feelings must be demonstrated: fear, love, excitement, doubt, embarrassment, despair become real only when they take the form of events.
>
> John Gardner, *On Becoming a Novelist*

Back around 2008 or 2009, the game design community was talking a lot about the resurgence of procedurally generated content. I was playing games like *Dwarf Fortress, Thrustburst, Spelunky Classic,* and *Captain Forever* at the time, and fellow designers were talking about the capacity these games have for generating new "player stories." A lot of designers were claiming that these games were essentially "story generators," and there was a lot of evidence for this, with players excitedly explaining unpredictable and surprising incidents they experienced in the games.

I didn't know it at the time, but LARPing (Live Action Role-Playing) communities already had their own term for this: froth. Froth is a succinct way of acknowledging the way we tell each other stories after a match and the way we construct narratives about all the cool stuff that happened during the game—that whole phase of play that is sort of after the game but sort of not. It was only recently that I realized that the hilarious long-form blog posts I'd been reading about doomed *Dwarf Fortress* colonies were the digital equivalent of this same phenomenon. Before Bekah and I had kids, we were avid *Pandemic* players and used to do the same thing after a close game. "I can't believe we saved Lagos! Sacrificing Paris seemed so risky but spending all those points the next turn really paid off!" And so on. To me, it seemed like games that were good at generating stories had good froth, and froth is fun.

In 2014, I began work on *Overland,* a turn-based video game about some folks on a post-apocalyptic road trip. While talking about design goals with our new team, one thing we kept coming back to was wanting to make a game that had good "froth." We wanted to make a game that generated interesting and surprising player stories—stories that were so interesting and so surprising that players would want to tell their friends later. So we made a new item on the to-do list: "story generator."

Thankfully, I knew all about those from playing all those other procedural games. But it took me a long time to realize that for games like this, the *player* is the story generator, and what we actually needed in the game was a *plot* generator.

Plot: the actions and events that take place in a story or narrative. Keep the verbs and nouns, throw everything else away. For example: "Alice got an avocado at the store." Or "Jeff crashed his car near the lake." Or "Morgan fell and got a scrape." Subjects verbing nouns at locations. You get the idea.

Story: the sequencing and "editing" of the plot and the prose that is used to communicate the nature of these sequences to the reader, including character motivations and so on. For example: "Alice nudged the stem of the avocado out of the way to check if it was still ripe, a trick she learned from her mom. She winced but put it in the basket anyway." Please note: These definitions are not intended to be used outside of this chapter, ever. These are clarifications of tools, not theoretical structures.

Plot is made up of the events and materials of the story, whereas the *story* is the whole enchilada, sentences and everything. *Overland* is not unique or special for needing to be a plot generator. In fact, quite the opposite—realizing that other games like ours were plot generators, and *not* story generators, is what led us to this conclusion in the first place.

I was excited about this change of plans. Plot generators have a lot of advantages. You don't have to write as many tricky sentences, for one. Localization is much, much easier, and we could completely sidestep the uncanny valley of trying to generate a believably written story, that humane *prose*, with all the complexity and nuance that comes with it. On some level, all games are plot generators already, so it was a matter of refinement, as opposed to pure creation. Plot generators have a lot of things in common with the way story telling works on a lower level. Think of the way a skilled author might omit certain details of a conversation, having confidence that the reader can fill in the blanks in a way that is powerful and evocative and still gets the idea across just the way the author wanted. Think of the way a good film montage connects two previously unrelated images to invoke in the viewer a startling realization.

Good plot generators function much the same way, finding surprising and interesting ways to arrange the actions and events of our game. Previously unrelated interactions butt up against each other and create new meanings. Earlier, opening the car door meant nothing, but now, *now* it means something. And plot generators leverage the players themselves to be the story generators. The prose, the sequencing, the motivations, the causes and effects—these things are left up to real live people. The generated plot is like a scaffolding or framework upon which players weave the story in their own words.

So, the good news is that if things happen in your game, your game is a plot generator; good job; that was easy; everybody take five; we're done here! For example, *Tetris* is a plot generator. "An L block fell. Then a T block fell. It fell in a bad spot. Then a square fell. It had been a long time since an I block appeared." *NBA Jam* is a plot generator: "Detroit scored two points. Then Houston scored two points. Then Houston scored three points." I wouldn't say these are bad plot generators, as they serve these games well, but they're definitely repetitive plot generators.

A repetitive plot generator can only generate a handful of actions or events. Of course, the context can shift or change in meaningful ways that add a bit of complexity. After all, the three-pointer that wins the game is on some level a fundamentally different three-pointer than some random shot in the first quarter, but the main actions or events for most video games are pretty limited. For example, in the earliest versions of *Overland*, players did not have a ton of options at their disposal. You could smack monsters with a stick, get nibbled on by said monsters, maybe heal up with a first aid kid, look for some stuff in that dumpster over there, die, or drive away. Those were all the options, and most of the time, it was even more limited and repetitive than that. Driving away and getting healed up were pretty rare events … and dying would end the game. So most of the time the "plot" that was coming out of an *Overland* playthrough was "smack with stick, look in dumpster, smack with stick, smack with stick, look in other dumpster, smack with stick," ad infinitum. Ad nauseam, even. But that's not that bad a starting place. A lot of games, including mine, struggle to get past just an endless string of "smack with stick." Deriving an interesting, human story from the output of our repetitive plot generator—"smack, search, smack, smack, search, smack"—was a chore. Maybe if the plots our game generated were less repetitive, then the story the player wanted to tell would be less of a chore. Maybe it would be an interesting and integral part of the game. Maybe then we would get that sweet, sweet *froth*.

So we started looking for things that both fit into our game and meaningfully altered the plot. Sometimes these things were obvious, like bringing a character back to life with CPR. Sometimes these things were not so obvious, like how patting a dog is totally worth an action point even if you don't get anything from it. Sometimes these things were second-order discoveries, like how changing player movement to include diagonals allows for emergent narrow escapes between kitty-corner obstacles.

We also looked at how story telling worked in related games. For example, in both the modern rogue-like *FTL: Faster Than Light*, and classic edu-game *Oregon Trail*, scenarios and encounters may be prefaced by popup dialogs with a narrative choice or a player choice. For example, maybe someone is stranded and you can choose between having them join your crew or killing the person and taking their ... jewels, or something. We thought about a lot of scenarios like these and tried to make the associated setups, actions, and outcomes be things that could happen in the game, in the level, instead of just in the dialog popup.

In *Overland*, when you meet a stranger who can join your team, there's no popup dialog with a couple of paragraphs of generated story. Instead, the stranger shouts a brief greeting. "I got left behind, please take me with you!" maybe, or, if there's a wrecked car nearby, "She's running on fumes, can I join up?" or, if the stranger is trapped behind a barricade, "Get me outta here!" It's practically Shakespeare, I know.

Next, we take the events that would normally be in a story-based popup dialog and break them up into different atomic actions: Move, Invite, Attack, Loot, and so on. Rather than simply clicking a button on a popup, players maneuver their characters across the gameplay grid, click on the stranger, and use the Invite action to have them join the group, use the Attack action to fight the stranger, or use the Invite action but only to grab their inventory items and then abandon the stranger. Suddenly, we have a little bit of new granularity here: "Dupe stranger into giving up items" is emergent, rather than just a button on a menu. It's something that players can invent on their own (and tell a story about later).

That's neat, but what I think is even better and more important is the space this approach provides for unexpected disasters and the resulting improvisations. For example, players might decide "I shall save this lost soul, noble traveler that I am," and then absolutely fail to accomplish this. Maybe they can't get to them in time. Maybe a wildfire blows downwind and engulfs them and/or the person they're trying to save. Maybe a player decides to attack the stranger but realizes too late the stranger wasn't traveling alone, and now there's trouble. Maybe the stranger doesn't even want to join the player's group, but after the player helps with injuries, the stranger has a change of heart.

As we expand this approach to things like meddling with other scavengers, trading at camps, and visiting special sites, it keeps getting richer. These new actions and events all contribute to the *plot* generated by an *Overland* playthrough. Moments and sequences like these help construct the scaffolding that players use to tell their stories. They help players make their adventures more interesting, more relatable, and more human.

For a while, though, it felt like no matter what we did, making the game actions better, and thus making the plot better, didn't actually pay off unless players were emotionally invested in the little characters. Some game actions reinforced that need, like patting the dog, but most things you could do were still basically resource-oriented. Ultimately, our art director just made all new character models that were cuter than our old stoic characters, and suddenly players were able to close the gap. They were having an easier time connecting with their group now. We even changed the UI to foreground your group and double down on that connection. Then, and only then, did all this work on generating cooler plots start giving better results.

In the meantime, though, I did a few other experiments. The first thing I tried was coding up a system for generating post-apocalyptic backstories, for when you meet strangers along the way. I used a simple find-and-replace type of formula, with some support for nesting, and the output was pretty distinct and interesting after a single day of development.

There just didn't seem to be any place to put it in the game. When were players going to stop and read a paragraph or two about the backstory of some rando they scooped up en route? This seemed like an unrealistic expectation for a lot of the future players of the game, and thus something that would be hard to justify (and localize). So I removed anything and everything remotely resembling a written story and instead gave characters lots of "traits"—their age, their home-town—and then some adjectives like "lonely" or "angry" or whatever. This was sure to be a home run, as the characters now had relatable emotions.

Surprise! It turns out that's not how writing works. We eventually figured out that if we wrote a couple of very short stories for each player, we might get somewhere. Inspired by Hemingway's six-word micro-story, "For sale: baby shoes, never worn," we worked on replacing the adjectives with micro-stories that would evoke the feelings of those adjectives. Even cheap attempts, like "Grew up an orphan," or "Used to attend anger management classes," were huge improvements. Later, I discovered the John Gardner quote I used at the front of the chapter and felt quite silly about my epiphany. Apparently, this is old news to actual writers.

For *Overland,* two is a good number of micro-stories per character, and we are currently getting some mileage out of randomly selecting a micro-story about a character's "past" and another about the "present." Together we call these "couplets," and they've been really helpful. An example couplet might be something like "Skipped prom to watch the new monster movie. Hoping to find a dog." Past and present combine in a montage-like way to evoke feelings and transitions, and, we hope, to emphasize the difference in characters' lives before and after the end of the world.

It might seem like it would be a problem if the randomly selected micro-stories were accidentally contradictory, but it turns out those combinations are the funniest or most unsettling. For example, if an *Overland* character's couplet is something like "Hated camping as a kid. Sleeps under the stars now," players can imagine this character is frustrated, has grown up, or is afraid, or all three. So while these two micro-stories are a bit contradictory, they are more interesting for it.

Basically, database collisions can be a good thing. Rather than keep up some complicated system of filters or weighting or anything, we just work on writing micro-stories that can combine with anything from the other column. Even though occasionally it'll produce something creepy like "Tortured squirrels when younger. Hoping to find a dog," which leaves a lot of uncomfortable ideas to the player's powerful imagination.

The other somewhat notable feature of these "micro-stories" is that the only real generative component is the mashing together of the two columns. Within each sentence, there are only gentle nudges to correct gendered pronouns. Earlier, when we were working on the plot generator, it was all about getting rid of all the words and making everything into systems. Here, we were getting the best results by removing almost all the systems and essentially drawing pre-written "cards" out of two separate "decks." The parallel that I enjoy as well is that all of these little sentences are mostly about plot points. They're about losing something, finding something, hiding something, missing something. The emotions and abstract feelings are derived from the described events and the juxtaposition of the two "cards."

Ultimately, these little background story couplets aren't earth-shaking features, but combined with the cute new character models, they go a long way toward strengthening that player-character connection, and that strong connection is the thing that makes the generated plots resonate and makes the bigger variety of events actually matter.

As I move on to new projects in other genres, all these weird little discoveries (mostly re-discoveries) about plot generators and how they work when real live meat-people are playing your game and what kinds of scaffolding we should be providing, these are the things I am thinking about the most. What is it about visual arts, written language, music, and UI that help players feel connected to their in-game counter-parts? What sorts of actions and events would be interesting to include? Will absolute strangers build stories around the frameworks we've provided in our weird little game? Will these same strangers tell their friends about the adventures they had with us?

CHAPTER 24

Generating Personalities in *The Shrouded Isle*

Jongwoo Kim

Kitfox Games

T he Shrouded Isle is a human sacrifice cult simulator that uses generated personalities to depict moral quandaries. The player is the high priest of a small island village that makes ritual sacrifices to a slumbering dark god in preparation for his prophesied awakening. The core gameplay revolves around maintaining the villagers' faith by investigating, manipulating and killing the possible sinners in the community. Using a minimal, trait-based approach to personality generation, *The Shrouded Isle* creates a cast of flawed, believable characters in each playthrough. By having the characters' behaviour conflict with the player's goals, the game procedurally presents the player with difficult moral choices.

The project began as a game jam entry for Ludum Dare 33 in August 2015, the theme of which was "You are the monster". Rather than depict a literal or physical monster, we wanted to explore why someone chooses to be an "administrative" monster, ostensibly serving the greater good but nonetheless harming the people in their community. Our entry, *The Sacrifice*, was well-received for its unique aesthetic and theme, so we decided to rebuild and expand the game for commercial release. Two years later, in August 2017, we released the original version of *The Shrouded Isle* for Windows and OSX. Due to positive critical and player reception, we released a free expansion called *Sunken Sins* in December 2017.

The challenge in designing *The Shrouded Isle* was two-fold. First, we needed to humanize the townspeople so that the player perceived them as individuals with personalities, rather than stat sheets to be optimized. Second, the player needed compelling reasons to make harsh decisions. Although we could have accomplished our goal with extensive scripted content, we decided early on to take a systemic approach, generating the townspeople and depicting the theme through the player's interactions with the characters. This would better immerse the player and present in each playthrough, making the player engage with the townspeople in earnest and own the consequences of each choice. Ultimately, character generation in *The Shrouded Isle* owes its success to the effective use of few core elements to create gameplay situations in which the player could interpret the character's personality.

CHARACTER GENERATION

Character generation in *The Shrouded Isle* has three main elements: family, traits and aesthetics. A character's family establishes social context (Figure 24.1). Every character belongs to one of the five Great Houses: Kegnni, Iosefka, Cadwell, Efferson and Blackborn. At the start of the playthrough, each House is assigned an average of six characters, for a total of 30 generated characters for the town. While the family members' relationships are not explicitly defined, each House is given at least one male and one female member with elderly portraits to represent the parents, and two to five young members to represent the children. No new characters can be gained during the playthrough. The limited number of characters and the implied family relations create a sense of permanence and history for the generated characters.

Each House has a unique role in the cult, which requires its members to perform a particular ritual when employed as the player's advisor (Table 24.1). The cult follows five values—Ignorance, Fervour, Discipline, Penitence and Obedience—and each house is responsible for one of them. For example, an Efferson advisor will always perform "Flagellate Sinners" to improve the town's Penitence. In the rare case that a character's personal traits match the family specialty, the character becomes an exceptionally effective or

FIGURE 24.1   Generated family tree in *The Shrouded Isle*.

ineffective advisor, making them either the favourite child or the black sheep of the family. Thus, family specialty adds a layer to a generated character's personality by representing public persona and reputation.

A character's private behaviour is represented through traits. Each character is assigned two traits: a virtue, which improves one of the cult's five values, and a vice, which impedes it. Characters cannot gain any more traits, though randomly triggered events and new mechanics

TABLE 24.1 Great Houses, Cult Values and Associated Rituals

Great House	Kegnni	Iosefka	Cadwell	Efferson	Blackborn
Cult Value	Ignorance	Fervour	Discipline	Penitence	Obedience
Ritual	Burn Books	Build Monument	Confiscate Goods	Flagellate Sinners	Investigate Heresy

added in the *Sunken Sins* expansion may replace an existing virtue or vice. The generation algorithm avoids assigning the same trait to multiple characters, usually resulting in a unique set of traits per character. Thus, each generated character has a clear, essential and unique strength and weakness that constantly affects the core gameplay.

Traits also have two levels of severity—minor and major—which determine their impact. For example, "Imaginative" is a Minor Vice that lowers Ignorance by 10 points, while "Morbid" is a Major Vice that reduces Fervour by 30 points. Characters may be assigned any combination of major and minor traits, as long as they have a virtue and a vice each. This can result in lopsided combinations such as a character with a Minor Virtue + Major Vice. While this may be unbalanced at the individual level, major traits are limited in number and therefore balanced at the town level. Furthermore, the lop-sidedness makes the character's impact on the town more visible, accentuating personality in the player's mind. Beyond this, the player has means to reverse or circumvent the impact of a character, which will be discussed later. This simplistic approach guarantees that every generated character is morally flawed but situationally useful to the player.

The final aspect of a generated character is aesthetic identity, which is composed of their name and portrait. While neither of these has any impact on gameplay, they are necessary to establish the characters' individuality. In a game with a fixed number of characters per playthrough, having any two characters share the same name or portrait breaks immersion. Furthermore, players tend to extrapolate character behaviour from simply how a character looks. During playtesting, we observed that players would employ characters as advisors simply because they looked attractive or choose them for sacrifice because they looked maniacal. Ideally, we would have modified portraits or made certain portraits exclusive to certain traits to incorporate this impulse with the core gameplay. Even as is, the aesthetic identity of a given character is a visible anchor for the player, allowing them to more easily extrapolate their personality.

INTERACTION

In this section, we will examine how the gameplay systems in *The Shrouded Isle* allow the player to interact with the generated characters in a way that makes their personalities memorable. The player's ostensible goal is to survive five years while maintaining the five values of the cult and maintaining control over the five Great Houses. Each of these goals is complicated by the fact that every action in *The Shrouded Isle* involves the townspeople as either proxy or target. This makes the player utterly dependent on the characters and their behaviour, which forms the bedrock of the gameplay.

Each playthrough of *The Shrouded Isle* is organized in terms of years, seasons and months. Within a given season, there are three main phases: Town, Work and Sacrifice. The Town phase serves as a preparatory and investigative phase. The player has two main tasks:

1. To investigate the townspeople to reveal their traits

2. To appoint an advisor from each family to use in the subsequent Work phase

The Work phase (Figure 24.2) is when the characters and their behaviours affect the town the most. Among the five advisors, the player selects one to three each month to perform various rituals to improve

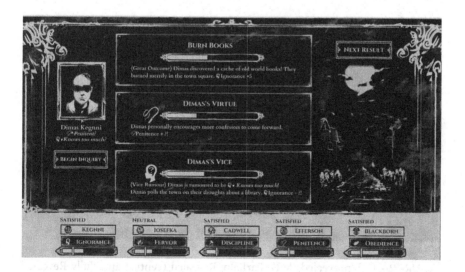

FIGURE 24.2   The Work Phase.

the cult's religious values. As the advisors perform the rituals, their traits also affect the religious values, encouraging players to use advisors with the most beneficial virtues and the least harmful vices.

The Sacrifice phase is the final phase of a season. The player selects one of the five advisors to be killed in ritual sacrifice. Since the sacrifice is intended as an example for the townspeople, the impact of a selected character is the inverse of the Work phase - the worse their vice, the greater the benefit to the town, but the better their virtue, the worse the loss.

Player actions in each phase revolve around the characters, their traits and their families. Yet, in order for the characters to seem like individuals, and not merely resource gathering automata, there needed to be risk in using them. Since characters' impact on the town was completely predictable, they felt overly mechanical. Thus, we added elements of random chance and hidden information to humanize the characters further.

In the final version of *The Shrouded Isle*, character traits can be in one of three states of knowledge—unrevealed, partially revealed and fully revealed (Figure 24.3). While the actual impact of a trait remains the same regardless of player knowledge (i.e. a Scholar will lower

FIGURE 24.3 Unrevealed (left), Partially Revealed (centre) and Fully Revealed (right) States.

Ignorance regardless of whether the player has knowledge of being a Scholar), the way that the player engages with a character changes based on how much has been revealed. By obscuring most traits, the player has to make a leap of faith when selecting advisors, trusting that a character will not be detrimental to the town as an advisor. This sets up player expectations towards a character's behaviour. For example, players often assume that a character with an unrevealed vice is benign, which is an irrational but understandable belief given limited knowledge. When a character is eventually revealed to have a Major Vice, we observe that players react with a sense of betrayal, as though the character actively chose to sabotage the plans.

Random modifiers to Work phase rituals were added to create further nuance, even when all the traits have been discovered. Though characters generally perform their family ritual at the normal magnitude, there is a 15% chance of triggering a Great or Poor Outcome, which applies a 1.5x or 0.5x modifier respectively. The modifiers are not significant enough to cause game-ending situations in earlier seasons. However, in the late game, they can unexpectedly cause one of the religious values to fall below the critical threshold, creating cascading consequences that throw a wrench in the player's survival plan. As for the rate, the higher chance compared to more typical "Critical Hit" rates causes characters to surpass or disappoint player expectations frequently. These randomized outcomes (Table 24.2) caused players to extrapolate character competence from the work results, overusing pet advisors who were merely lucky, or punishing poor performers by killing them in the Sacrifice phase.

A side effect of adding uncertainty to character behaviour was that skilled players would be risk averse in their character selection. While hidden information and random chance forced players in the initial seasons in the game to interact with non-optimal characters, eventually they would tend to exclusively use characters that they could fully vet.

TABLE 24.2 Work Phase Outcomes

Outcome	Great	Average	Poor
Chance	15%	70%	15%
Multiplier	1.5x	1x	0.5x

Thus, the game needed to provide compelling motivation and nuanced circumstances that allowed each character to be situationally useful.

The family opinions system during the Work phase was added to encourage players to use each character. Using an advisor from a given family will improve the opinion toward the player, while not using the advisor reduces it. Since the player can only use up to three advisors per month, two to four families are inevitably scorned. In order to avoid revolt, the player is compelled to use advisors from each family for at least one of three months during a season, even if their contribution to the cult's values may be questionable or clearly detrimental. As a result, characters the player might otherwise ignore are given chances to display their personalities.

The Sacrifice phase (Figure 24.4) is a more explicit attempt to draw attention to flawed characters. A mechanical inversion of the Work phase, the selected person's vice increases the cult's values, while virtue decreases them. Narrative wise, this represents the moral example the sinner's death sets for the townspeople—worse the vice, better the example. With this dynamic in mind, players are motivated to select at least one character with a Major Vice as a seasonal advisor for the sake of having a convenient scapegoat.

FIGURE 24.4   The Sacrifice Phase.

Another aspect of the Sacrifice phase is the severe opinion penalties applied on the dead character's family. Understandably, families do not take kindly to having their members killed, even for religious reasons. While the penalty can be mitigated by thorough investigation of a character's traits using Inquiries, repeatedly targeting the same family imposes a massive opinion penalty that risks revolt. The penalty adds further nuance to the player's choice in that sacrificing the ostensibly worst sinner among the advisors is not necessarily the most politically astute choice. Indeed, skilled players may sacrifice someone with a Minor Vice, or in rare cases someone with a Major Virtue, in order to preserve stability.

TRAIT MODIFICATION

While the near immutability of a character's traits was by design, we found that players expected some dynamism in the generated personalities beyond the aforementioned interactions. In the original release of the game, this desire was addressed through random events, presented either as a letter or visit by one of the townspeople, asking for the player's advice or decision on an important matter. The player choices usually were political or moralistic in nature, primarily affecting family opinions and cult values. However, some choices had personal outcomes, replacing a character's existing trait with another one. This approach allowed us to create character arcs focusing on trauma and redemption, such as someone overcoming the sacrifice of a loved one to become more resilient, or a sceptical scholar regaining her faith in the cult. Some traits triggered a chain of events that took place over multiple seasons. For example, an Artist may repeatedly ask for approval to put on performances, each show being more deranged than the last. While event chains allowed for more extensive character development, they were also more fragile, because the player had to avoid killing any characters involved to continue triggering the events. As a result, we relied more on singular events for trait modification.

Despite these event-driven character arcs, players still felt characters were too static. Once a character's traits were fully revealed and their associated events exhausted, only the stat values of the traits and the family specialty mattered from a gameplay standpoint. Since players would frequently reuse favourite characters with good trait pairings, the final year of a given playthrough was repetitive.

FIGURE 24.5 The Purification Tower screen, showing purification in progress (left cell).

In the *Sunken Sins* expansion, contagions were added to retain trait dynamism throughout the playthrough. The intent was to surprise the player by having a character behave differently even if the player had previously discovered everything about them. In the first autumn in a playthrough, a random character was selected to be the carrier of a "spiritual contagion" that replaced their virtue with a partially discovered trait that reduced a cult value, much like a vice. In every season afterwards, either the contagion spread to another character in the same family or another contagion was spawned in a different family. Given the potential penalties, contagions were useful in making the players pay more attention to the characters throughout the playthrough. Similar to how players blamed characters for Work phase failures, players blamed characters affected by contagions for spreading them to otherwise useful and virtuous members of their family.

To counterbalance the randomness of contagions, we added the Purification Tower (Figure 24.5), which gave the player active means to modify character traits. During the Town phase, the player can choose to confine up to three characters in the tower and try to improve them through submerging them in seawater. While there are no immediate costs to purification, confined characters are unable to serve as advisors, and the action takes a full season to complete. Furthermore, the success rate is dependent on how much the player has inquired about contagion, having a 100% rate if fully revealed. For afflicted characters, successful purifications would remove the contagious trait and restore the underlying virtue. However, failure would result in the drowning of the character, which would result in major opinion loss with the family. Given the opinion cost and limited availability of inquiries, the player needed to consider whether the benefit of curing someone immediately was worthwhile compared to the risks of killing a virtuous person as well as angering their family. Depending on the situation, the player may decide that they cannot afford to wait until the next season to have enough inquiries, in order to curb the spread of the contagion. On the other hand, the player could decide to ignore an afflicted character for now, if their underlying virtue was unimpressive anyway. Thus, active trait modification in the Purification Tower created a tension similar to the Sacrifice phase, in that the player must judge the moral worth of the townspeople.

A secondary purpose of the Purification Tower is that it can randomly modify non-contagious traits, creating more opportunities for characters to surprise the player. When an unafflicted character is purified, there is a moderate chance that either their virtue or vice will be replaced with one with a higher magnitude and a low chance that the character will drown (Table 24.3). In essence, purified characters become exaggerated versions of themselves, for better or worse. As purifying the unafflicted is optional, players feel responsible for the outcome, resulting in a greater sense of satisfaction or disappointment in the compared to the similarly randomized Work phase.

For characters that already have a Major Virtue, purification triggers a literal transformation. They are turned into the Awoken, unintelligible mushroom-like mutants who are thought to be blessed by Chernobog. The virtue is replaced with the Awoken trait (Table 24.4), which has no statistical value, and the character's portrait is also replaced. In order to unlock the secret ending in the *Sunken Sins* expansion, the player must transform all surviving townspeople into the Awoken by the end of the playthrough.

TABLE 24.3 Purification Outcomes for Characters Afflicted with Contagion

Contagion Reveal State	Cure Chance	Vice Worsening Chance	Death Chance
Fully Revealed	100%	0%	0%
Partially Revealed or Unrevealed	40%	40%	20%

TABLE 24.4 Purification Outcomes for Unafflicted Characters

Virtue Type	Virtue Improvement Chance	Vice Worsening Chance	Death Chance	Awoken Transformation Chance
Major Virtue	0%	0%	0%	100%
Minor Virtue	40%	40%	20%	0%

In gameplay terms, becoming Awoken makes characters nearly useless during the Work phase as they lack virtues. Furthermore, in the Sacrifice phase, they cost the player an immense amount of cult values when killed, as they are living symbols of the cult's faith. Thus, the Awoken are functionally similar to victory point cards in deck building games like *Dominion* in that they are necessary for unlocking a secret ending but can constrain the player's options if collected too early.

In narrative terms, the transformation represents loss of personality caused by forced conformity. Characters no longer behave as they used to behave and are literally inhuman. Since only characters with a Major Virtue can be turned into the Awoken, the player must decide whether turning the most virtuous members of the community into gibbering monstrosities is worth whatever new possibility the ending might contain. In this context, the Purification Tower was a success in encouraging players to consider the townspeople's personalities and providing motivation for acts of administrative evil.

ANALYSIS AND CONCLUSION

Unfortunately, players moved past the moral quandaries of the sacrifice and purification quickly, embracing their inner tyrants. During playtesting, we found that players no longer approached the Sacrifice phase with trepidation after one or two seasons. One failed attempt to encourage self-reflection was allowing the player to not kill anybody during the Sacrifice phase. However, playtesting showed that players were underwhelmed with the option as it was rather anticlimactic compared to making a sacrifice. Furthermore, balancing the "No Sacrifice" option was difficult for both thematic and economic reasons. Defying Chernobog's will should result in a heavy punishment for the player, but representing the punishment as cult value loss or family opinion loss seemed arbitrary and confusing, because they both represent worldly, if subjective, values. Even if the punishment were framed in a believable way, the "No Sacrifice" option needed to be balanced against economic outcomes for sacrifices, so that it was neither the obvious, easy way out nor the useless, never worthwhile option. Therefore, we removed the option so that the moral quandary focuses on who should be killed rather than whether anyone should be killed at all.

Another shortcoming of personality generation in *The Shrouded Isle* is that there are too many characters at the start of the playthrough. As 30 characters were present at the beginning, some players felt overwhelmed by choice paralysis during the Town phase and had difficulty emotionally connecting with the characters in the first few seasons. The game could have started with fewer townspeople and added more as time progressed, representing them as new arrivals to the village or children coming of age. However, the new characters would have raised questions that undermined the narrative, such as "Do other communities exist?" or "Why did I not know about these children earlier?" While the questions were not insurmountable, they added unnecessary complications. Furthermore, the demographic decline of the town gave the game a distinct, desperate feel, compared to other simulators that focus on growth and prosperity. If *The Shrouded Isle* had a non-apocalyptic setting, we might have chosen a more gradual approach to personality generation.

The Shrouded Isle's character generation was successful in humanizing the townspeople to the player while using aspects of their personality to dynamically create difficult choices. To establish social context, each character was assigned to one of five families that serve a specific role in the village. Flawed but distinct personalities were created through giving each character a unique pair of traits. Each character also had a clear aesthetic identity by being given unique name and portrait. Once the game began, the gameplay systems maximized the opportunity for the characters to depict their personalities by requiring the player to trust and depend on the characters in order to rule the village. In the Work phase, elements of random chance and hidden information created opportunities for characters to act as independent agents, surpassing or betraying the player's expectations. In having family opinions be affected by advisor usage, players were given further motivation to tolerate or engage with deeply flawed characters that would otherwise be side lined for optimal strategic play. Finally, the Sacrifice phase, through inversion of virtues and vices and dramatic family opinion penalties, motivates the player to re-examine each advisor, considering both the personal behaviour and the political consequences of killing them. Through a combination of generating flawed characters and game mechanics that motivate players to engage with them, *The Shrouded Isle* creates circumstances in which the player must choose to become an "administrative monster" in order to survive.

CHAPTER 25

Dialog

Elan Ruskin

"Healthkit here!"

"There's a monster behind you, Fred!"

C haracters that seem to understand and remark on the state of the world add a lot to a game, but as the amount of relevant gamestate and available dialog grows, selecting one line out of thousands with an immense if/else script becomes daunting.

I came to think about this problem when working on *Left 4 Dead*, a cooperative shooter game that relies heavily on characters responding to the environment and each other for its storytelling. The player-controlled *Left 4 Dead* characters autonomously comment in response to tactical situations (such as warning of zombie attacks and calling out useful resources) but can also be directed to say context-specific things from voice menus. Because any character in *Left 4 Dead* can die at any time, we needed a system that could adapt to choosing the best available conversation from whomever is alive. Furthermore, because there is an AI director randomizing circumstances, a building that might contain an ambush in one playthrough could be innocent in another, and so location-based speech triggers would be inadequate for "Hey! An ambush!" and the like.

In this chapter, I'll describe one approach to dialog that evolved in response to those requirements then proved to be a very powerful and simple framework for any project in which characters need to be aware of world state, remember history, cascade from special to general cases, and select the best available dialog/script/animation in context. By keeping things straightforward, it also provides writers a data-driven way to make special cases, running gags, back-and-forth conversations, and anything else that depends on persistent character memory.

USE CASES

In this context, "dynamic" dialog simply means character speech that responds to players' actions based on the state of the world around them and previous events. This has been a part of games since early parser-based text adventures such as *Deadline* and *Witness*, which had NPCs that could carry on simple conversations and remember players' previous actions, but as games grew more complex the quantity of state and dialog to manage grew as well.

Many roleplaying games support back-and-forth conversation with players via conversation trees. This familiar idiom provides a clear cause-and-effect relationship between player choices and character dialog. The most common implementation is essentially a state machine with player input driving the character from one state to another, which is simple to author:

```
STATE_GREETING: say "Have you seen the village clocktower?"
if PLAYER_RESPONSE == "yes" : goto STATE_SEEN_TOWER
if PLAYER_RESPONSE == "no" : goto STATE_DECLINED_TOWER
STATE_SEEN_TOWER: say "Nicest one in the whole county,
isn't it."
    End
STATE_DECLINED_TOWER: say "Here, I'll show you the way."
    End
```

and so on. But this rapidly becomes unwieldy when characters must remember players' prior actions and other events in the game—the larger the game, the more burnt villages and slain dragons there are for characters to keep track of:

```
STATE_GREETING: say "Have you seen the village clocktower?"
 if PLAYER_RESPONSE == "yes" and VILLAGE_DESTROYED == false
 : goto STATE_SEEN_TOWER
 if PLAYER_RESPONSE == "no" and VILLAGE_DESTROYED == false :
    goto STATE_DECLINED_TOWER
 if PLAYER_RESPONSE == "yes" and VILLAGE_DESTROYED == true :
    goto STATE_SEEN_TOWER_DESTROYED
```

```
if PLAYER_RESPONSE == "no" and VILLAGE_DESTROYED == false :
   goto STATE_DECLINED_TOWER_DESTROYED
STATE_SEEN_TOWER_DESTROYED: say "Glad you were able to see it
   before it burned down."
End
STATE_DECLINED_BURNING_TOWER: say "That's a shame, it was
   the nicest one in the county."
End
```

which is hard to keep up for thousands of possible bits of state.

Another common type of responsive dialog is event-driven barks. For example, NPCs in most stealth games will say things like "What's that I saw over there?" or "Did I just hear a noise?" or "That light went out!" and so forth to convey the AI's state to the player. Shooters' teammate NPCs yell warnings like "Incoming, right flank!"; sports games often have extensive play-by-play commentary. Some titles further this into an artistic device, such as *Bastion*'s narrator commenting on everything the player does. This sort of dialog can also be implemented via a tree of if-else statements but becomes unwieldy as the possible combinations of events and conditions multiply.

All these cases share a need to track state about the world in a uniformly manageable way, use that state to select just the right line from a big database of character speech, and remember what was said before when selecting the next line. Here I'll present one possible system for handling this in a simple yet powerful way, by thinking of dialog as a system of general rules with increasingly specific exceptions.

The easiest way to understand the system presented here is to build it up one step at a time from the use cases that motivate it. For the sake of example, let's say we're working on a team-based competitive shooter game. We want characters to vocalize

- in response to specific events, such as being shot at,

- when the player hits a key for a specific vocalization, such as calling for a medic, or

- when the player hits the general "vocalize" key, in which case something context-specific should play depending on what the player is looking at, such as "step on that capture point!"

CONTEXT-SENSITIVE VOCALIZATION

Our first implementation will be a simple list of possible character responses, with rules determining which one plays when, for example, the player hits the "vocalize" button. Every rule is associated with some response—both the audible line and the animation that goes with it—that I'll henceforth treat as a single unit. In principle, the script would look something like this:

```
rule Voc_Grenadier_CallForMedic
{
   criteria
{ Event=OnVocalizeKey ; LookingAt=Medic ;
SpeakingCharacter=Grenadier }
   Response
   { Grenadier_Medic_Call // "hey doc, come help me" }
}
rule Voc_Grenadier_Announce_Capture_Point
{
   criteria
{ Event=OnVocalizeKey ; LookingAt=CapturePoint ;
SpeakingCharacter= Grenadier }
   Response
 { Grenadier_Do_Capture_Point // "someone stand on that
capture point!" }
}
```

The Vocalize() function then walks through each of the rules in turn, finding the one that matches the speaking character, the trigger event (in this case the player hitting a key), and the object under the player's cursor. We can use the same approach for game-triggered events such as a character hitting full charge on their special attack:

```
rule Bark_Laserguy_Announce_Megacharge
{
   criteria
{  Event=OnFullyCharged ; SpeakingCharacter=Laserguy }
   Response
   { Laserguy_Report_Charge // "My laser is fully
   operational!" }
}
```

And so on. This is a convenient way to create lines that are context-sensitive variations on the same basic idea. The character controller only needs to emit a generic "OnVocalizeKey" event, and then the rules database can select the most appropriate line based on context.

If we add a new kind of object to the game, we need only add a new response rule with the relevant LookingAt for the character to address. Making rules more specific is easy as well; a character can, for example, distinguish between specific capture points Alpha and Bravo by adding a criterion to the relevant rules:

```
rule Voc_Laserguy_Announce_Capture_Point_Alpha
{
  criteria
{ Event=OnVocalizeKey ; LookingAt=CapturePoint ; Cap-
PointId=A ; SpeakingCharacter=Laserguy }
  Response
  { Laserguy_Do_Capture_Point_Alpha // "stand on point A!" }
}
rule Voc_Laserguy_Announce_Capture_Point_Bravo
{
  criteria
{ Event=OnVocalizeKey ; LookingAt=CapturePoint ; CapPoin-
tId=B ; SpeakingCharacter=Laserguy }
  Response
    { Laserguy_Do_Capture_Point_Bravo // "stand on point
B!" }
}
```

If we keep the basic LookingAt=CapturePoint rule as well, we then have a scenario where *two* rules match when the player triggers the vocalization: both the generic one with criteria {Event=OnVocalize-Key; LookingAt=CapturePoint;} and the more specific one with the additional CapPointId=A criterion. In this case we choose the rule that has more criteria: the one that is more specific. This means we always have the general line to fall back to if a specific one can't be found. If a new map includes a capture point G, the general "Stand on that capture point!" line will play if we haven't recorded a specific response.

AUTOMATIC TRIGGERS

Let's extend this idea to support characters automatically commenting on objects in their field of vision—useful for wisecracking NPC sidekicks. We can get there with three more bits of machinery: a way to tag objects in the world with specific names; a way for rules to set flags on themselves; and a timer that dispatches onSee events to each character at regular intervals, with an additional context for whatever object is in the character's field of vision.

The simplest approach to tagging objects is to put a string field on each actor, so that, for example, cats would have a "cat" tag, barrels a "barrel" tag, and so on. In a component-driven engine such as Unity, this could be as simple as creating a Vocalization Target component that has a simple string field on it. (For more on the power of tags to organize your content, see Chapter 22.)

Then we can write rules for specific objects, so when the character receives an "onSee" event and it happens to be facing a cat, it will choose the relevant rule. Because we have that timer triggering this event automatically every few seconds, it will create the illusion that the character is spontaneously noticing things around it (Figure 25.1).

Conversely, if no rule matches for the currently looked-at object (a chair, let's say), the character will remain silent.

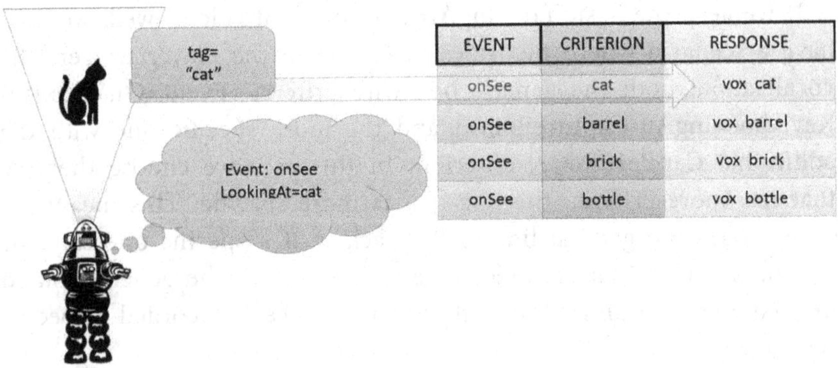

	EVENT	CRITERION	RESPONSE
	onSee	cat	vox cat
	onSee	barrel	vox barrel
	onSee	brick	vox brick
	onSee	bottle	vox bottle

tag= "cat"

Event: onSee
LookingAt=cat

FIGURE 25.1

The next piece is for rules to have a way of setting a "said once" flag on themselves, so that the character doesn't repeatedly make the same comment. This is easily achieved by adding a callback that runs when the line of dialog has finished playing. Something like:

```
rule Fred_LookingAt_Cat
{
  criteria
{ Event=onSee ; LookingAt=cat ; SpeakingCharacter=Fred ;
this.SaidOnce=false }
  response
    { Fred_Comment_Cat // "A cat! The Internet must be
nearby." }
callback
{ this.saidOnce := true }
}
```

That's all we needed to adapt our prior system to make characters utter some context-specific remark whenever they walk past something interesting.

MEMORY

Next, we want characters to remember *which* things have been said previously, so that we can implement things like running gags. We can get there with rules that write, increment, or modify arbitrary bits of context into an associative array on the character. So, a simple running gag could be implemented like:

```
rule Fred_LookingAt_Barrel_0
{
  criteria
{ Event=onSee  ;  LookingAt=Barrel  ;  SpeakingCharac-
ter=Fred; speaker.BarrelsSeen=0 }
  response
    { Fred_Comment_Barrel0 // "I  wonder  what's  in  this
barrel." }
callback
{ speaker.BarrelsSeen += 1 }
}
rule Fred_LookingAt_Barrel_1
{
```

```
 criteria
{ Event=onSee ; LookingAt=Barrel ; SpeakingCharac-
ter=Fred; speaker.BarrelsSeen=1 }
 response
 { Fred_Comment_Barrel1 // "I heard these barrels store
vast quantities of marinara sauce." }
callback
{ speaker.BarrelsSeen += 1 }
}
rule Fred_LookingAt_Barrel_2
{
 criteria
{ Event=onSee ; LookingAt=Barrel ; SpeakingCharac-
ter=Fred; speaker.BarrelsSeen=2 }
 response
 { Fred_Comment_Barrel2 // "All this sauce and no pasta in
sight." }
callback
{ speaker.BarrelsSeen += 1 }
}
```

We can also expand the notion of context to include the state of the world beyond the characters' own memories. If the world has an associative array of state like the characters do, then rules can test that information in their criteria like any other bit of context. For example, a character may have different lines about their village square depending on whether the dragon has visited:

```
rule Jane_LookingAt_Square_NoDragon
{
criteria
{ Event=onSee ; LookingAt=VillageSquare ; global.Dragon-
Freed=false ; SpeakingCharacter=Jane }
response
{ Jane_LookingAt_Square_NoDragon_1, // "It looks like the
farmer's market is open."}
}
rule Jane_LookingAt_Square_WithDragon
{
criteria
{ Event=onSee ; LookingAt=VillageSquare ; global.Dragon-
Freed=true ; SpeakingCharacter=Jane }
```

```
response
{Jane_LookingAt_Square_WithDragon_1,  //  "Gosh, that's
much more fire than usual."}
}
```

REPARTEE

How about characters having back-and-forth conversations with each other? The most straightforward way is to treat each line of dialog as a separate rule and event. When one character has finished speaking, it sends an event to the other character, along with a bit of context indicating *which* dialog has just finished playing.

```
rule Fred_LookingAt_Barrel_1
{
 criteria
{ Event=onSee  ;  LookingAt=Barrel  ;  SpeakingCharac-
ter=Fred; speaker.BarrelsSeen=1 }
 response
 { Fred_Comment_Barrel1 // "I heard these barrels store
vast quantities of marinara sauce." }
callback
{
speaker.BarrelsSeen += 1 ;
SendFollowupEvent( target:Jane,  event:onReply,  Pre-
viousLine: Fred_Comment_Barrel1 );
}
}
rule Jane_ReplyTo_Fred_Barrel1
{
 criteria
{ Event=onReply ; SpeakingCharacter=Jane; PreviousLine=-
Fred_Comment_Barrel1 }
 response
 { Jane_ReplyTo_Fred_Barrel1 // "Oh no, I'm allergic to
tomatoes!" }
callback
{
SendFollowupEvent( target:Fred,  event:onReply,  Pre-
viousLine: Jane_ReplyTo_Fred_Barrel1 );
}
}
```

In the example above, SendFollowupEvent() takes two main parameters, along with an optional number of additional parameters that become context to the next query. The key pieces are the event name and a notion of to *whom* to send the event. In this case, the event goes directly to Jane, who then tests her rule to find one with a PreviousLine criterion matching "Fred_Comment_Barrel1".

If we have multiple characters, we can also develop a notion of broadcasting onReply to everyone nearby—instead of target:Jane, it would be target:Anyone. **All** nearby characters would search their databases for some follow-up remark to Fred_Comment_Barrel1. The one with the most specific response (i.e., the rule with the most criteria) wins. This is useful for situations where you can't predict which characters will be present in every scene or for improving variety so that either Jane or Pierre or Kim might reply to Fred in any given playthrough.

We can string together conversations simply by adding rules to the database—to provide Fred with a reply to Jane's reply, he just needs an onReply rule with a PreviousLine=Jane_ReplyTo_Fred_Barrell criterion. We could also use target:Self to cut up a long monologue into shorter pieces.

COMPLEX RESPONSES

To increase variety, we can turn the Response field into a list of lines and select one at random every time the rule matches:

```
rule Fred_LookingAt_Bottle
{
criteria
{ Event=onSee ; LookingAt=bottle ; SpeakingCharac-
ter=Fred ; this.SaidOnce=false }
response
{
Fred_Comment_Bottle1, // "This place is full of litter."
Fred_Comment_Bottle2, // "Hey, a refreshing beverage!"
}
callback
{ this.saidOnce := true }
}
```

The response field could also include replay policies to determine whether each line is said only once or whether selection is round robin until all lines have been said, at which point it starts over again, or so on. Round-robin behavior is useful for events that are encountered repeatedly, such as a stealth AI's barks: you could have five lines for the OnSawPlayer event, but as the event will surely come up more than five times in the game, you want to recycle those lines once they've all been used.

DATA-DRIVEN CONTEXT

Using an associative array to store context allows callbacks to specify *any* key for writeback, even creating entirely new bits of context without needing any programmer support. This means that every bit of conversation can store an arbitrary piece of memory, which provides you with a lot of flexibility to define entirely new conversations and running gags.

For example, a writer could create a running gag in which every character comments about seeing cats but has a different response depending on how many other people have said something already. If the writer can invent and increment a global CatsSeen counter simply by mentioning it in a rule callback, this sort of interaction can be built entirely in data without needing programming support. (For more on tools design, see Chapter 28.)

USABILITY

The primary goal here is a flexible, usable, understandable, and data-driven tool for scripting arbitrarily complex dialog. One advantage of a rule-based system such as this one is that it collects all the possible states that could be used to select a line of dialog into a single pile of facts. From the programmer's point of view, the information necessary to decide which line gets played may be strewn across many objects hither and yon, for example, a code-driven approach to playing a line when a character is in a specific town and has killed more than 7 trolls and a key character is alive and the player has equipped a magic sword with at least four charges left on it and there are no dragons nearby might look something like:

```
if (
( globals->GetCurMap()->name == "Town1" ) &&
( globals->GetKilled( kENEMY_TROLL ) > 7 ) &&
(   savedstate->GetCharacter->Get("Sheriff")->m_isAlive
) &&
( !savedstate->GetPlace("Town1")->m_isOnFire ) &&
( player->GetInventory()->Get( "MagicSword" ) != NULL
) &&
( player->GetInventory()->Get( "MagicSword" )->m_Charges
>= 4 ) &&
( world->FindEntitiesNear( player->GetLoc(),
kTYPE_DRAGON ).count() == 0 )
) { ... }
```

There are several things painful about this.

First, the context available for dialog is poorly discoverable. If you didn't know there was an m_IsOnFire field on place objects, you wouldn't know that you could write dialog specific to local urban flammability. Second, it's not obvious how you get information from all these sources: there may be a complex chain of members and functions between wherever you're triggering the dialog and the information you need to select it. Third, the information may be strewn across many different classes with different programmers responsible for them; on a large project, it's impossible to keep track of all the state that's being managed by other people. Fourth, giant conditional blocks are confusing, messy, and easy to screw up, especially when you later add new conditions. Most importantly, this leaves the writer completely dependent on programmer support to add any dialog to the game—this data is only discoverable by reading through the source code and headers, so either writers must also be programmers, or programmers need to exhaustively document every bit of available context (and of course any such document will rapidly go out of date). In our implementation, it's more useful to think of the world as a merged pile of facts. We can imagine each query as containing every bit of available information in a dictionary (divided into namespaces if you like), conceptually like:

```
{
CurrentMap : "Town1",
EnemiesKilled_ : { kENEMY_TROLL : 9, kENEMY_SOLICITOR :
2, etc },
```

```
  PlayerInventory : { MagicSword : { NumCharges : 5 },
MagicPants : {} },
  World : { Town1 : { OnFire : false, TaxDay : true } },
  NearbyEnemyCount : 0,
  // and so on
}
```

This makes it easy for the rule-matching algorithm to find any field it wants to filter; it's a simple key lookup. It also means you can use any bit of context in any rule. If you want a character's comment upon the town clock tower to change depending on what happened in a nearby village, that information is already available to you in that context dictionary. If you want to alter a character's barks based on how much danger they perceive themselves to be in, you could pass in the global count of active enemy characters. It creates opportunities for serendipity: you may have added a "TotalFruitPurchased" context for use by the fruit-vendor in village A, but if it's available globally, it may come in handy if you're struck with sudden inspiration for a character in town B to comment on their cousin's burgeoning fruit empire.

Also, combining all the contexts into one place makes them self-documenting to an extent. If you build a diagnostic printing all the context attached to every query into the dialog system, in addition to a useful debugging feature you'll also have a convenient list of contexts that is always complete and up to date. On *Left 4 Dead*, this diagnostic served as the writers' primary index.

In practice, merging every piece of state in the universe into a flat dictionary for every lookup is very computationally expensive. Next, we'll consider some data structures and simple optimizations that can keep this manageable.

DATA STRUCTURES AND THEIR IMPLEMENTATION

To review the key data structures in the approach mentioned earlier:

- A **context** is a single key-value pair such as PlayerHealth:72 or CurrentMap:Village5. For performance reasons it's best to use numeric values as much as possible, so for string values such as names, consider internally replacing them with unique symbols or hashes.

- A **query** is a group of contexts accumulated together into a single flat vector (or associative array). When a function wants to query the system, it assembles contexts from several places:

  - The function itself—for example, your UseMagicItem() function might supply MagicItem:wand and ChargesLeft:8, which are both specific to that piece of code. You will probably always have some top-level event context that identifies the general category of line to be played, such as CastSpell, SeenEnemy, Injured, and so on.

  - The speaking character's state, such as its current health, what object it is looking at, and other information that varies moment to moment.

  - The character's memory, including all the writebacks from previous rules. For example, a count of how many times the player healed this character, or how many times they've commented upon the weather in some running gag.

  - Global state, such as which map is loaded, the disposition of other characters, any pertinent ongoing effects.

- A **criterion** is a single comparison on a **context's** value, such as PlayerHealth > 50 or NearestObject=Barrel.

- A **rule** is a list of criteria; if all of them are true, the rule matches. Several rules may match at once, in which case you choose the most specific (the one with the most criteria). Each rule should at least have a criterion for that top-level event function, both for organizational purposes and for an optimization mentioned below.

- A **response** is the outcome when a rule matches, including

  - the line (or animation or whatever) to play,

  - writebacks to the character's memory or the world's state, or

  - follow-up events to dispatch to other characters for them to respond.

Building a Query

Function parameters (*e.g.*) Character.FindDialog(Event=OnHit, Attacker="Knight", Damage=12.4, ...)	
Event	"OnHit"
Attacker	"Knight"
Damage	12.4

+

Character state	
Name	"Odo"
Hitpoints	78
Nearest_Ally	"Wital"
Current_Weapon	"Mace"

+

Character memory	
Weather_Remarks	4
Saxons_Bludgeoned	7

+

Global	
Current_Map	"Hastings"
Remaining_Dragons	0
Quest5_Complete	false

With these data structures in place, choosing a line of dialog is essentially the following:

1. Construct a query (an associative array of contexts) by merging together function-specific context, character state, character memory, global context, and whatever else.

2. For each rule in the database,

    a. Test each criterion. If any criterion fails, skip this rule.

    b. If all criteria match, add this rule to the list of matching rules.

3. Select the highest-scoring rule (e.g., the one with the most criteria)

The naïve algorithm—looping over every criterion in every rule—runs in quadratic time but a few optimizations can make it much better.

First, sort the criteria in each rule, and the contexts in each query, by their keys. This lets you replace the random access step of each criterion looking up the corresponding fact in the query. With sorted keys, you can march pointers through the query vector and the rule's criterion vector in parallel, rejecting early as soon as any criterion fails to match. The rules' criteria can be sorted by an offline build step.

Second, merging multiple data sources (function call, character state, world state) into a single query vector doesn't need to be done literally. You can maintain each of those sources of context as a separate vector and have the rule's criteria test against all of them. If you're sorting your contexts as mentioned above, you can maintain separate index pointers into each array of contexts and move them all in parallel (Figure 25.2).

Third, you can hierarchically partition your rules database by high-level criteria, essentially a nested table of tables. For example, if every rule in your system has a SpeakingCharacter criterion, you can store a table from every possible speaker name to only the rules pertaining to that speaker, and so narrow down the number of rules to test considerably. By applying this recursively to other criteria (such as event and so on) you can reduce the number of rules that really need to be tested by quite a lot. (Theoretically, you could take this to its logical conclusion and represent the

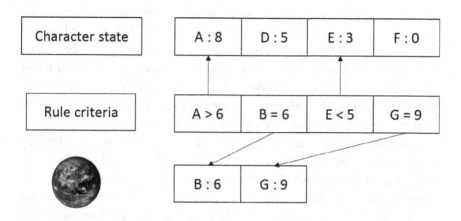

FIGURE 25.2

whole database as an interval tree with one dimension for each possible criterion, but this is much more complicated than it is worth.)

Fourth, if your game is divided up into regions or levels, and some rules are pertinent only in certain levels, you can store those rules inside those levels like any other asset, adding them to the database when the level is loaded and evicting them afterwards. This once again reduces the number of rules that need to be tested, as well as the memory footprint.

Fifth, sort the rules in each subdivision of the database by the number of criteria they have, in descending order. Once a high-scoring rule has been found, there is no need to test any rules that could only produce a lower score.

AUTHORING TOOLS

When it comes to writing the tool that lets writers get dialog into the game, there are many options, and the most important thing is to choose one that's suited to your team and circumstances. One possibility is to simply script rules directly using a syntax similar to the examples above. This is straightforward but grows unwieldy when you've got more than a few hundred rules to manage.

Another is to use a spreadsheet, exporting from that into game-readable asset. The advantage of this approach is that spreadsheets are familiar tools; you can use the spreadsheet's sorting tools to see all the lines for a given character at a glance, and it's quick to add additional bits of dialog simply by adding new rows to the spreadsheet. The downside is that you will need a separate column in the spreadsheet for each possible criterion, which becomes unwieldy when you have many special-purpose criteria for running gags and the like. Specifying context writebacks (RunningGag+=1) is also cumbersome.

Another possibility is to store the rules in some sort of relational database and write a front end that lets you author, search, and manage it. Campo Santo games did this to great effect for *Firewatch*,[1] with a unified database that managed not only dialog rules, but also tracked localization info, voice-over recording status, and content files. The downside here of course is that you must write such a tool. As with the spreadsheet there's also the question of how you store the criterion array—either you use one column in the database for every possible criterion, with the same shortcomings as the spreadsheet, or you have a TEXT field that contains all the criteria like "{Event=onSee; LookingAt=VillageSquare; global.DragonFreed=false; SpeakingCharacter=-Jane}" in which case searching is more cumbersome.

Another interesting approach is to look at rules as increasingly specific exceptions to earlier rules and use a scripting language built around the idea. For example, the Inform 7 text-adventure authoring language has a natural language syntax for this:

```
The cat behavior rules is a rulebook producing an object.
A cat behavior rule when the cat can touch the catnip:
say "The cat frolics with the catnip until nothing remains
of it.";
rule succeeds with result catnip.
A cat behavior rule when the cat can touch the cream:
say "The cat laps up the cream.";
rule succeeds with result cream.
A cat behavior rule when the cat can touch the ball of wool:
say "The cat makes the ball of wool into a useless tangle.";
rule succeeds with result ball.
```

That particular syntax would be unwieldy for rulebooks of any considerable size, but the general idea may be adapted into something more manageable.

Finally, spare a thought or three for debugging features. You can save many hours of frustration with techniques like (for example) a visualization that prints out a query as it's sent into the system, along with the origin of all its contexts, all the rules it tests, and which ones pass or fail.

CONCLUSION

In summary, the key takeaways are:

1. Keep it simple. This whole apparatus is just a rule-matching engine (or a *production system* in computer science parlance). Every feature presented here was an incremental step on a basic idea.

2. Queries are simply lists of facts, treated as a key-value dictionary.

3. Every query into the system includes as many facts about the world as possible. Throwing all that state at the database for every query enables writers to add new rules for new specific circumstances without requiring programmers to go and add additional data to the query.

4. Responses have a way to trigger follow-up queries on other characters, for back-and-forth conversations.

5. Responses have a way to write back state, into either characters' or the global memory.

6. Context names are arbitrary—code will define some, but writers should be able to invent new ones just by writing to an unused name from a response callback.

7. Rules are additive—you can start with a few general-case "OnBark" lines that have no special criteria and then add increasingly specific ones.

8. Because rules are additive, you can add new characters, scenarios, quests, etc., to the game just by loading additional rules into the database.

But most of all: keep it simple.

NOTE

1 William Armstrong and Patrick Ewing (2017, March). "Do you copy? The dialog system in Firewatch." Game Developers' Conference, San Francisco, CA.

5

Resources

I f interactive storytelling is almost as old as language itself, we should
expect to find it everywhere. In previous chapters, we've seen examples in
interactive dramatic works and roleplaying games. Here we'll share some
wider perspectives on interactive and procedural storytelling.

Specifically, we'll consider esoteric tarot divination from the view of
procedural storytellers, as well as the ways that automated bots on Twitter
can be seen through our lens in their astounding variety. Finally, we will
close with a practical guide on creating tools for procedural storytelling, for
those readers inspired enough to get started immediately.

It's important to choose the right tool for the job, as they say, and
this profession is no different, even if you sometimes build the tool
yourself. Thanks for reading, and happy generating!

This page intentionally left blank

CHAPTER 26

Tarot as Procedural Storytelling

Cat Manning

It's easy to think of procedural generation as a process that occurs digitally, mediated by an algorithm that displays the results on a screen, and this book is filled with examples of methods to create dynamic, rich procedurally generated digital content. I find that one of the richest tools for procedural storytelling is not digital at all but analogue and has existed in one form or another for centuries. That method is the tarot.

In the contemporary English-speaking world, tarot reading may be the best known of all cartomantic methods of divination. The reader uses a 78-card deck, comprised of a 22-card Major Arcana and a 56-card Minor Arcana, to draw anywhere from 1 to 10 cards in a spread to answer a particular question posed by a querent (Figure 26.1). Each card in the deck has several associated meanings, and the reader determines which are most relevant to the querent and the rest of the spread by associational construction. Tarot, then, is a procedural algorithm: cards are drawn and placed into position according to the system the reader has chosen. The results are then read as a whole, both meanings of individual cards and the interplay of patterns coalescing to form the final impression of the reading. What emerges is an interpretation: possibly a nebulous one and possibly quite solid. The outcome can depend on a number of factors: how familiar the reader is with tarot in general and the particular deck specifically, the pre-existing

FIGURE 26.1 Selections of some Major Arcana cards from the Rider-Waite-Smith deck.

relationship, if any, between the reader and the querent, and the phrasing of the question being posed.

Regardless of one's belief in the divinatory power of tarot, it's both a quick method for building intimacy and a powerful procedural generator, for the same reasons. There exists no objectively correct reading of a particular tarot spread; it's left to the querent and the reader to decide when and how they're satisfied with the reading. Tarot readers can perform another spread for clarity or draw an additional clarifying card if results seem ambiguous or unsatisfactory to the querent. The number of cards suggests an enormously boggling range of possibilities: there are 4.675×10^{21} possible 10-card Celtic Cross spreads. Yet, tarot manages to avoid the oatmeal problem that Kate Compton writes about in Chapter 1.

This is due to several aspects, some of which can be duplicated in digital procedural generation, and some that would prove more difficult or outright impossible. Meaning in tarot reading is constructed through a complex and layered associational structure of intersecting meanings and through the reader's associations with that structure. A traditional tarot deck contains several overlapping taxonomies; the deck is divided between Major and Minor Arcana, and the latter is subdivided into suits. Within those suits, numbered cards and court cards are separate.

Even within these overarching taxonomies, there are some small but narratively salient variations: the suit of Pentacles is represented in some decks as Coins or Disks, and Wands is occasionally Staves or Clubs. The court cards often see the most variation: Page / Knight / Queen / King are traditional, but Prince / Princess / Queen / King also occur, ostensibly to add more of a binary gender balance. There are court variants like Son / Daughter / Mother / Father in the Wild Unknown deck and the Amazon / Siren / Witch / Hag in the Dark Goddess deck.

The expressive range of the individual deck adds another layer of meaning: certain decks lend themselves more to particular shades of a card's interpretation.[1] Some decks have variant suits: the Slow Holler deck has Branches, Stones, Knives, and Vessels; the PoMo tarot has Bottles, Bills, TVs, and Guns. Others have extra suits, as in the Fifth Dimension's addition of "ether" to supplement the four traditional elements or the Silicon Dawn's partial Void suit. Aleister Crowley's Thoth deck adds an additional Major Arcana card of the Aeon, to represent a new age of humanity. Words and imagery of the cards themselves can lend readers toward or away from potential interpretations: Crowley's Thoth tarot, and decks based on it, have evocative one-word prompts printed at the bottom of their Minor Arcana, priming readers and querents to see a specific angle to the problem, where other decks leave associational meaning nonverbal (Figure 26.2).

The deck's expressive range, while directed by the creators, is also subject to the reader's response to that expressive range. Though the Rider-Waite-Smith deck is the most well-known deck, hundreds of variants exist, and readers chooses the deck or decks they feel are most suited to the situation at hand. A deck that has no or few human figures may feel to one reader as though it's ill-suited to questions of romance and intimacy; another reader may welcome that lack of leading imagery. Each reader brings their own pre-existing associations with imagery and cards, and each reader has their own taxonomy based on skill, prior knowledge, and individual practice. A tarot reader who does not know the difference between the Page and the Knight of a suit, for instance, can still decide on an interpretation of each card and devise their own

FIGURE 26.2 From left to right: Marseille, Thoth, Rider-Waite-Smith, Golden Thread interpretations of the Four of Wands.

pattern that will drive interpretive methods. Because tarot allows for so much interpretive agency on the part of the reader, it engages the attention of both the person asking the question and the reader of the cards.

To illustrate in detail how tarot succeeds at creating this framework of nearly infinite possibilities, all of which feel salient, unique and personal, I'm going to do several sample readings using my own associational structures and then examine my methods from a narrative design perspective. Other tarot readers may have different associations than the ones I bring to these readings, which indicates the different construction of meanings this method of storytelling offers. In order to talk about the wide variations the tarot provides, I'll first choose not only the number of cards to draw, but the spread and thus the narrative range of possibilities. In tarot, a spread is a particular number and geometric arrangement of cards, which assigns particular meanings such as "hopes and fears" or "advice" to cards depending on their position. A one-card spread is the easiest and bluntest of instruments, best used for focus and brief flashes of insight. I drew "Justice" about how an upcoming project meeting will go, which could suggest the need for fairness, clarity, and openness in that conversation, but could also serve as a potential warning that I'll only get back as much as I put in.

Three card spreads provide slightly more context. A past-present-future spread offers a perspective on what is happening: what has occurred in the past to bring the querent to the current position, what the situation is in the present moment, and what to expect. A situation-outcome-action spread offers slightly more agency to the querent, by offering an action that would change the current situation and an outcome if that action is taken; there is no sense that the action must be taken, only of a path that leads forward from the middle card. Both offer a linear narrative progression for the reader to construct. 10-card spreads offer less linear forward momentum than three 3-card spreads, but the former provides a contextual overview of a situation.

The usual past-present-future is crossed here (Figure 26.3) with a "situation" card, which indicates a complicating factor or a new piece of information. The subconscious and hopes and fears may seem similar, but "subconscious" relates more to the querent's general present

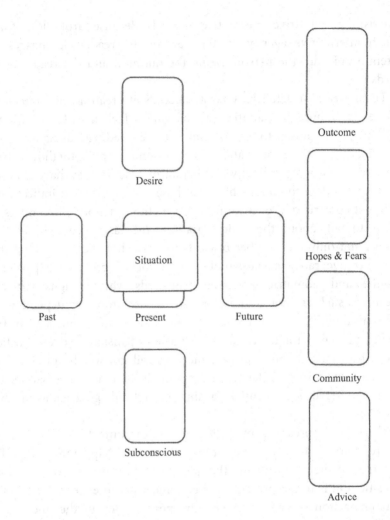

FIGURE 26.3 Some readers invert the order of the long "cross" to the side, and some use slightly different card labels to describe the interplay between internal and external states of the querent.

state of mind, while "hopes and fears" projects that present subconscious onto the future and thus ties back to the central part of the cross.[2] 10-card spreads are best for complex problems with a variety of factors influencing the querent; they can, however, bog down a novice reader or querent with too much information, particularly if there aren't multiple clear associations in the spread. By introducing a number of additional cards that aren't chronological, the Celtic Cross spread allows for more "hooks" for both querent and reader to draw connections and for a more salient and personal picture to arise. The complexity of the reading increases as more cards are introduced, but because of associational structures within the tarot deck and within the spread, more pathways for emergent meaning are possible. Those pathways won't always be relevant to other interpretations, and some will contradict, but it's up to the reader and querent to decide which structures to bring to the surface as they piece together possible associations.

Here, we'll start with a fairly simple three 3-card spread (Figure 26.4) and a situation-action-outcome reading within that. We'll use a hypothetical common question: "should I look for a safe and stable job or pursue a riskier but more creatively and emotionally fulfilling path?" By surfacing a specific, concrete question, we have already significantly constrained our narrative possibility space and made it easier for a reader to focus on constructing a narrative that can be focused to provide greater personal meaning to the querent. But even within that narrower possibility space, already we run into narrative variants: our querent might be in a situation in which a practical job is necessary to pay rent, loans, or medical bills; she also may have

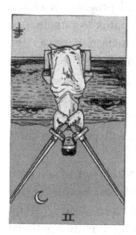

FIGURE 26.4 A spread of three tarot cards.

resources and connections that allow more of a safety net. The reader may not always be aware of the asker's situation, and while a skilled reader may be able to pick up on a querent's enthusiasm or fear, it can't be assumed as a factor that will always surface during a reading.[3]

When the cards are drawn, we have the Two of Swords reversed in the situation, the Ten of Cups in the action, and the Wheel of Fortune in the outcome. At this moment, intersections of meaning are the most relevant aspect. The cards can be interpreted individually, and then, to provide our reading, in a multiply overlapping semantic web. Two of Swords in the present could suggest, rudimentarily, conflicting options, a bifurcated path, or the twin severing blades of scissors; with the reversal, it suggests a difficult decision imposed from without. Given the question, it seems to reflect the querent's uncertainty about which path would be best in the medium to long term for overall quality of life. Swords is the suit of air and of the mind, of rational decisions weighed. The presence of Cups in the action card suggests a departure from that rationality is necessary, a move to the emotional and intuitive qualities of the water suit; a trusting of the heart and the gut. The Ten of this suit in particular suggests a joy and fulfilment caused by harmony, of community, of real connection after false indulgence. We then move to the Wheel of Fortune in the outcome position. The Wheel alone suggests the inevitability of change; of cycles beyond human control; of forward motion. It could signify forward progress or chaos. Instead of telling our querent which of two career paths to pursue, one interpretation of this narrative possibility space instead suggests she embrace her conflicting and real feelings of the moment and become at peace, that there is never "enough" information to make the one correct choice. Taken all together, the reading suggests a difficult decision that has to be made between two options and that choosing the path of emotional fulfilment and listening to one's heart will provide a third path with its own set of joys and challenges.

My querent here will probably have a fairly good idea of which path is the best for her heart, without my needing to advise her toward one option or another and my doing that would close down certain possibility sets of the reading that the ambiguity of our associational meaning structure allows.

So how do I, as the reader, put together the associational meaning structures of these cards to get a coherent and meaningful story, beyond simply memorizing "Two of Swords means a difficult decision," etc.? The answer lies in intersecting taxonomies of meaning and symbolism, and the ability to read them in layers rather than choosing only one to focus on. Individual card meanings are actually only one taxonomy— arguably the most important, but without paying attention to other taxonomies such as number, Minor vs. Major Arcanas, and art and how they layer, a great deal of interesting and personal meaning can be lost. The first thing I look to is the presence of suits in the reading—does one dominate? A reading that's heavy in Swords, for example, can suggest a command of reason and the mind over the situation, in addition to warning about rigidity, while Pentacles would suggest that the matter is very much grounded in the material, that situations like bills, rent, and economic ties in relationships are on the querent's mind or should be considered. The Major Arcana also has its own sphere; it suggests a sense that these matters speak to a querent's profound self-conception or a spiritual component, that an aspect of the situation will aid the querent in their personal growth. Progression also matters: the tarot suits ascend in order from Pentacles to Cups to Swords to Wands, and so a progression or regression, especially in a three 3-card linear reading, can be interesting. Here, we have a move from Swords to Cups, the sense that the "lower" suit actually represents progress: that going backward actually might be going forward. It asks us to reconsider, to double back on our assumptions.

Number also plays a role here. While Cups is a "lower" suit on the hierarchy than Swords, the Ten is a higher card than the Two: we have two different intersecting taxonomies to read against each other here. Tens in the Minor Arcana signify a culmination of a cycle; in the suits of Cups and Coins, they suggest a deeper reconnection after struggle, while in Wands and Swords, they imply a matter that becomes too much to bear. Though meaning varies across each individual card, each numerological card in the Minor Arcana shares a general narrative position with the other. To move from the Ten, the end of a cycle fulfilled, to the card of perpetual cycles in the Major Arcana suggests a move of progression upward in numeric terms.

In this case, Cups as a "lower suit" is overwritten by the linear numerological progression from Two to Ten to Major Arcana and from inverted to upright: that reading still exists, but other meanings layer over it. I'm personally inclined to favor a numeric progression over a suits progression, though other readers might find the latter's salience more significant and account for that more heavily in their own reading of these three cards. The reading's complexity stems from these multiple category intersections: they don't conflict or collapse into one dominant linear progression. Even with a reading in which all the tarot's taxonomies did proceed neatly in one direction, that itself would feel salient and be another piece of data.

But more fun comes in when we think about narrative positioning and how easy it is to shift the meaning of a tarot spread by ostensibly small variants. What happens if we switch our action and outcome cards? We retain the sense that our querent faces a difficult decision, but now the action suggested is to surrender to the whims of fortune, to accept that both paths will have their difficulties or perhaps to take the riskier, more challenging path! But then the outcome is the Ten of Cups—the sense that giving into risk will provide great emotional fulfillment. Where the first reading exhorts listening to one's heart to find a new and unexpected path, the second suggests giving into chaos and that the result will provide emotional fulfillment. The elements of unpredictability and attachment remain, but the narrative we tell ourselves about how to reach the point is quite significantly shifted, even though the spread contains the same individual cards.

Less significant in terms of variation, but still meaningful, is switching the position of a card from upright to reversed. The Wheel of Fortune is the only card in the tarot deck that can't be read either upright or reversed, so we'll switch the Two of Swords to upright. With this, we get the sense that the decision is imposed internally rather than externally—our querent's situation materially hasn't changed, obviously, but our thinking about it may well have. She may be inclined to consider her own agency in this decision more, rather than the external factors imposing on her with a reversal. It's a subtle shift, but one that can change how the querent and reader view the cause of the situation.

The greatest variation comes when an entirely new card is substituted for one of our initial three; this shifts not only the meaning of that position but the entirety of the spread. Let's substitute the Seven of Swords for the Wheel of Fortune: in this case, our upward progression is lost, and we have a Swords-heavy spread that suggests that, despite moves toward getting in touch with her emotions, our querent's situation will be dominated by dispassionate reasoning and carefully measured choices. The Seven of Swords signifies subterfuge, shrewdness, and betrayal; occurring in response to the Ten of Cups, it suggests to me a retreat from open emotion into self-protection and possibly even paranoia. Whatever path the querent chooses, the Seven of Swords in this position suggests a need for caution, wariness, and the potential for betrayal: a departure from the surrender to a third, exciting path the Wheel of Fortune previously signified.

This interpretive quality allows tarot to avoid the oatmeal problem: the substitution of even one card asks readers to consider what multiple aspects of the card might be implying without giving concrete answers. It's up to the readers to fill in the gaps and thus supply the most narratively satisfying piece of the procedural system themselves.

Certain individual aspects of tarot can be duplicated digitally or in narrative design: the Golden Thread tarot has an accompanying app that seems to be one of the most popular digital decks and allows readers to log daily cards, spreads, and moods associated with both analog and digital readings from a pre-selected list. As of this writing, Emily Short is in the process of designing a *Tarot of the Parrigues*, which is currently accessible in a publicly available draft form.[4] Outside of constructing allusive, layered structures of meaning in a way that requires readers to apply their own personal meanings, tarot is difficult to translate directly into a digital sphere, as the process of reading so often depends on a back and forth (among the reader, the querent, and the cards) that's difficult to capture in real time digitally. What tarot can offer narrative designers is a strong model for how to create meaningful, personal, and unique stories.

By using multiple co-existing layers of meaning and symbology, and not insisting that one take precedence over the other, tarot asks the reader to choose from multiple modes of interpretation to construct a coherent meaning. This narrative construction is often more personally satisfying than unstructured advice might be because of the investment of selecting and curating meaning from a large set of possibilities.

NOTES

1 For an excellent article on expressive ranges of tarot decks, see Emily Short's https://emshort.blog/2018/05/03/favorite-tarot-decks/#more-38151

2 Some readers label "desire" and "subconscious" as "above" and "below" respectively, suggesting both the position of the cards and the aspirational nature of the querent's struggle contrasted with what might be hidden in the depths of their mind. Some incorporate self-image and resources; some use the long axis of the cross to project 3, 6, 9, and 12 months ahead of the situation.

3 There are also situations in which a querent will not ask the question verbally but will focus on it; in these situations, the reader can only look for larger narrative patterns.

4 The project in its current form, as of this article's writing, can be found here: https://emshort.blog/2018/06/26/parrigues-tarot-draft/

CHAPTER 27

Things You Can Do with Twitterbots

George Buckenham

Twitter, unlike most social media platforms, has a rich history of openly automated accounts. Any social media platform of a significant size will have automated accounts posting spam—but Twitter also has automated accounts posting generated poetry, art, fiction and much more not easily categorized. A big reason this is the case is Twitter's early focus on encouraging developers to work with its APIs (and subsequent legacy of permissive policies towards automated accounts)—but it's also because of the format of Twitter. Each tweet is a small thing, jumbled into the timeline. It's easier to generate something meaningful and interesting if it's short and can gain strength from the tweets surrounding it.

One genre of generated text that is a surprisingly good fit for tweets is worldbuilding. While in games generative worldbuilding is often very concerned with building an intricate self-consistent world model, Twitterbots are free to just create short fragments of evocative description. @neighbour_civs tweets every 3 hours, each time with a short description of a people. For example:

> The Wasteland-Lizard Tribe. A great poet of theirs composed an epic about the Great Rancher. They colour their snouts with red paste.
>
> or

The "Red Antler" Society. They regard the current era as lasting from the destruction of the Extravagant Tower to the disappearance of the Goose City. Their longships are recognizable by their green sails.

The more details you give, the harder you have to work to keep them all consistent. Each tweet contains just a name for the tribe and two details, so there's not much chance of conflict. What is there is evocative, giving hooks that allow you to expand the world in your head. Who is the Great Rancher? Why did the Goose City disappear? Each tweet sits free of every othe—there's a consistent tone but no insistence that all of these places are in the same world.

Just as it's possible to use small fragments of worldbuilding as part of a larger system, it's possible for tweets to exist as part of a larger project. @unfamiliar_city takes after a travel guide, with tweets such as:

Don't miss Dadoe, our favorite spot for Lourhou-style cuisine https:// unfamiliar.city/city/150001778968
   and
To say "sorry" in the iyzhthar language, say "shachrukthai" (ɪɒcɟʌkθe) https://unfamiliar.city/city/150001422085

Each of these links will take you to a larger page, with a brief rundown of useful facts about the city in question. Following the link in the first tweet, I find some basic words and phrases ("Hello: redou", "Thank you: derhou", "Sorry: bouboubou"), current exchange rate to the US Dollar ("$1 USD = 4.28 ladoudou"), 7-day weather forecast (as I write this, it's forecast to snow all week) and some tourist advice—in this case, a fuller description of the restaurant in the tweet:

Dadoe: Owner Rhoerhourhe Bäthe has given Lourhouian-style cuisine a modern edge while still staying true to the regional style. The venue is stunning, stylish stone and wood third-floor room with world-renowned charm. Be sure to try the "bfougou" (a light soup made with rhoubou and a vegetable called boebagou).

This achieves impressive internal consistency—for example, the name of the restaurant, Dadoe, is also given elsewhere as the translation of the word "tasty". These details, technically, exist outside the world of

Twitter—but in much the same way that a human's feed can be valuable because it links to a lot of interesting stuff, @unfamiliar_city's tweets are valuable as a portal to and a way of surfacing the richness of the generator powering the unfamiliar.city website.

As well as containing text and links to external content, tweets can contain embedded images and videos. My bot, @soft_landscapes, generates a pastel mountainscape every six hours. Each image contains a series of mountain-top crests, receding into the mist. Its tweets work in much the same way as @unfamiliar_city or @neighbour_civs—each tweet exists in its own beautiful, isolated world, evoking thoughts of what lies beyond the frame. While outputs from the bot have been exhibited as standalone artwork, they are more properly appreciated as an ongoing process, a sampling of an interestingly crafted probability space of possible landscapes.

For example, that probability space is focused on a region that generates delicate pastel views, but it also includes smaller, rarer slivers of very dark views, or very saturated views. Sometimes the haze is strong enough that no mountains are visible—while typically an image containing nothing but a flat, off-white, rectangle would be a failure of procedural generation, here the surrounding context (in a series of views of landscapes, on an account that claims to generate views of landscapes) just makes you think "oh! it's very foggy there", and this has been my reaction when I climb to the top of an actual mountain.

It's possible to focus on arresting images, even when creating a bot restricted purely to text. An early inspiration for me was the bot @tiny_star_fields, which produces tweets that look like this:

```
*.      .

   *  *

  ☆


*    *    ◇    ◆.


   *  *       . ·


      *        .    *
```

It's beautiful—both for its interest in and commitment to the glyphs it uses and for the way that you immediately extrapolate from those glyphs to the night's sky. I look at its 180 characters of assorted Unicode, and I think of sitting at a campfire in the desert, staring up at the vast sky and marvelling at all of the stars I can't see back home, seeing the Milky Way for the first time.

Within the wide fields of Unicode also live emoji. Every few hours, @skeletonsday posts an emoji skeleton going about its day. Each tweet is just a few symbols, but it's enough to construct a whole narrative. Skelly says no to a frog. Skelly goes to SeaWorld. Skelly discovers aliens. What an adventurous life Skelly leads, all suggested within a few characters, with the help of all the overloaded context we apply to emoji.

All the bots we've considered so far post a stream of independent tweets and so suggest a continuous, endless process. It is definitely interesting to work with an art form so readily suited to the infinite series, but there are obvious drawbacks when trying to convey a traditional narrative (with a beginning, middle and end). The complex state-tracking needed to form a coherent story using generative methods can be pretty daunting—but one of the best things about making Twitterbots is that they are small, bite-sized projects that can be made and released quickly. The form is necessarily one in which most of the content generated will be missed, and most of the viewers of the work will encounter it partway through. As a result of all these constraints, the Twitterbots that are best at conveying narrative do it by establishing a mood, giving interesting narrative details and then allowing the work to extend out within the viewer's mind.

Within these constraints, @ArpObservatory stands out for effectively conveying a specific narrative. It's the Twitter account of an astronomer based in the Atacama Desert, Chile, and the bio reads "In July we started receiving audio signals from outside the solar system, and we've been studying them since". Roughly every half hour, it tweets a mix of generated diagrams (waveforms, frequency response curves, etc.), links to actual generated audio (hosted on SoundCloud), comments on the nature of the waveforms received (sample: "During the last 40 mins we've received three confirmed audio-bursts and three more expected to be confirmed shortly".) and personal observations—often of the nearby wildlife ("I just watched a 'lava lizard' basking by the salt flat".), but sometimes more reflective ("Gazing up at the clear night sky, each star appears so close".). Viewed as a feed, repetitions become inescapable, and the bones of the grammars used for each part start poking through. But the experience you get when you follow the account and see a sprinkling of tweets within your feed is quite different—your normal Twitter feed is sprinkled with a sense of lonely purpose and everyday beauty from the Atacama.

As with @soft_landscapes, this is a project that is judicious about probability. The rarity of the more personal reflections makes each one feel special, a special insight into the scientist's mind set and situation. The continued ambiguity of the import of the signals (are these really messages from aliens? Scientific caution advises against jumping to any rash conclusions.) keeps a focus on the mood. Of course, it doesn't hurt that the generated images and audio are beautiful in their own right.

@ArpObservatory is also one of the best examples of making expressive use of the metadata Twitter allows you—each account has a stream of tweets and a profile with username, bio, website, location, profile and header image, etc. These are the first impressions a bot provides, and they set the framing for the actual tweets. There is, of course, much more context floating around for any particular viewers: how they found the account, who RTs the account, the replies, the followers; these are even more important to the experience of the bot and much harder to control for a botmaker. If you are creating bots, it's worth thinking carefully about any and all context you can set. Time spent thinking about the expectations of the viewers and how to manipulate them can be more effective than any amount of algorithm-tweaking.

In the same way that your bot should respond to the Twitter context it is part of, it sets a context for others. By making a bot, you are creating a machine that autonomously acts in a medium on an equal footing with human beings. You are responsible for what it posts, and for the results of that, in the same way that you're responsible for posts you make manually. This responsibility comes through in basic ways like filtering any corpuses used for slurs, or not @-notifying users without consent. But there are also larger ethical issues, such as you and your bots' relationship to Twitter the company and Twitter the platform. You are creating art with a commercial platform, and that is a complicated relationship. The people running Twitter have a different set of goals to you; it's worth thinking about where they align, and what happens when they don't.

Thoughts like this have led many prominent creators of bots to rethink their ongoing presence on and creation of works for Twitter. Everest Pipkin, creator of @tiny_star_fields, recently stated baldly "i do not want my work to serve them; i don't want to to increase their prestige" (https://twitter.com/everestpipkin/status/1010585694400417792) but even so has not stopped making bots entirely. While Twitter is not a neutral platform, it is still a platform with reach, a platform with power. They vowed, "from now to the death of this platform, protest bots are the only bots i will make" (https://twitter.com/everestpipkin/status/1010588540978098177) and created @Abolish_ICE_Now, a bot listing US detention facilities holding immigrants, together with statistics on the facilities, the communities surrounding them and images taken from satellite photography or Google Images.

Bedford Municipal Detention Center jails immigrants at 2121 L Don Dodson Drive, Bedford, TX. Its last inspection rating was 'Acceptable'. Bedford has a population of 47,617 and an elevation of 601.38 ft. Homes are 3.8% vacant, 41.2% rented, and 55.1% owned.

(attached is a satellite photo of Bedford Municipal Detention Center) https://twitter.com/Abolish_ ICE_Now/status/1043717973242871808)

The bot follows each tweet with a translation into Spanish.

Bedford Municipal Detention Center tiene inmigrantes encerrados en 2121 L Don Dodson Drive, Bedford, TX. La última calificación de inspección que obtuvo fue 'Acceptable'. Bedford tiene una población de 47,617 y una elevación de 601.38 ft. El ingreso medio por hogar es $65,579.

The bot comes from a sense of anger and wants to effect change, but it is still thoughtfully composed and still has the care and aesthetic sensibility that runs through all of Everest's work. This bot does not playfully pretend at being anything other than a bot; its sentences are clearly templates, and this serves to emphasize the cold anger that drove its creation.

Of course, for many other creators, Twitter is still a playground. Twitter is an effective medium for news and protest, but it is also used as a medium for jokes. @vg_erotica, is a bot that, as the name suggests, combines videogames and erotica. A few sample tweets:

> He lifted his lips from where they played at the place where his neck met his shoulder and placed them at his ear, speaking, the words low and dark and full of wicked intent. "Tell me."
>
> "Back my game on Kickstarter." - https://twitter.com/vg_erotica/status/999635191596544001
>
> She lifted her chin and pressed a single, soft kiss on her lips, trying not to notice when she leaned into the touch, when she breathed a little sigh as she lifted her head. "Screenshot saved." - https://twitter.com/vg_erotica/status/1002443995040055296

Even from two tweets, you can infer the format. Hot, breathless prose, brought down to earth with a bump by a worn-out phrase from games. The length of tweets is perfect for this: long enough to establish a rhythm before interrupting it. None of these tweets would be funnier if they spent longer setting up or dwelled longer on the videogames. The incongruity that generates the humour comes naturally from the procedural rhetoric— sampling randomly from the space of "erotic" and "videogames" always works, because anything sampled from one set will juxtapose against anything from the other. Sometimes the juxtaposition works perfectly, sometimes it falls flat, but that's okay, because the average is good enough, and the probability space also includes some that are very good.

Working on the same logic is @darndesttruisms, which combines "my small child said a thing which backs up my political arguments" and "statements taken from the American artist Jenny Holzer's works". A sample tweet:

> My 5-yr old kid just whispered "the desire to reproduce is a death wish" in my ear. - https://twitter.com/darndesttruisms/status/1014696925809930240

This is even simpler: the setup is less elaborate, and the Jenny Holzer statements are taken from a single corpus and would've required less effort to assemble. It's a less funny bot, but its aims are broader than just comedy. It triggers a sense of unease at hearing these incongruous statements from fictional children, an interrogation into the use of rhetoric, a juxtaposition of the grand universal statement with the small and particular. I like to think Jenny Holzer (who displayed her truisms on posters, cinema hoardings, LED screens, T-shirts and other public spaces) would approve of this bot, and see it as an extension of her practice.

@everyword was a long-running Twitterbot; as the name suggests, it posted every word (in the English language). At a rate of once every half hour, it took seven years to complete its task. Over the years, it built up tens of thousands of followers, including me. I remember a real sense of excitement in the replies as it started to near the end of the alphabet. What would be the final word? What would it do when it reached the end: stop or start again at the start? Finally, it reached "zymurgy" … and then rolled immediately onto "éclair". The English language has borrowed a few words from French, and the word list's sorting put those starting with "é" after those starting with "z".

This again follows the structure of a joke. A context was established, an expectation was set—at the end of "z", the bot will complete its task. This expectation was built up over a full 7 years of patient iteration into our feeds. We lived with a slow advance through the alphabet. And then, the twist, the punchline: "z" was not actually the end. As with all good jokes, the punchline follows naturally on from the setup, but it's not what you expected beforehand. It's the twist of having your mental model realigned that makes a joke satisfying, and I still treasure the twist @everyword provided.

As well as using bots to create jokes, botmakers can also use them to destroy jokes. Darius Kazemi is a renowned botmaker, who regularly takes a current Twitter joke or meme and creates a bot that automates its creation. Examples include @choppermemebot (which fits movie scripts into the American Chopper format), @expandingbot (which generates expanding brain image macros) and @BracketMemeBot (which takes Wikipedia categories and makes elimination brackets out of them). These bots are all created after a particular meme has reached a point of saturation, where surveying your Twitter feed can feel like everyone is just cramming arbitrary combinations of concepts into the format *du jour*. By automating that process and creating a greater swell of tweets than the format can sustain, Darius hastens the death of that particular format (at least within the circles exposed to the bot). This can be a good thing, as every joke has a shelf life after which it becomes tiresome.

@everyword was a very popular bot, and it inspired many imitators. An imitator I especially enjoyed was @everyboolean. It has posted just two tweets: first, the single word "true". Then, the single word "false". What made @everyboolean so satisfying was the gap of many years between the two tweets. During that time, the content of the second tweet could be easily inferred, but the posting schedule could not be. Where @everyword delivered a great twist by setting a regular posting schedule, but delivering unexpected content, @everyboolean delivered a years-long sense of suspense by having a tweet whose contents could be inferred but not the timing. You need two instances to establish a pattern.

That long period of suspense is interesting, because it ties back to the durational aspect of Twitter. Unlike many digital spaces, it is a place where things can exist for a long time. It's a way to experience art as an ongoing process, to sit with it until it becomes background noise. @everyword lived in people's timelines; @everyboolean didn't but always threatened to send that concluding tweet. I don't follow many of Darius's bots, but still they circulate through my feed via retweets. Part of what's good about Twitterbots is how they are best when they respond directly to the conditions of Twitter itself: the social conventions, the rhythms of interaction and even the specific technical constraints on the platform.

Another take on @everyword was @everyletter123. Let me briefly recap its tweets:

A

(*20 March 2013* -https://twitter.com/EveryLetter123/status/314416 396341743616

B

(*20 March 2013* -https://twitter.com/EveryLetter123/status/314416 420333166592)

C

(*20 March 2013* -https://twitter.com/EveryLetter123/status/314416 396341743616) at which point it stopped tweeting, presumably forever. Now, obviously, bots break all the time. It's hard to maintain software on the Internet; it's a place with constantly changing standards, every system jury-rigged on top of five others. But this failed for a simple and conceptually satisfying reason: it is impossible to create a tweet containing the single letter "D". This is because "D username message" is the shorthand syntax for sending a direct message to someone, so any tweet starting with D and then a space is interpreted as a command to send a DM, instead of a tweet. This was developed when Twitter's main interface was SMS, but the history lives on and the restriction is still present today.

I like to think of @everyletter123 patiently trying every day to send the next tweet in the series. Every day, Twitter rejects it, it acknowledges the rejection and goes back to sleep, ready to try again tomorrow.

Similarly, I like to think about the broken bot @wa_k (bio: "I want you to know COOL kanji. Let's learn Japanese, especially Kanji."), which became stuck and tweeted out "吐—MEANING: disgorge, vomit, confess PRONUNCIATION: to, ha(ku)" six times a day until it finally broke.

There is something about the ways that bots can break, can get stuck in robotic patterns of behaviour, their very inhuman-ness, that asks that you take them seriously as independent entities. Now, to be clear, all bots are ultimately someone's responsibility, broken or not, but I find myself more ready to play along with the personhood of those bots that display their artifice most transparently.

A well-functioning bot, tended to by human hands, is hard to think of as anything but the creation of a person. It takes a broken, forgotten bit of code, valiantly disgorging six times a day, to inspire true wonder.

CHAPTER 28

Creating Tools for Procedural Storytelling

Emily Short

T his chapter assumes that you have built, or are building, a storytelling system that procedurally determines how and in what order to show content to the player. It also assumes that "writing" for this system involves hand authoring or importing a significant amount of data, together with whatever meta-data is required to allow your system to properly process it.

This is a very broad definition. It would encompass

- text adventure design systems that include object-oriented representations of objects in the game world,

- dungeon layout systems that associate any amount of narrative with the dungeon rooms,

- storylet-based games like *Fallen London*, and

- narrative systems with extensive text generation that rely on significant corpora of words.

Not all of the observations here will apply equally to all systems; they're meant more as a framework for thinking about challenges that I've encountered many times as I've built and rebuilt systems of this kind.

WHAT CAN AUTHORING TOOLS FOR PROCEDURAL STORYTELLING DO?

Creating Content

The majority of procedural storytelling systems require the developer to create the elements of storytelling herself—whether these are lines of dialogue with trigger conditions, storylets associated with preconditions and effects, branching conversations, grammars for creating generative text, or world models designed for use in a text adventure. Different phases of the work often have different support needs.

The First Five Minutes

Often, a new system needs to be primed with some content before it can produce any playable experience at all. This stage doesn't matter too much for systems that are designed to work on a single studio project. Usually by the time you're building a dedicated content creation tool, you've already got a prototype off the ground, and new content creation is destined to be additive. However, for any system that is meant to be used for new work on a regular basis—and especially for systems you expect to be used by non-professionals—it's critical to think about how quickly a user can get from opening the software to trying out a playable experience. For StoryNexus, the quality-based narrative system used by Failbetter Games, you need a sequence of storylets for the player to get acquainted with the system and play through some basic mechanics. That might take hours of construction, configuration, and uploading art files. For the average text adventure, you need a room or two and some initial inventory items and actions. For a grammar-based system, the minimum might consist of one or more top-level nodes to expand.

A tool providing default implementations can do a lot to get a first-time author up and running. The text adventure development system Inform comes with a default library that implements almost everything you need to get a playable first room, for instance. There's almost nothing in it, but as a new author you can compile and run within the first five minutes of using the tool and already have something that's ready for interaction. Spirit AI's dialogue tool Character Engine provides default projects that have a few basic lines of dialogue rigged up, so you can have a (very rudimentary) conversation almost as soon as you start. Twine and Texture allow for playable experiences from the moment you've built your first links.

Developing a Structure

So, the first interaction is in place. The next task is to make a playable chunk: a tutorial, a chapter, or even the arc of a whole game. I often find it useful to build an initial skeleton for the story in a fairly linear fashion, then to come back and add branches, variants, and alternative content. Or, if it's a grammar-based project, I might be creating a single baseline sentence in a generative grammar, and I expect to come back later and add variants.

In Twine, developing structure might mean making nodes that stand in for the start and end of each scene, with the actual content of the passage to be elaborated later between those points. In Character Engine or Inform (very different tools sharing a concept of scenes), that might mean describing how scenes start and end.

Quality-based narrative tools like StoryNexus, where the system is selecting freely from a group of available storylets, can make this a bit harder, because given a selection of storylets with prerequisites and consequences, it's more difficult for the user to anticipate all the possible stat combinations the player might reach, and there's no explicit model of narrative content.

Matching Fiction to Mechanics

Suppose I need to make sure I have appropriate content variants to correspond to each category in a system. Perhaps I'm writing a game about the traditional elements, and I need an Earth, Air, Water, and Fire version of each item of clothing. Or I'm writing storylets for a storylet-driven narrative system, and I need three ways of advancing the player's relationship with a character, one based on each of the three major relationship skills of Kindness, Cunning, and Humor. Or I'm creating cards for a narrative deck-building game and I need to construct six randomized disaster events. Here the author's job is to come up with a fictional wrapper for already-defined mechanical content. This work becomes grinding or dull, especially if you have a large number of predefined systems elements you need to fill in. It's easy to fall into a rut and produce no interesting variations.

There are several ways that a tool can help with this. One is by tracking content that still needs to be created and offering mechanical writing prompts to the author in random order. Writing fictional elements for different pieces of the system means the author is less likely to burn out on a particular concept. It's hard to write fifty closely related bits of fiction in a row without falling into a bit of a rut. Tools that can track and assign content-creation tasks like this are also useful in collaborative projects, where different authors might be contributing fictional tidbits for recombination.

Another option is to have the tool actually propose randomized fiction prompts. Once I had the job of writing a number of storylets for *Fallen London*. Other designers had already defined the mechanical parameters: what player stats would unlock the storylet, what stat levels would determine success and failure, what the value of success rewards should be, and so on. *Fallen London* also has a richly developed lore that associates different parts of the city and characters with particular player stats. To help myself come up with appropriate mini stories about all of these scenarios, I built a small generative grammar to build storylet premises around particular stat combinations. Given a request for a story about applications of the Watchful stat, it would invent lines like:

> You keep a watchful vigil on your mark's home to gain an introduction to your mark's relatives, at the risk of going mad.
> You try to decipher an encrypted collection of notes from a sea voyage to gain information about your mark's childhood, at the risk of seeing a warped version of a priest in your dreams

The grammar would give me three of these at a time. They weren't always particularly good, but that didn't matter: there was usually at least one in the three that gave me an idea I could flesh out into a more fully formed fiction that was thematically aligned to the assigned mechanics.

Elsewhere, some research suggests that writers are more likely to come up with inventive text to match predefined meanings if they're prompted with sample images rather than words. It would be easy to imagine designing prompts that relied on composited pictures rather than text.

Accretive or Sculptural Writing Processes

Once an initial skeleton of content is in place, I often like to read or play the generated game until I reach a point at which I can imagine a cooler response, dialogue line, or event, and I add that element in that location. For a conversation game, that might entail finding a moment where a character could answer a question I hadn't considered previously. For a story game, that might mean noticing a particular twist outcome that has become possible based on the events leading up to that point.

The appeal of this kind of writing is that it puts the author in sympathy with the experience of the player: you're thinking in a player mode about the narrative, and that often leads to some of the most satisfying insights about content.

The challenge is that not all tools are equally good at supporting this creation mode, and some make it very difficult indeed. Tools that help with sculptural authoring are those that

- allow a tight play/replay cycle. Inform, for instance, lets the author play to a given point, make some changes in the source code, and recompile and replay to the same point in the story. In some cases, this may require retaining and reusing random seeds as well as the history of play up to that point in the story.

- allow the author to tell a running game instance that we want to copy all of the current state and associate it with a new piece of content. This cuts the authoring burden and capacity for error considerably.

During the content-building phase, my multi-author conversation game *Alabaster* included a feature that let the player/co-author try interactions like ASK (THE NPC) ABOUT LILITH. Any time the player reached a point at which there was no answer already defined, the game changed to an authoring mode, allowing the player to specify how the NPC should respond at this point.

The game would then ask a few questions to flesh out what that line of dialogue should look like and automatically write to a file all of the data required to instantiate that dialogue in exactly that point in the narrative. This allowed different authors working on the system to build out their own areas of content—or even riff on each other's content—without having to learn the underlying procedures or memorize a content tagging system.

Adding Variety

The previous authoring action was about adding more chunks of content in order to reflect world state more completely and accurately. This one is about adding more internal variety to content in order to support a richer replay experience.

> I love chocolate cake.
> And replacing it with a token that gives alternate flavors, like
> I love [chocolate/vanilla/strawberry] cake.
> Though it might just as well be a replacement for the entire dish ...
> I love [chocolate cake/mushroom omelets].
> ... or for the verb ...
> I [love/hate/feel ambivalent about] chocolate cake.

Elaborating a section of content like this can be fun—and in many projects, it's possible to do almost an infinite amount of it. In my procedural text project *Annals of the Parrigues*, I developed a complex grammar for describing towns and travel but often brought in lists of specific objects from outside. *Annals of the Parrigues* knows about several hundred varieties of apple, simply because Darius Kazemi's procgen corpus repository[1] offered me a source file that was easy to use.

There are two big traps for authors here. One is that they will work extensively on something that is not going to be seen much. If a given piece of content is only going to be seen in 5% of playthroughs, elaborating that content with hundreds of variants is likely a bad use of time. Tools can help here by highlighting the most frequently accessed pieces of content, either by doing some static analysis on the available material or by taking statistics from automated testing.

The other trap, subtler and more difficult to capture, is that by introducing variants they will actually make the average output more boring. Suppose my initial sentence was

I love apple spice cake with goat cheese frosting.
That's a pretty specific cake. If I then add variants
I love [apple spice/vanilla/chocolate/strawberry] cake with [goat cheese/buttercream/vanilla] frosting.
... then the majority of generated lines will be things like
I love vanilla cake with buttercream frosting.I love strawberry cake with vanilla frosting.

These are significantly less interesting ideas than the cake I started with. By adding variants, I've actually decreased the average quality of the output. A tool can't necessarily capture and correct this, unless we have well-defined metrics for the quality of generated output (in which case, we could be filtering out bad output automatically). One facility it can offer is to show example generations using the new grammar in real-time. This gives the author instant feedback about whether the new generations are better or worse than the original.

Importing Content

Not *all* procedural storytelling systems are about building the components from scratch. A few experimental works in interactive storytelling draw on crowd-sourced data to create the model of a story world. The Scheherazade project at Georgia Tech, for instance, invites workers on Mechanical Turk to submit short stories about familiar events such as a trip to the movies or a bank robbery.[2] From hundreds of example stories, they build a model of how a typical trip to the movies might go and what sorts of actions are typical at any given stage of the movie-going experience.

Jeff Orkin's *Restaurant Game* project took a similar approach: Orkin posted a two-player game in which one could act the role of a waitperson at a typical restaurant and the other played the customer. Each person could speak freeform dialogue or interact with a 3D environment, for instance by sitting down in a chair or carrying a plate of food. He then used this collection of data to build a model of how people act in restaurants. The model captured not only the types of behavior one might expect when authoring such a scenario—ordering food, paying the bill—but also some of the extraordinary tricks played by human players, such as a customer who walked back into the kitchen and attempted to steal the restaurant's microwave oven.

Meanwhile, Gabriella Barros and other researchers working in data-driven game creation make games that draw on Wikipedia and similar publicly available data sources, filling in characters and situations in previously developed templates.

Approaches driven by crowd-created or web-sourced data are less common in commercial game production, at least so far: the quality of the stories and the ability of the designer to control where they go is typically not at the required level. Even in more heavily authored work there can often be times where some form of localized import is useful.

Import and Curate

On one past project, I needed characters in the story to have fallback remarks available if they ran out of other things to say—lines that would feel flavorful and fit with what they'd already been saying but wouldn't advance the story further.

To that end, I imported a couple of hundred common proverbs from Internet data sources, culled the list to remove things that were too specific to our culture or too offensive to include, and then did some quick tagging to associate the proverbs with particular themes, such as "wealth" or "love," as well as a positive/negative valence. I could then deploy these as needed when the story had defined what the situation was about and whether the line should express a positive or negative outlook on it.

Supporting importation like this often requires nothing more than *getting out of the author's way*, by offering a tool in which large amounts of delimited data can be pasted. But one can extend this by offering import tools that neatly extract content from online sources like DBpedia. As one gets more sophisticated, one might also want to offer some automated data cleaning or tools that might suggest data tags and allow the author to correct them. When importing my proverbs, I looked for certain keywords as indicators that the proverb was about money, for instance.

Depending on how much of this kind of work you expect authors to do, you might provide keyword-based tools, regular expressions, or even machine-learning based classifiers to help sort external materials according to whatever criteria are important in your particular story-telling system. Human correction will likely still be needed, but the correction may still be less work than hand-tagging from scratch.

Revising Content

The more complex the procedural system, the more unwieldy and unpredictable revisions are likely to become. If the shape of the story depends on a particular set of progress stats, then minor changes here or there could drastically change how the story plays.

Refactoring an Existing System

I've often realized my corpus was the wrong size or that elements were in the wrong places. Or I have two meta-data tags that are doing very similar work and I need to consolidate them into one. Or maybe there's a variable that's only checked in a handful of places in the story, and it would be most efficient to remove it entirely, because it's not pulling its weight. The ability to search and replace or to move significant portions of content from one area to another becomes critical in these circumstances.

THINGS TO THINK ABOUT WHILE PLANNING A NEW TOOL

Think about What Kind of Procedural Aesthetic You're Going For

Whether you realize it or not, your work is driven by aesthetic principles as well as technical ones. What are those?

- What kinds of experiences are you eager to facilitate?
- What would you recognize as good quality?
- Is it okay or even desirable for the output to look generated, or are you going for something that appears human-created?
- Are humorous incongruities desirable or to be avoided?

Know Your Intended Users and Their Technical Sophistication

- Are you building the tool for yourself or for others?
- Are the people you're recruiting paid or volunteers?
- How much experience do they have building this kind of project? Playing this kind of project?

I've seen a number of tools developed as part of publishing platforms, with the business model that the developer will make a tool and then authors flock to create work on that platform, and both parties will share the profits. This model only works if the platform is easy enough to learn and attractive enough in its output that authors are motivated to take on the job of learning it.

Tools designed for in-house studio use can afford to be more clunky. Speaking about the timed-dialogue tooling she developed for *Ladykiller in a Bind*, Christine Love acknowledges that the tool is both unsuitable for anyone but herself to use—and exactly what she needed.[3] There's nothing wrong with developing a tool for entirely personal use, with idiosyncrasies tuned to the needs of the individual creator, if the purpose is to support the creation of a single project.

The more expert the expected user, the less time you need to spend building documentation, tool tips, and examples. But expert users can still benefit from time-saving shortcuts, strong testing, and good visualization—and they may be *less* inclined than novices to request those features, because they figure they can just forge ahead. If you are in the position of supporting a single expert user or small group of experts, you may want to observe their creation process to figure out what might be slowing them down. Do they have to follow certain templates every time they create a new element? How might that be automated?

Investigate and Mirror the Creative Terminology of Your Users

Your software is trying to meet them as closely as possible to their own natural paradigm. Interactive narrative tends to be counterintuitive for many people, and it places a considerable cognitive load—holding the whole structure in your head and remembering how different world states can proliferate and affect later outcomes, can be overwhelming.

AS YOU'RE BUILDING

Don't Design Only for What Looks Good with a Small Amount of Data

What works for a small project is rarely the same thing that works for a large one.

Anticipate the Founder Principle

The first significant works using this software will make a big impression on those who follow and establish the kind of work that's done with it for a long time (perhaps permanently). This was certainly the case for old-school text adventures, where the brilliant classic *Adventure* set a precedent for underground adventuring, mazes, and light puzzles for many games to come. Subsequent commercial enterprises, especially Infocom, intentionally explored how other genres could be realized in text adventure form, but certain conventions from *Adventure* (and then *Zork*) persisted for many years, even when there were tool sets available allowing for much more varied development.

Along the same lines, many visual novels adopt an anime style and presentation not because they have to, but because these are the examples that guide their development. Many works created with Choice of Games' ChoiceScript tool recapitulate the style and design of Alter Ego (the original 1980s work that inspired ChoiceScript) and the first few Choice of Games branded games, especially *Choice of Dragons* and *Choice of Broadsides*. *Lifeline* games have tended to share the chatty style and episodic danger structure of the original game in the series.

Note that it's not necessarily a bad thing at all for new work to draw on the design example of previous material. Sometimes, if the tool is designed to build materials for a branded series, this is actually a good thing because the market for new work knows what to expect from a new piece.

What if you're trying to create a more general tool, one that could be used for many different purposes by many different users? In that case, it's worth producing multiple examples in different styles as early as possible in the lifecycle of the tool. When we wrote the documentation for Inform 7, we included several hundred code examples that could be compiled and played, and we intentionally developed these to cover a wide range of genres, styles, and types of gameplay. We wanted new readers of the Inform manual to feel that whatever their game concept might be, it was worth pursuing, and they didn't need to make their idea conform to previous genre norms.

Don't Build GUI Tools Too Soon

If you're building an engine to produce a procedural narrative, you're likely discovering new kinds of data you need to represent or new structures that allow you to be more expressive. A GUI tool usually constrains you to the data structures you've anticipated. Starting with something more flexible—an extensible XML or JSON data structure, a domain-specific language—will allow room to iterate on what you expect the system to do.

If you're working with enough novice content creators that you absolutely must have a GUI early in the process, then give yourself the option of adding free-text custom tags so that people can continue to add hooks of their own as they go.

Expect to Accommodate Hacks

No matter how genius your system, there will always be some point in the project where you want to do something peculiar that isn't otherwise accounted for: an Easter egg interaction, a special consequence that doesn't happen anywhere else, whatever. Make sure your tool allows you to add arbitrary tags or hooks to data, outside of the normal structure. This is useful for things that turn out to be one-offs, and it's also useful for prototyping new functionality to which you haven't yet decided to commit.

Beware Complexity Cost

When you find yourself building a hack into your system in order to accommodate new behavior, it's often tempting to decide you need to add a whole new layer to the system. In practice, sometimes it's better to live with a handful of hacks—not just because you have finite time, but because the more moving parts the system has, the more work the author is likely to have to do. In systems where the quality of the experience correlates with the amount of total content available (and that is often true at least to some degree for procedural storytelling systems), creating authoring friction *is making your output worse* because you're accepting a hit to the amount of content you can produce. So when introducing a new system feature, you have to consider whether that feature is making the experience *enough* better to compensate for the costs.

Collect Feedback in Writing Workshops

At Spirit, where I now work on the procedural dialogue system Character Engine, we introduced a tradition of writers' workshops, which are meant to emulate the writing workshops of short story authors. The idea is to get people talking about what they're building, what their aesthetic aims are, and where they're running into problems. It's not a testing venue *per se*, and we leave the more judgmental feedback at the door. The aim here is to find out what authors *want* to create, and what's stopping them.

Before we instituted this custom, we found that authors would often not raise issues about tool problems they encountered immediately because they assumed there was a solution and they were just "being stupid" in not realizing how to solve something.

No Tool Is Ever Ready until It's Been Used to Write a Sizable Project

... and probably not until it's been used to write two or three projects.

Port Related Work to Your System

If you're building a system with similar aims to an existing tool, it can be very instructive to get permission to port work from other systems to yours. In the 1990s and 2000s, the interactive fiction community developed a simple standard game, *Cloak of Darkness*, that was ported to dozens of different interactive fiction tools, as a way of demonstrating their functionality and giving authors a sense of the strengths and weaknesses of different systems.[4]

In my own projects, I've ported my early parser IF game *Galatea* from Inform 6 to the Versu and Character Engine systems and ported short pieces written for Inform 6 to the very different Inform 7. There are several major advantages to doing this. First, it helps deal with the problem of having sizable projects in your new system: porting can be faster than inventing new content from scratch, and this gives you the opportunity to develop quite a lot of new material relatively quickly. Depending on the details of each system, you may even be able to write a script to port some of the old material automatically.

Second, porting full-sized projects will highlight both the strengths and the weaknesses of your system. You are likely to find there are some effects in the old system that your new system doesn't replicate—but you may also discover that some formerly difficult things have become easy. Note that this doesn't replace the need to build new projects natively in your tool. Older projects may not test all aspects of what you've created!

Budget for Extensive Iteration

Usually, building the tool will reveal new levels of productivity that are possible once the tool baseline is available. This point is probably obvious to most people who work in games, where *iterate* is the baseline directive of all directives. But I've often seen production schedules that assume that once the initial set of specs is fulfilled, no more work will be required on the tool. As a consequence, you get studios working with tools that aren't *quite* fit to purpose, or that over the years have built up a tremendous technical debt, until they need to be scrapped and replaced entirely—and the replacement usually turns out to be a long, slow, and iterative process as well.

A better and more self-aware approach is to assign a certain amount of ongoing overhead to tool improvements and to keep in regular contact with your content-creation community about what new features it would like to see. Inform 7 users are still proposing improvements to a tool that has been under development for two decades.

Use the Tool to Reinforce Good Design Practices

As you build multiple projects using this tool, you'll start to get a sense of design idioms, of techniques that work or don't work.

Allow the Tool to Be Clever

We often expect to see AI techniques in games; we don't always expect to see them in the tooling itself, reducing authorial burden or suggesting new possibilities for development. There are fields of research that do address this—computational creativity research touches on ways for computers to assist in human design, and "mixed initiative" tools are those in which the computer and the human user take turns adding elements to a creation or bringing the design along in some way. Mike Cook's Danesh tool analyzes the expressive range of procedural generators, helping authors tweak their work toward a richer variety of output.[5]

Expect Users to Be Forgetful and Do Not Expect Them to Be Working Alone

Solo creators sometimes do enter a flow state where they have all the major concerns of their work in their heads at once—but this can be hard to maintain. It's impossible if the project belongs to a team rather than an individual or if someone is likely to go away from the project for a long time.

Help Your Users Test Their Work

For even the least procedural types of interactive narrative, world state can get so complex that quality assurance testers will never be able to explore every possible scenario. While one can't completely replace QA testers, it's often desirable to test the resulting system in an automated way, trying to answer questions such as

- Are there any points at which the engine runs out of viable content? Dead ends of the narrative where the player would be unable to proceed?

- Are there pieces of content that cannot be reached or that are reached very rarely?

- How long is the average playthrough relative to the total content size?

Help Your Users Define Their Own Tests and Metrics

Inform allows users to create a range of test commands that they can execute to verify the behavior of a specific command sequence.

Anticipate how your users will visualize the structure of their stories and the outcomes of their tests. In procedural narrative spaces, visualizations very often focus on narrative branching. But many of the types of games described in this book do not simply branch—or they may involve such a large and complex structure that a branching visualization will hide the forest with thousands of trees.

NOTES

1 https://github.com/dariusk/corpora
2 http://eilab.gatech.edu/open-story-generation
3 www.gdcvault.com/play/1024403/Micro
4 Roger Firth's website containing the specification for *Cloak of Darkness* and many example projects can still be found at www.firthworks.com /roger/cloak/.
5 www.danesh.procjam.com/

This page intentionally left blank

Index

Page numbers in *italic* indicate figure.
Page numbers in **bold** indicate table.

Printed in the United States
by Baker & Taylor Publisher Services